Table of Contents

Top 20 Test Taking Tips...4
Number Sense and Operations..5
Patterns, Relations, and Algebra...18
Geometry and Measurement..24
Data Analysis, Statistics, and Probability...53
Trigonometry, Calculus, and Discrete Mathematics...68
Practice Test..103
    Practice Questions..103
    Number Sense and Operations...103
    Algebra and Functions..107
    Measurement and Geometry...126
    Statistics, Probability, and Discrete Mathematics...140
    Constructed Response...147
    Answers and Explanations..149
    Number Sense and Operations...149
    Algebra and Functions..150
    Measurement and Geometry...154
    Statistics, Probability, and Discrete Mathematics...158
Secret Key #1 - Time is Your Greatest Enemy..163
    Pace Yourself...163
Secret Key #2 - Guessing is not Guesswork...163
    Monkeys Take the Test..163
    $5 Challenge..164
Secret Key #3 - Practice Smarter, Not Harder...165
    Success Strategy..165
Secret Key #4 - Prepare, Don't Procrastinate...165
Secret Key #5 - Test Yourself...166
General Strategies..166
Special Report: How to Overcome Test Anxiety...172
    Lack of Preparation...172
    Physical Signals...173
    Nervousness...173
    Study Steps..175
    Helpful Techniques..176
Additional Bonus Material...180

Top 20 Test Taking Tips

1. Carefully follow all the test registration procedures
2. Know the test directions, duration, topics, question types, how many questions
3. Setup a flexible study schedule at least 3-4 weeks before test day
4. Study during the time of day you are most alert, relaxed, and stress free
5. Maximize your learning style; visual learner use visual study aids, auditory learner use auditory study aids
6. Focus on your weakest knowledge base
7. Find a study partner to review with and help clarify questions
8. Practice, practice, practice
9. Get a good night's sleep; don't try to cram the night before the test
10. Eat a well balanced meal
11. Know the exact physical location of the testing site; drive the route to the site prior to test day
12. Bring a set of ear plugs; the testing center could be noisy
13. Wear comfortable, loose fitting, layered clothing to the testing center; prepare for it to be either cold or hot during the test
14. Bring at least 2 current forms of ID to the testing center
15. Arrive to the test early; be prepared to wait and be patient
16. Eliminate the obviously wrong answer choices, then guess the first remaining choice
17. Pace yourself; don't rush, but keep working and move on if you get stuck
18. Maintain a positive attitude even if the test is going poorly
19. Keep your first answer unless you are positive it is wrong
20. Check your work, don't make a careless mistake

Number Sense and Operations

Kinds of numbers

<u>Natural numbers</u>
Counting numbers, beginning with 1. (1, 2, 3, . . .)

<u>Whole numbers</u>
Zero and the natural numbers. (0, 1, 2, . . .)

<u>Integers</u>
The positive and negative values of the whole numbers. (-1, 0, 1, . . .)

<u>Rational number</u>
Any number that can be expressed as a fraction with an integer as the numerator, and a non-zero integer as the denominator.

<u>Irrational number</u>
Any non-terminating, non-repeating number that CANNOT be expressed as a fraction. For example, π.

<u>Real numbers</u>
The set of all numbers that fall into any of the above categories.

<u>Complex number</u>
Any number that contains the imaginary number i, where $i^2 = -1$ and $= \sqrt{-1}$.

Adding and subtracting signed numbers

Addition: If the signs are the same, add the absolute values of the addends and apply the original sign to the sum. If the signs are different, take the absolute values of the addends and subtract the smaller value from the larger value. Apply the original sign of the number with the greater absolute value to the difference.

Subtraction: Change the sign of the number after the minus symbol and then follow the rules for addition.

Multiplying and dividing signed numbers

Multiplication: If the multiplicand and multiplier have the same sign, either both positive or both negative, the product is positive. If the multiplicand and multiplier have opposite signs, the product is negative. When there are more than two factors multiplied together, count the number of negative factors. If there are an odd number of negative factors, the product is negative. If there are an even number of factors, the product is positive. If zero is a factor, the answer is zero.

Division: If the dividend and divisor have the same sign, the quotient is positive. If the dividend and divisor have opposite signs, the quotient is negative. If the dividend is zero, the answer is zero, unless the divisor is also zero. Any time the divisor is zero, the quotient is undefined.

Numeric problems

Solve inside any parentheses first; solve exponents second. Then do all multiplication and division in the order they appear, from left to right. Finally, do all addition and subtraction in the order they appear, from left to right.

Field properties for addition and multiplication

Additive Identity
$a + 0 = a; 0 + a = a$

Additive Inverse
$a + (-a) = 0; (-a) + a = 0$

Associative
$(a + b) + c = a + (b + c)$ for addition and $(ab)c = a(bc)$ for multiplication

Closure
In addition, $a + b$ is a real number. In multiplication, ab is a real number.

Commutative
$a + b = b + a$ for addition and $ab = ba$ for multiplication.

Distributive
$a(b + c) = ab + ac$ and $(a + b)c = ac + bc$

Multiplicative Identity
$a \cdot 1 = a$ and $1 \cdot a = a$

Multiplicative Inverse
$a \cdot a^{-1} = 1$ and $a^{-1} \cdot a = 1$

Field properties for subtraction and division

Subtraction
$a - b = a + (-b)$

Division
$a \div b = \dfrac{a}{b} = a \cdot b^{-1} = a \cdot \dfrac{1}{b}$

Properties of natural numbers

Prime
Counting numbers greater than 1 whose only factors are 1 and itself.

Composite
Counting numbers greater than 1 that are not prime.

Note: 1 is neither prime nor composite; 2 is the only prime even number.

Prime Factorization
According to the Fundamental Theorem of Arithmetic, every composite number can be uniquely written as the product of prime numbers.

Greatest Common Factor (gcf)
The greatest number that will divide evenly into each of two or more natural numbers. To find the gcf, factor each number and identify each common prime factor the least number of times it appears in any one of the natural numbers in the set. Find the product of the identified common prime factors. If there no common factors, the gcf is 1.

Greatest Common Divisor (gcd)
Signified by gcd(m, n), where m and n are both natural numbers, it is the same as the greatest common factor.

Least Common Multiple (lcm)
Signified by lcm(m, n), where m and n are both natural numbers, it is the lowest number that is a multiple of each of the natural numbers in the set. To find the lcm, factor each natural number and identify each common prime factor the most number of times it appears in any one of the natural numbers in the set. Find the product of the identified common prime factors.

Finding GCF

The greatest common factor of a group of algebraic expressions may be a monomial or a polynomial. Begin by factoring all the algebraic expressions until each expression is represented as a group of factors consisting of monomials and prime polynomials. To find the greatest common factor, take each monomial or polynomial that appear as a factor in every algebraic expression and multiply. This will give you a polynomial with the largest numerical coefficient and largest degree that is a factor of the given algebraic expressions.

Ratio, proportion, and cross products

Ratio: A comparison of two quantities; expressed in one of three ways: a to b; $a{:}b$; or $\frac{a}{b}$. The units in both terms must be identical to have a correct ratio. If it is not possible to convert to the same units, write the expression as a rate, such as miles per hour, or miles/hour.

Proportion: A statement of two equal ratios, such as $\frac{a}{b} = \frac{c}{d}$.
Cross Products: In a proportion, it is the product of the numerator of the first ratio multiplied by the denominator of the second ratio, and the denominator of the first ratio multiplied by the numerator

of the second ratio, or $\frac{a}{b} = \frac{c}{d} \Rightarrow ad = bc$. In a true proportion, the cross products will always be equal.

Percent

Percent means "hundredth" or "per hundred." To change a percent to a decimal, divide the number by 100. This is accomplished by moving the decimal point two places to the left. The percent of an amount, P, is the percentage rate, R, times the whole amount, or base, B. In other words, $P = RB$. To write a percent as a proportion, use the formula $\frac{R}{100} = \frac{\text{partial amount}}{\text{whole amount}}$.

Mean and weighted mean

Mean: The same thing as the arithmetic average. Use the formula
$$\text{mean} = \frac{\text{sum of all numbers in the set}}{\text{quantity of numbers in the set}}$$

Weighted mean: Weighted values, such as $w_1, w_2, w_3, \ldots$ are assigned to each member of the set $x_1, x_2, x_3, \ldots$. Use the formula
$$\text{weighted mean} = \frac{w_1 x_1 + w_2 x_2 + w_3 x_3 + \cdots + w_n x_n}{w_1 + w_2 + w_3 + \cdots + w_n}$$

Make sure there is one weighted value for each member of the set.

Monomials and polynomials

Monomial: A single constant, variable, or product of constants and variables, such as 2, x, $2x$, or $\frac{2}{x}$. There will never be addition or subtraction symbols in a monomial. Like monomials have like variables, but they may have different coefficients.

Polynomial: An algebraic expression which uses addition and subtraction to combine two or more monomials. Two terms make a binomial; three terms make a trinomial.

Degree of a Monomial: The sum of the exponents of the variables.

Degree of a Polynomial: The highest degree of any individual term.

Patterns of special products

Perfect Trinomial Squares
$x^2 + 2xy + y^2 = (x + y)^2$ or $x^2 - 2xy + y^2 = (x - y)^2$

Difference Between Two Squares
$x^2 - y^2 = (x + y)(x - y)$

Sum of Two Cubes
$x^3 + y^3 = (x + y)(x^2 - xy + y^2)$

Note: the second factor is NOT the same as a perfect trinomial square, so do not try to factor it further.

Difference Between Two Cubes
$$x^3 - y^3 = (x - y)(x^2 + xy + y^2)$$

Again, the second factor is NOT the same as a perfect trinomial square.

Perfect Cubes
$$x^3 + 3x^{2y} + 3xy^2 + y^3 = (x + y)^3 \text{ and } x^3 - 3x^2y + 3xy^2 - y^3 = (x - y)^3$$

Multiplying two binomials

First: Multiply the first term of each binomial
Outer: Multiply the outer terms of the binomials
Inner: Multiply the inner terms of the binomials
Last: Multiply the last term of each binomial
$$(Ax + By)(Cx + Dy) = ACx^2 + ADxy + BCxy + BDy^2$$

Dividing polynomials

Set up a long division problem, dividing a polynomial by either a monomial or another polynomial of equal or lesser degree. When dividing by a monomial, divide each term of the polynomial by the monomial.

When dividing a polynomial by a polynomial, begin by arranging the terms of each polynomial in order of one variable. You may arrange in ascending or descending order, but be consistent with both polynomials. To get the first term of the quotient, divide the first term of the dividend by the first term of the divisor. Multiply the first term of the quotient by the entire divisor and subtract that product from the dividend. Repeat for the second and successive terms until you either get a remainder of zero or a remainder whose degree is less than the degree of the divisor. If the quotient has a remainder, write the answer as a mixed expression in the form
$\text{quotient} + \frac{\text{remainder}}{\text{divisor}}$.

Factoring polynomials

First, check for a common monomial factor. When the greatest common monomial factor has been factored out, look for patterns of special products: differences of two squares, the sum or difference of two cubes for binomial factors, or perfect trinomial squares for trinomial factors. If the factor is a trinomial but not a perfect trinomial square, look for a factorable form, such as:

$$x^2 + (a + b)x + ab = (x + a)(x + b) \text{ or } (ac)x^2 + (ad + bc)x + bd = (ax + b)(cx + d).$$

For factors with four terms, look for groups to factor. Once you have found the factors, write the original polynomial as the product of all the factors. Make sure all of the polynomial factors are prime. Monomial factors may be prime or composite. Check your work by multiplying the factors to make sure you get the original polynomial.

Rational expressions

A rational expression is a fraction with polynomials in both the numerator and the denominator; the value of the polynomial in the denominator cannot be equal to zero. To add or subtract rational expressions, first find the common denominator, then rewrite each fraction as an equivalent fraction with the common denominator. Finally, add or subtract the numerators to get the numerator of the answer, and keep the common denominator as the denominator of the answer. When multiplying rational expressions, factor each polynomial and cancel like factors (a factor which appears in both the numerator and the denominator). Then, multiply all remaining factors in the numerator to get the numerator of the product, and multiply the remaining factors in the denominator to get the denominator of the product. Remember – cancel entire factors, not individual terms. To divide rational expressions, take the reciprocal of the divisor (the rational expression you are dividing by) and multiply by the dividend.

Complex fractions

A complex fraction is a fraction that contains a fraction in its numerator, denominator, or both. Simplify it by rewriting it as a division problem, or multiply both the numerator and denominator by the least common denominator of the fractions in the complex fraction.

Square root

A square root is a number which, when multiplied by itself, yields a real number. Positive real numbers have exactly one real positive n^{th} root, and n could be even or odd. Every real number has exactly one real n^{th} root when n is odd. Negative numbers only have real n^{th} roots if n is odd.

Working with exponents

A positive integer exponent indicates the number of times the base is multiplied by itself. Anything raised to the zero power is equal to 1. A negative integer exponent means you must take the reciprocal of the result of the corresponding positive integer exponent. A fractional exponent signifies a root. The following formulas all apply to exponents:

$$x^0 = 1$$
$$x^{-n} = \frac{1}{x^n}$$
$$\left(\frac{a}{b}\right)^{-1} = \frac{b}{a}$$
$$(x^a)^b = x^{ab}$$
$$(xy)^n = x^n y^n$$
$$\left(\frac{x}{y}\right)^n = \frac{x^n}{y^n}$$

0^0 is undefined.

Terms relative to equations

Equation: Shows that two mathematical expressions are equal; may be true or false.

One Variable Linear Equation: An equation written in the form $ax + b = 0$, where $a \neq 0$.

Root: A solution of an equation; a number that makes the equation true when it is substituted for the variable.

Solution Set: The set of all solutions of an equation.

Identity: A term whose value or determinant is equal to 1.

Empty Set: A situation in which an equation has no true solution.

Equivalent Equations: Equations with identical solution sets.

Solving one variable linear equations

Multiply all terms by the lowest common denominator to eliminate any fractions. Look for addition or subtraction to undo so you can isolate the variable on one side of the equal sign. If the side with just variable terms is a polynomial, factor that side so one of the factors is just the variable. Divide both sides by the coefficient of the variable. When you have a value for the variable, substitute this value into the original equation to make sure you have a true equation.

Absolute value

Absolute Value: The distance a number is from zero; always a positive number or zero. The absolute value of a number, x, is written $|x|$.

Inequalities

Inequality: A mathematical statement showing that two mathematical expressions are not equal. Inequalities use the > (greater than) and < (less than) symbols rather than the equal sign. Graphs of the solution set of inequalities are represented on a number line. Open circles are used to show that an equation approaches a number but is never equal to that number.

Conditional inequality: An inequality that has certain values for the variable that will make the condition true, and other values for the variable that will make the condition false.

Absolute inequality: An inequality that can have any real number as the value for the variable to make the condition true, and no real number value for the variable that will make the condition false.

To solve an inequality, follow the same rules as solving an equation. However, when multiplying or dividing an inequality by a negative number, you must reverse the direction of the inequality sign. Double Inequality: A situation in which two inequality statements apply to the same variable expression.

When working with absolute values in inequalities, apply the following rules:

$$|ax + b| < c \Rightarrow -c < ax + b < c$$

$$|ax + b| > c \Rightarrow ax + b < -c \text{ or } ax + b > c$$

One-variable quadratic equations

A one-variable quadratic equation is an equation that can be written in the form $x^2 + bx + c = 0$, where a, b, and c are the coefficients. This is also known as the standard form of an equation. The solutions of quadratic equations are called roots. A quadratic equation may have one real root, two different real roots, or no real roots. The roots can be found using one of three methods: factoring, completing the square, or using the quadratic formula. Any time you are solving a quadratic equation, never divide both sides by the variable or any expression containing the variable. You are at risk of dividing by zero if you do, thus getting an extraneous, or invalid, root.

Solving quadratic equations

Begin by rewriting the equation in standard form, if necessary. Factor the side with the variable. Set each of the factors equal to zero and solve the resulting linear equations. Check your answers by substituting the roots you found into the original equation. If, when writing the equation in standard form, you have an equation in the form $x^2 + c = 0$ or $x^2 - c = 0$, set $x^2 = -c$ or $x^2 = c$ and take the square root of c. If $c = 0$, the only real root is zero. If c is positive, there are two real roots—the positive and negative square root values. If c is negative, there are no real roots because you cannot take the square root of a negative number.

Completing the square root

To complete the square, rewrite the equation so that all terms containing the variable are on the left side of the equal sign, and all the constants are on the right side of the equal sign. Make sure the coefficient of the squared term is 1. If there is a coefficient with the squared term, divide each term on both sides of the equal side by that number. Next, work with the coefficient of the single-variable term. Square half of this coefficient, and add that value to both sides. Now you can factor the left side (the side containing the variable) as the square of a binomial. $x^2 + 2ax + a^2 = C \Rightarrow (x + a)^2 = C$, where x is the variable, and a and C are constants. Take the square root of both sides and solve for the variable. Substitute the value of the variable in the original problem to check your work.

Quadratic formula

The quadratic formula is used to solve quadratic equations when other methods are more difficult. To use the quadratic formula to solve a quadratic equation, begin by rewriting the equation in standard form $ax^2 + bx + c = 0$, where a, b, and c are coefficients. Once you have identified the values of the coefficients, substitute those values into the quadratic formula $= \frac{-b \pm \sqrt{b^2 - 4ac}}{2a}$. Evaluate the equation and simplify the expression. Again, check each root by substituting into the original equation. In the quadratic formula, the portion of the formula under the radical $(b^2 - 4ac)$ is called the discriminant. If the discriminant is zero, there is only one root: zero. If the discriminant is positive, there are two different real roots. If the discriminant is negative, there are no real roots.

Systems of equations

System of Equations: A set of simultaneous equations that all use the same variables. A solution to a system of equations must be true for each equation in the system.

- 12 -

Consistent System: A system of equations that has at least one solution.

Inconsistent System: A system of equations that has no solution.

Systems of equations may be solved using one of four methods: substitution, elimination, transformation of the augmented matrix and using the trace feature on a graphing calculator.

Solving systems of two linear equations by substitution

To solve a system of linear equations by substitution, start with the easier equation and solve for one of the variables. Express this variable in terms of the other variable. Substitute this expression in the OTHER equation, and solve for the other variable. The solution should be expressed in the form (x, y). Substitute the values into both of the original equations to check your answer.

Solving systems of equations by elimination or addition

To solve a system of equations using elimination or addition, begin by rewriting both equations in standard form $Ax + By = C$. Check to see if the coefficients of one pair of like variables adds to zero. If not, multiply one or both of the equations by a non-zero number to make one set of like variables add to zero. Add the two equations to solve for one of the variables. Substitute this value into one of the original equations to solve for the other variable. Check your work by substituting into the other equation.

Trace feature of a graphing calculator

Using the trace feature on a calculator requires that you rewrite each equation, isolating the y-variable on one side of the equal sign. Enter both equations in the graphing calculator and plot the graphs simultaneously. Use the trace cursor to find where the two lines cross. Use the zoom feature if necessary to obtain more accurate results. Always check your answer by substituting into the original equations. The trace method is likely to be less accurate than other methods due to the resolution of graphing calculators, but is a useful tool to provide an approximate answer.

Graphing two-variable linear inequalities

Whenever you have an inequality using the symbol < or >, always use a dashed line for the graph. If the inequality uses the symbol ≤ or ≥ , use a solid line since equal is an option. All graphs of linear inequalities require that one side of the line is shaded. To determine which side to shade, select any point that is not on the line (the origin is an easy point to use if it is not on the line) and substitute the x- and y-values into the inequality. If the inequality is true, shade the side with that point. If the inequality is false, shade the other side of the line.

Intersect, coincident, and parallel

Intersect: Exactly one solution that satisfies both equations. It is represented by a single point where the two lines intersect on a graph.

Coincident: An infinite number of solutions that satisfy both equations. It is represented by a single line, since all points are in common for both linear equations.

Parallel: No solutions satisfy both equations. It is represented by parallel lines on the graph, since the lines never intersect.

Cartesian coordinate plane

The Cartesian coordinate plane consists of two number lines placed perpendicular to each other, and intersecting at the zero point, also known as the origin. The horizontal number line is known as the x-axis, with positive values to the right of the origin, and negative values to the left of the origin. The vertical number line is known as the y-axis, with positive values above the origin, and negative values below the origin. Any point on the plane can be identified by an ordered pair in the form (x,y), called coordinates. The x-value of the coordinate is called the abscissa, and the y-value of the coordinate is called the ordinate. The two number lines divide the plane into four quadrants: I, II, III, and IV.

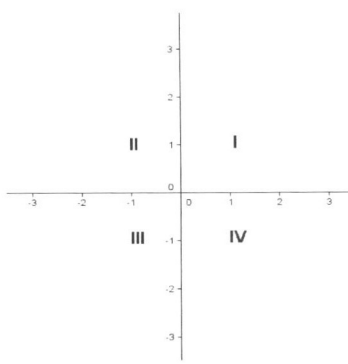

Line equations

Standard form
$Ax + By = C$; the slope is $\frac{-A}{B}$ and the y-intercept is $\frac{C}{B}$.

Slope-Intercept form
$y = mx + b$, where m is the slope and b is the y-intercept.

Point-Slope form
$y - y_1 = m(x - x_1)$, where m is the slope and (x_1, y_1) is a point on the line.

Two-Point form
$\frac{y-y_1}{x-x_1} = \frac{y_2-y_1}{x_2-x_1}$, where (x_1, y_1) and (x_2, y_2) are two points on the given line.

Intercept form
$\frac{x}{x_1} + \frac{y}{y_1} = 1$, where $(x_1, 0)$ is the point at which a line intersects the x-axis, and $(0, y_1)$ is the point at which the same line intersects the y-axis.

Parabola

The standard form of a parabola is $= ax^2 + bx + c$, where a, b, and c are coefficients and $a \neq 0$. In this form, if the value of a is positive, the parabola opens upward. If the value of a is negative, the parabola opens downward. The axis of symmetry is the line $= \frac{-b}{2a}$. The vertex of the parabola is the point $\left(\frac{-b}{2a}, \frac{4ac-b^2}{4a}\right)$. The vertex form of a parabola is $= a(x - h)^2 + k$, where a, h, and k are coefficients. In this form, if the value of a is positive, the parabola open upward. If the value of a is negative, the parabola opens downward. The vertex of the parabola is the point (h, k).

Circle and sphere

The standard form of a circle is

$$(x - h)^2 + (y - k)^2 = r^2$$

where h, k, and r are coefficients. The center of the circle is the point (h, k), and the radius is r units. The general equation of a sphere is

$$(x - a)^2 + (y - b)^2 + (z - c)^2 = r^2$$

where a, b, c, and r are coefficients. The center of the sphere is the point (a, b, c), and the radius is r units.

Ellipse

The standard form of an ellipse is $\frac{(x-h)^2}{a^2} + \frac{(y-k)^2}{b^2} = 1$, where a, b, h, and k are coefficients. The center of the ellipse is the point (h, k). The ellipse has four vertices at points $(h + a, k)$, $(h - a, k)$, $(h, k + b)$, and $(h, k - b)$. The ellipse has two lines of symmetry. The horizontal axis of symmetry is the line through points $(h + a, k)$ and $(h - a, k)$. The vertical axis of symmetry is the line through the points $(h, k + b)$ and $(h, k - b)$. When these lines are drawn, the longer axis is the major axis, and the shorter axis is the minor axis. The lengths of the two axes are given by $2|a|$ and $2|b|$. If $a^2 > b^2$, the ellipse will be longer in the x-direction. If $a^2 < b^2$, the ellipse will be longer in the y-direction.

Hyperbola

The hyperbola has two standard forms. The first standard form of a hyperbola is $\frac{(x-h)^2}{a^2} - \frac{(y-k)^2}{b^2} = 1$, where a, b, h, and k are coefficients. The center of the hyperbola is the point (h, k), and it opens to the left and right along a line having the equation $y = k$. The vertices are the points $(h - a, k)$ and $(h + a, k)$. The asymptotes are lines which the hyperbola approaches but never reaches, and are defined by the equations $y = k + \frac{b}{a}(x - h)$ and $= k - \frac{b}{a}(x - h)$. The asymptotes are also described as the diagonals of a rectangle with center at the center of the hyperbola and legs of length $2|a|$ and $2|b|$. The second standard form of a hyperbola is $\frac{(y-k)^2}{b^2} - \frac{(x-h)^2}{a^2} = 1$, where a, b, h, and k are coefficients. The center of the hyperbola is the point (h, k), and it opens upward and downward along a line having the equation $x = h$. The vertices are the points $(h, k - b)$ and $(h, k + b)$. The asymptotes are lines which the hyperbola approaches but never reaches, and are defined by the equations $= k + \frac{a}{b}(x - h)$ and $y = k - \frac{a}{b}(x - h)$. The asymptotes are also described as the diagonals of a rectangle with center at the center of the hyperbola and legs of length $2|a|$ and $2|b|$. Note that the only difference between the equation of an ellipse and the equation of a hyperbola is the symbol between the two fractions.

Slope, horizontal, vertical, parallel, and perpendicular

Slope: A ratio of the change in height to the change in horizontal distance. On a graph with two points (x_1, y_1) and (x_2, y_2), the slope is represented by the formula $m = \frac{y_2 - y_1}{x_2 - x_1}$; $x_1 \neq x_2$. If the value of the slope is positive, the line slopes upward from left to right. If the value of the slope is negative, the line slopes downward from left to right. If the y-coordinates are the same for both points, the slope is 0 and the line is a horizontal line. If the x-coordinates are the same for both points, there is no slope and the line is a vertical line.

Horizontal: Having a slope of zero. On a graph, a line that is the same distance from the x-axis at all points.

Vertical: Having no slope. On a graph, a line that is the same distance from the y-axis at all points.
Parallel: Lines that have equal slopes.

Perpendicular: Lines that have slopes that are negative reciprocals of each other: $\frac{a}{b}$ and $\frac{-b}{a}$.

Finding midpoint and distance of two points

To find the midpoint of two points (x_1, y_1) and (x_2, y_2), average the x-coordinates to get the x-coordinate of the midpoint, and average the y-coordinates to get the y-coordinate of the midpoint. The formula is

$$\text{midpoint} = \left(\frac{x_1 + x_2}{2}, \frac{y_1 + y_2}{2}\right)$$

The distance between two points is the same as the length of the hypotenuse of a right triangle with the two given points as endpoints, and the two sides of the right triangle parallel to the x-axis and y-axis, respectively. The length of the segment parallel to the x-axis is the difference between the x-coordinates of the two points. The length of the segment parallel to the y-axis is the difference between the y-coordinates of the two points. Use the Pythagorean Theorem $a^2 + b^2 = c^2$ or $c = \sqrt{a^2 + b^2}$ to find the distance. The formula is:

$$\text{distance} = \sqrt{(x_2 - x_1)^2 + (y_2 - y_1)^2}$$

Calculating simple and compound interest

Simple Interest: Interest that is paid once per year for the principal amount. The formula is $I = Prt$, where I is the amount of interest, P is the principal, or original amount, r is the annual interest rate, and t is the amount of time, in years.

- 16 -

Compound Interest: Interest that is paid multiple times per year for the amount of the principal plus accrued interest. The formula is $P = P_0 \left(1 + \frac{r}{n}\right)^{nt}$, where P is the total value of the investment, P_0 is the initial value, t is the amount of time in years, r is the annual interest rate, and n is the number of times per year the interest is compounded.

Relationship between distance, rate, and time

Distance is achieved by moving at a given rate for a given length of time. The formulas that relate the three are $d = rt$, $= \frac{d}{t}$, and $t = \frac{r}{d}$, where d is the distance, r is the rate of change over time, and t is total time. In these formulas, the units used to express the rate must be the same units used to express the distance and the time.

Distance from a line to a point not on the line

When the line is in the format $Ax + By + C = 0$, where A, B, and C are coefficients, use a point (x_1, y_1) not on the line and apply the formula
$$d = \frac{|Ax_1 + By_1 + C|}{\sqrt{A^2 + B^2}}$$

Scalars and vectors

Scalar: A quantity represented by a real number. It always shows magnitude, but never direction.

Vector: A quantity having both magnitude and direction. A vector (PQ) is represented by the symbol $\overrightarrow{PQ}$, where P is the tail and Q is the head. A unit vector in the direction of the x-axis is represented by the symbol $\vec{\imath}$. A unit vector in the direction of the y-axis is represented by the symbol $\vec{\jmath}$.

Speed is a scalar quantity. (Drive 55 miles per hour.) Velocity is a vector. (Drive north at 55 miles per hour.)

Solving radical equations

Begin by isolating the radical term on one side of the equation, and move all other terms to the other side of the equation. Look at the index of the radicand. Remember, if no number is given, the index is 2, meaning square root. Raise both sides of the equation to the power equal to the index of the radical. Solve the resulting equation as you would a normal polynomial equation. When you have found the roots, you MUST check them in the original problem to eliminate extraneous roots.

Patterns, Relations, and Algebra

Functions

A function is an equation that has exactly one value for *y* (the dependent variable) for each member of *x* (the independent variable). The set of all values for *x* is the domain of the function, and the set of all corresponding values of *y* is the range of the function. When looking at a graph of an equation, the easiest way to determine if the equation is a function or not is to conduct the vertical line test. If a vertical line drawn through any value of x crosses the graph in more than one place, the equation is not a function.

Properties of functions

In functions with the notation $f(x)$, the value substituted for *x* in the equation is called the argument. The domain is the set of all values for *x* in a function. Unless otherwise given, assume the domain is the set of real numbers that will yield real numbers for the range. This is the domain of definition. The graph of a function is the set of all ordered pairs (x, y) that satisfy the equation of the function. The points that have zero as the value for *y* are called the zeros of the function. These are also the *x*-intercepts, because that is the point at which the graph crosses, or intercepts, the *x*-axis. The points that have zero as the value for *x* are the *y*-intercepts because that is where the graph crosses the *y*-axis.

Horizontal and vertical shift

Horizontal and vertical shift occur when values are added to or subtracted from the *x* or *y* values, respectively. If a constant is added to the *y* portion of each point, the graph shifts up. If a constant is subtracted from the *y* portion of each point, the graph shifts down. This is represented by the expression $y = f(x) \pm k$, where *k* is a constant. If a constant is added to the x portion of each point, the graph shifts left. If a constant is subtracted from the x portion of each point, the graph shifts right. This is represented by the expression $y = f(x \pm k)$, where *k* is a constant.

Stretch, shrink, and reflection

Stretching, shrinking, and reflecting occur when a function is multiplied by a constant. If the function is multiplied by a real number constant greater than 1, the graph is stretched. If a constant greater than 1 is multiplied by the *x* portion of each point, the graph is stretched horizontally. If a constant greater than 1 is multiplied by the *y* portion of each point, the graph is stretched vertically. If the function is multiplied by a real number constant greater than zero but less than 1, the graph shrinks. If a positive real number constant less than 1 is multiplied by the *x* portion of each point, the graph shrinks horizontally. If a positive real number constant less than 1 is multiplied by the *y* portion of each point, the graph shrinks vertically. If the *x* portion of each point is multiplied by a negative number, the graph is reflected across the *x*-axis. If the *y* portion of each point is multiplied by a negative number, the graph is reflected across the *y*-axis.

Exponential functions and logarithmic functions

Exponential functions are equations that have the format $y = b^x$, where base $b > 0$ and $b \neq 1$. The exponential function can also be written $f(x) = b^x$. Logarithmic functions are equations that have the format $y = \log_b x$ or $(x) = \log_b x$. The base b may be any number except one; however, the most common bases for logarithms are base 10 and base e, also known as the natural logarithm. On the test, any logarithm that does not have an assigned value of b is assumed to be base e. Exponential functions and logarithmic functions are related in that one is the inverse of the other. If $f(x) = b^x$, then $f^{-1}(x) = \log_b x$. Also, the equation $y = b^x$ is the same as $= \log_b y$. The following properties apply to logarithmic expressions:

$$\log_b 1 = 0$$
$$\log_b b = 1$$
$$\log_b b^p = p$$
$$\log_b MN = \log_b M + \log_b N$$
$$\log_b \frac{M}{N} = \log_b M - \log_b N$$
$$\log_b M^p = p \log_b M$$

Linear functions

In a linear function, the rate of change (the slope) is constant throughout. Linear functions are straight line graphs and are used to describe things such as distance, where the *rate of change* does not change. The standard form of a linear equation is $Ax + By = C$, where A, B, and C are real numbers. Other forms of linear equations make solving problems easier. The slope-intercept form $y = mx + b$ (m and b are real numbers, m is the slope, $m \neq 0$, and b is the y-intercept) is useful for finding the zeros of the function. Solve the equation $mx + b = 0$ for x to get $= -\frac{b}{m}$, which is the only zero of the function. The domain and range are both the set of all real numbers.

Constant and identity functions

Constant functions are given by the equation $y = b$ or $f(x) = b$, where b is a real number. There is a single variable y in the equation, so there are no zeros unless $b = 0$, in which case every point is a zero. The graph of a constant function is a horizontal line of slope 0 that is positioned b units from the x-axis. If b is positive, the line is above the x-axis; if b is negative, the line is below the x-axis. Identity functions are identified by the equation $y = x$ or $(x) = x$, where every value of y is equal to its corresponding value of x. The only zero is the point (0, 0). The graph is a diagonal line with slope 1.

Quadratic function

A quadratic function follows the equation pattern $= ax^2 + bx + c$, or $f(x) = ax^2 + bx + c$, where a, b, and c are real numbers and $a \neq 0$. The domain of a quadratic function is the set of all real numbers. The range is also real numbers, but only those in the subset of the domain that satisfy the equation. To determine the number of roots of a quadratic equation, solve the expression $b^2 - 4ac$. If this value is positive, there are two unique real zeros. If this value equals zero, there is one root, which is a double root. If this value is less than zero, there are no real roots. To find the roots of a quadratic equation, solve the equation $x^2 + bx + c = 0$. In a quadratic function, the rate of change varies throughout, but there is a maximum or a minimum value for the amount of change.

Quadratic functions are useful in determining things such as how changing the price of something will affect its sales and profit margin.

Graphs of quadratic functions

A quadratic function will always form a parabola when it is graphed. In the equation $(x) = ax^2 + bx + c$, if a is positive, the parabola will open upward. If a is negative, the parabola will open downward. The axis of symmetry is a vertical line that passes through the vertex. To determine whether or not a parabola will intersect the x-axis, check the number of real roots. An equation with two real roots will cross the x-axis twice. An equation with one real root will have its vertex on the x-axis. An equation with no real roots will not contact the x-axis.

Fundamental Theorem of Algebra and Remainder Theorem

The Fundamental Theorem of Algebra states that every function, when set equal to zero, has a solution, and that every polynomial has at least one root. Every polynomial will have as many roots as the largest integer exponent in the polynomial. For example, if x^4 is the largest exponent of a term, the polynomial will have exactly 4 roots. Some roots may be double roots, so those must be counted twice. The Fundamental Theorem of Algebra does allow for complex roots, so do not expect to find all real roots for every function. The Remainder Theorem is useful for determining the remainder when a polynomial is divided by a binomial. The Remainder Theorem states that if a function $f(x)$ is divided by a binomial $x - a$, where a is a real number, the remainder will be the value of $f(a)$. If $f(a) = 0$, then a is a root of the polynomial at the point $(a, 0)$.

Factor Theorem and Rational Root Theorem

The Factor Theorem is related to the Remainder Theorem and states that if $f(a) = 0$ then $(x - a)$ is a factor of the function. Rational Root Theorem: A function $f(x) = a_n x^n + a_{n-1} x^{n-1} + a_{n-2} x^{n-2} + \cdots + a_1 x + a_0$ with integral coefficients will have a rational root that, when reduced to lowest terms, will be a fraction such that the numerator is a factor of a_0 and the denominator is a factor of a_n. The Rational Root Theorem also deals with complex roots. If a function has a complex root $p + qi$, where i is the imaginary number, then its conjugate, or $p - qi$, is also a root of the function. One way to help determine approximations of roots is to evaluate functions with different values. If $f(p)$ and $f(q)$ have opposite signs, you know there must be a zero somewhere between those two numbers.

Rational functions

A rational function is a fraction such that $f(x) = \frac{p(x)}{q(x)}$, $p(x)$ and $q(x)$ are both polynomials and $q(x) \neq 0$. The domain is the set of all real numbers EXCEPT any number for which $q(x) = 0$. The range is the set of real numbers that satisfies the function when the domain is applied. Whenever you graph a rational function, you will have vertical asymptotes wherever $q(x) = 0$. If the polynomial in the numerator is of lesser degree than the polynomial in the denominator, the x-axis will also be a horizontal asymptote. If the numerator and denominator have equal degrees, there will be a horizontal asymptote not on the x-axis. If the degree of the numerator is exactly one greater than the degree of the denominator, the graph will have an oblique, or diagonal, asymptote.

Square root functions

A square root function is a function that contains a radical and is in the format $(x) = \sqrt{ax + b}$. The domain is the set of all real numbers that yields a positive radicand or a radicand equal to zero. Because square root values are assumed to be positive unless otherwise identified, the range is all real numbers from zero to infinity. To find the zero of a square root function, set the radicand equal to zero and solve for x. The graph of a square root function is always to the right of the zero and always above the x-axis.

Absolute value functions

An absolute value function is in the format $(x) = |ax + b|$. Like other functions, the domain is the set of all real numbers. However, because absolute value indicates positive numbers, the range is limited to positive real numbers. To find the zero of an absolute value function, set the portion inside the absolute value sign equal to zero and solve for x. An absolute value function is also known as a piecewise function because it must be solved in pieces – one for if the value inside the absolute value sign is positive, and one for if the value is negative. The function can be expressed as
$$f(x) = \begin{cases} ax + b & \text{if } ax + b \geq 0 \\ -(ax + b) & \text{if } ax + b < 0 \end{cases}$$

This will allow for an accurate statement of the range.

Polynomial functions

A polynomial function is a function with multiple terms and multiple powers of x, such as
$$f(x) = a_n x^n + a_{n-1} x^{n-1} + a_{n-2} x^{n-2} + \cdots + a_1 x + a_0$$
where n is a positive integer that is the highest exponent in the polynomial, and $a_n \neq 0$. Like quadratic equations, the domain is the set of all real numbers. If the greatest exponent in the polynomial is even, the polynomial is said to be of even degree and the range is the set of real numbers that satisfy the function. If the greatest exponent in the polynomial is odd, the polynomial is said to be odd and the range, like the domain, is the set of all real numbers.

One-to-one functions

In a one-to-one function, each value of x has exactly one value for y (this is the definition of a function) *and* each value of y has exactly one value for x. While the vertical line test will determine if a graph is that of a function, the horizontal line test will determine if a function is a one-to-one function. If a horizontal line drawn at any value of y intersects the graph in more than one place, the graph is not that of a one-to-one function. Do not make the mistake of using the horizontal line test exclusively in determining if a graph is that of a one-to-one function. A one-to-one function must pass both the vertical line test and the horizontal line test.

Monotone, even, and odd functions, and discontinuities

A monotone function is a function whose graph either constantly increases or constantly decreases. Examples include the functions $(x) = x$, $f(x) = -x$, or $f(x) = x^3$. An even function has a graph that is symmetric with respect to the y-axis and satisfies the equation $(x) = f(-x)$. Examples include the functions $f(x) = x^2$ and $(x) = ax^n$, where a is any real number and n is a positive even integer. An odd function has a graph that is symmetric with respect to the origin and satisfies the equation $(x) = -f(-x)$. Examples include the functions $f(x) = x^3$ and $(x) = ax^n$, where a is any real number and n is a positive odd integer. Any time there are vertical asymptotes or holes in a graph, such that the complete graph cannot be drawn as one continuous line, a graph is said to have discontinuities. Examples would include the graphs of hyperbolas that are functions, and the function f(x)=tan x.

Variables that vary directly and inversely

Variables that vary directly are those that either both increase at the same rate or both decrease at the same rate. For example, in the functions $f(x) = kx$ or $(x) = kx^n$, where k is a positive constant and $n > 0$, the value of y ($f(x)$) increases as the value of x increases and decreases as the value of x decreases. Variables that vary inversely are those where one increases while the other decreases. For example, in the functions $f(x) = \frac{k}{x}$ or $f(x) = \frac{k}{x^n}$ where k is a positive constant, the value of y increases as the value of x decreases, and the value of y decreases as the value of x increases. In both cases, k is constant of variation.

Algebraic and transcendental functions

Algebraic functions are those that exclusively use polynomials and roots. These would include polynomial functions, rational functions, square root functions, and all combinations of these functions, such as polynomials as the radicand. These combinations may be joined by addition, subtraction, multiplication, or division, but may not include variables as an exponent. Transcendental functions are all functions that are non-algebraic. Any function that includes logarithms, trigonometric functions, variables as exponents, or any combination that includes any or all of these is not algebraic in nature, even if the function includes polynomials or roots, and therefore a transcendental function.

Equal functions

Equal functions are those whose domains are equal, and whose ranges are equal for all corresponding values in the domain. In other words, $f(x)$ and $g(x)$ are equal if every value of $f(x)$ is equal to every corresponding value of $g(x)$. To find the sum of the functions f and g, assuming the ranges are all real numbers, solve each function individually and add the results: $(f + g)(x) = f(x) + g(x)$. To find the difference of the functions f and g, assuming the ranges are all real numbers, solve each function individually and subtract the results: $(f - g)(x) = f(x) - g(x)$.

Product, quotient, and composite of two functions

To find the product of the functions f and g, assuming the ranges are all real numbers, solve each function individually and then multiply the results: $(f \cdot g)(x) = f(x) \cdot g(x)$. This is much easier, and less prone to mathematical error, than trying to multiply two polynomials together before applying the value of x. To find the quotient of the functions f and g, assuming the ranges are all real numbers, solve each function individually and then divide the results: $\left(\frac{f}{g}\right)(x) = \frac{f(x)}{g(x)}$; $g(x) \neq 0$.

The composite of two functions f and g, represented by the symbol $(f \circ g)(x)$ or $f(g(x))$, is found by substituting $g(x)$ for all instances of x in $f(x)$ and simplifying. It is important to note that $(f \circ g)(x)$ does not always equal $(g \circ f)(x)$. The process is not commutative like addition or multiplication expressions. If $(f \circ g)(x)$ does equal $(g \circ f)(x)$, the two functions are inverses of

- 22 -

each other. This is one of the easiest tests to determine if two functions are inverses. If the two functions are graphed, the graphs will be reflections of each other with respect to the line $y = x$.

Geometry and Measurement

Altitude, height, concurrent, and orthocenter

Altitude of a Triangle: A line segment drawn from one vertex perpendicular to the opposite side. In the diagram below, $\overline{BE}$, $\overline{AD}$, and $\overline{CF}$ are altitudes.

Height of a Triangle: The length of the altitude, although the two terms are often used interchangeably.

Concurrent: Lines that intersect at one point. In a triangle, the three altitudes are concurrent.

Orthocenter of a Triangle: The point of concurrency of the altitudes of a triangle. Note that in an obtuse triangle, the orthocenter will be outside the circle, and in a right triangle, the orthocenter is the vertex of the right angle.

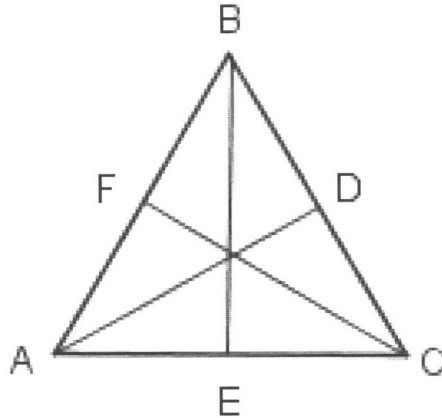

Median and centroid

Median of a Triangle: A line segment drawn from one vertex to the midpoint of the opposite side. This is not the same as the altitude, except the altitude to the base of an isosceles triangle and all three altitudes of an equilateral triangle.

Centroid of a Triangle: The point of concurrency of the medians of a triangle. This is the same point as the orthocenter only in an equilateral triangle. Unlike the orthocenter, the centroid is always inside the triangle. The centroid can also be considered the exact center of the triangle. Any shape triangle can be perfectly balanced on a tip placed at the centroid. The centroid is also the point that is two-thirds the distance from the vertex to the opposite side.

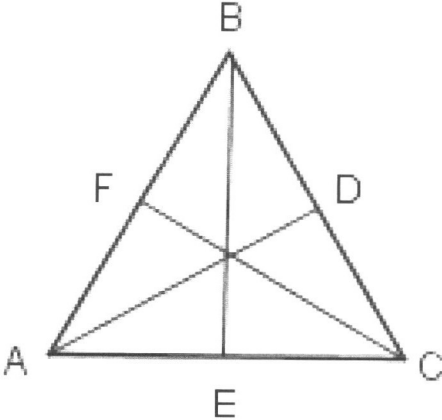

Perpendicular and angle bisectors

Perpendicular bisector: A line that bisects the side of a triangle at a right angle. The perpendicular bisectors of a triangle are concurrent at a point called the circumcernter that is equidistant from the three vertices. The circumcenter is also the center of the circle that can be circumscribed about the triangle.

Angle bisector: A line that divides the vertex angle of a triangle into two equal parts. The angle bisectors are concurrent at a point called the incenter that is equidistant from the three sides. The incenter is also the center of the largest circle that can be inscribed in the triangle.

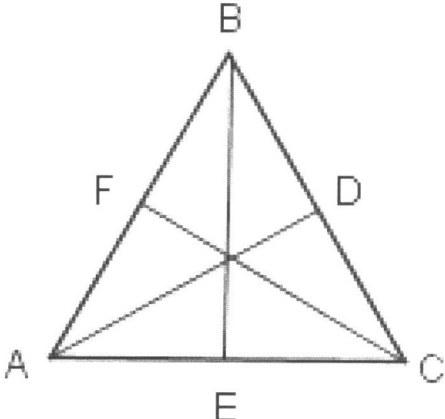

Congruent and similar figures

Congruent figures are geometric figures that have the same size and shape. All corresponding angles are equal, and all corresponding sides are equal. It is indicated by the symbol ≅.

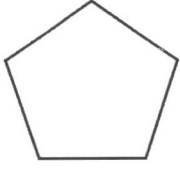 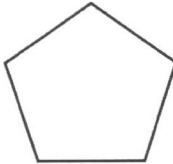

Congruent polygons

Similar figures are geometric figures that have the same shape, but do not necessarily have the same size. All corresponding angles are equal, and all corresponding sides are proportional, but they do not have to be equal. It is indicated by the symbol ~.

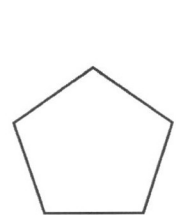 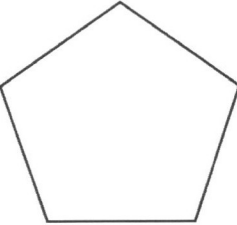

Similar polygons

Note that all congruent figures are also similar, but not all similar figures are congruent.

Symmetry, symmetric, and line of symmetry

Line of Symmetry: The line that divides a figure or object into two symmetric parts. Each symmetric half is congruent to the other. An object may have no lines of symmetry, one line of symmetry, or more than one line of symmetry.

No lines of symmetry   One line of symmetry   More than one line of symmetryb

Quadrilaterals, parallelograms, and trapezoids

Quadrilateral: A closed two-dimensional geometric figure comprised of exactly four straight sides. The sum of the interior angles of any quadrilateral is 360°.

Parallelogram: A quadrilateral that has exactly two pairs of opposite parallel sides. The sides that are parallel are also congruent. The opposite interior angles are always congruent, and the consecutive interior angles are supplementary. The diagonals of a parallelogram bisect each other. Each diagonal divides the parallelogram into two congruent triangles.

Trapezoid: Traditionally, a quadrilateral that has exactly one pair of parallel sides. Some math texts define trapezoid as a quadrilateral that has at least one pair of parallel sides. Because there are no rules governing the second pair of sides, there are no rules that apply to the properties of the diagonals of a trapezoid.

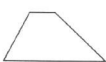

Rectangles, rhombuses, and squares

Rectangles, rhombuses, and squares are all special forms of parallelograms.

Rectangle: A parallelogram with four right angles. All rectangles are parallelograms, but not all parallelograms are rectangles. The diagonals of a rectangle are congruent.

Rhombus: A parallelogram with four congruent sides. All rhombuses are parallelograms, but not all parallelograms are rhombuses. The diagonals of a rhombus are perpendicular to each other.

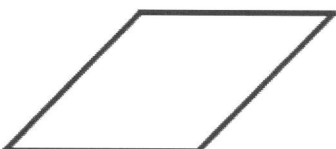

Square: A parallelogram with four right angles and four congruent sides. All squares are also parallelograms, rhombuses, and rectangles. The diagonals of a square are congruent and perpendicular to each other.

Ray, angle, and vertex

A ray is a portion of a line extending from a point in one direction. It has a definite beginning, but no ending. Rays are represented by the symbol $\rightarrow$. An angle is formed when two rays meet at a common point. It may be a common starting point, or it may be the intersection of rays, lines, and/or line segments. Angles are represented by the symbol $\angle$. The vertex is the point at which the two rays meet to form an angle. If the angle is formed by intersecting rays, lines, and/or line segments, the vertex is the point at which four angles meet. The opposite angles are called vertical angles, and their measures are equal.

Types of angles

An acute is an angle with a degree measure less than 90º. A right angle is an angle with a degree measure of exactly 90º. An obtuse angle is an angle with a degree measure greater than 90º but less than 180º. A straight angle is an angle with a degree measure of exactly 180º. This is also a semicircle. A reflex angle is an angle with a degree measure greater than 180º but less than 360º. A full angle is an angle with a degree measure of exactly 360º. This is also a circle.

Complementary, supplementary, and adjacent angles

Complementary: Two angles whose sum is exactly 90º. The two angles may or may not be adjacent. In a right triangle, the two acute angles are complementary.

Supplementary: Two angles whose sum is exactly 180º. The two angles may or may not be adjacent. Two intersecting lines always form two pairs of supplementary angles. Adjacent supplementary angles will always form a straight line.

Adjacent: Two angles that have the same vertex and share a side. Vertical angles are not adjacent because they share a vertex but no common side.

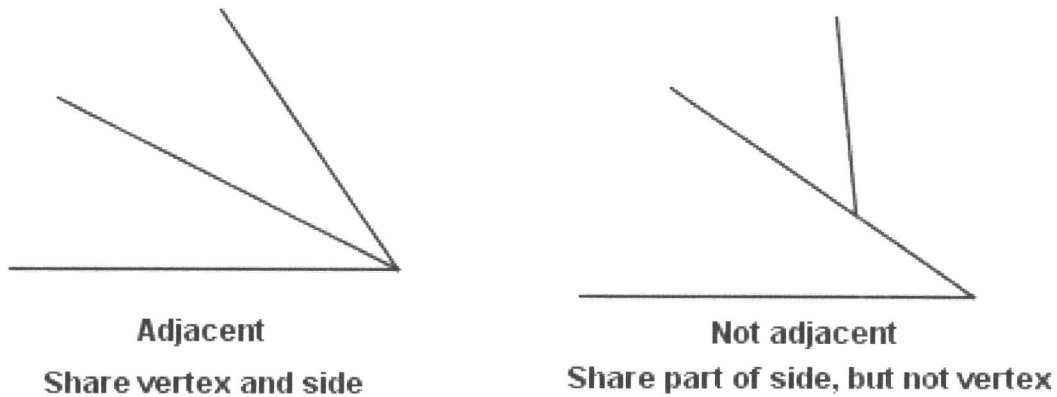

Adjacent
Share vertex and side

Not adjacent
Share part of side, but not vertex

Plane

A plane is a two-dimensional flat surface defined by three non-collinear points. A plane extends an infinite distance in all directions in those two dimensions. It contains an infinite number of points, parallel lines and segments, intersecting lines and segments, as well as parallel or intersecting rays. A plane will never contain a three-dimensional figure or skew lines. A plane may intersect a circular conic surface, such as a cone, to form conic sections, such as the parabola, hyperbola, circle or ellipse. Two given planes will either be parallel or they will intersect to form a line.

Intersecting lines, parallel lines, vertical angles, and transversals

Intersecting Lines: Lines that have exactly one point in common.

Parallel Lines: Lines in the same plane that have no points in common and never meet. It is possible for lines to be in different planes, have no points in common, and never meet, but they are not parallel because they are in different planes.

Vertical Angles: Non-adjacent angles formed when two lines intersect. Vertical angles are congruent. In the diagram, $\angle ABD \cong \angle CBE$ and $\angle ABC \cong \angle DBE$.

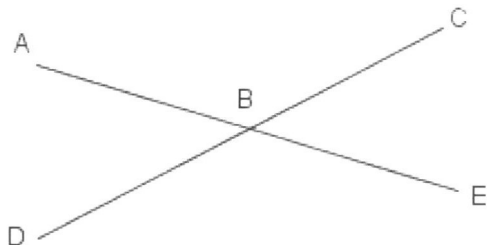

Transversal: A straight line that intersects at least two other lines, which may or may not be parallel.

Interior angles, exterior angles, and corresponding angles

Interior Angles: When two parallel lines are cut by a transversal, the angles that are between the two parallel lines are interior angles. In the diagram below, angles 3, 4, 5, and 6 are interior angles.

Exterior Angles: When two parallel lines are cut by a transversal, the angles that are outside the parallel lines are exterior angles. In the diagram below, angles 1, 2, 7, and 8 are exterior angles.

Corresponding Angles: When two parallel lines are cut by a transversal, the angles that are in the same position relative to the transversal and one of the parallel lines. The diagram below has four pairs of corresponding angles: angles 1 and 5; angles 2 and 6; angles 3 and 7; and angles 4 and 8. Corresponding angles formed by parallel lines are congruent.

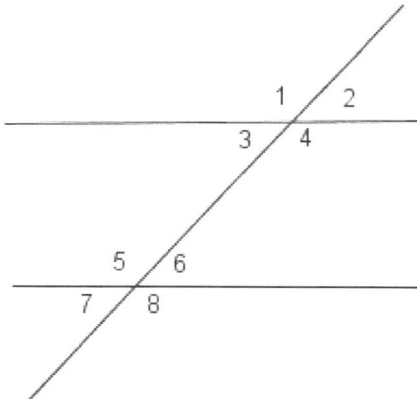

Alternate interior angles and alternate exterior angles

Alternate Interior Angles: When two parallel lines are cut by a transversal, two interior angles that are on opposite sides of the transversal and on opposite parallel lines are congruent opposite interior angles. In the diagram below, there are two pair of alternate interior angles: angles 3 and 6, and angles 4 and 5. Alternate interior angles formed by parallel lines are congruent.

Alternate Exterior Angles: When two parallel lines are cut by a transversal, two exterior angles that are on opposite sides of the transversal and on opposite parallel lines are congruent opposite exterior angles. In the diagram below, there are two pair of alternate exterior angles: angles 1 and 8, and angles 2 and 7. Alternate exterior angles formed by parallel lines are congruent.

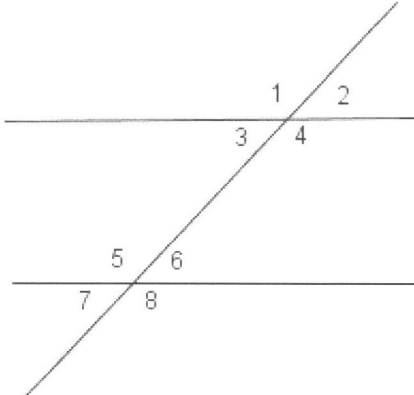

Perpendicular lines and bisectors

Perpendicular lines are lines that intersect at right angles. They are represented by the symbol ⊥. The shortest distance from a line to a point not on the line is a perpendicular segment from the point to the line. In a plane, the perpendicular bisector of a line segment is a line comprised of the set of all points that are equidistant from the endpoints of the segment. This line always forms a right angle with the segment in the exact middle of the segment. Note that you can only find perpendicular bisectors of segments.

Side, vertex, regular polygon, apothem, and radius

Each straight line segment of a polygon is called a side. The point at which two sides of a polygon intersect is called the vertex. In a polygon, the number of sides is always equal to the number of vertices. A polygon with all sides congruent and all angles equal is called a regular polygon. A line segment from the center of a polygon perpendicular to a side of the polygon is called the apothem. In a regular polygon, the apothem can be used to find the area of the polygon using the formula $A = \frac{1}{2}ap$, where a is the apothem and p is the perimeter. A line segment from the center of a polygon to a vertex of the polygon is called the radius. The radius of a regular polygon is also the radius of a circle that can be circumscribed about the polygon.

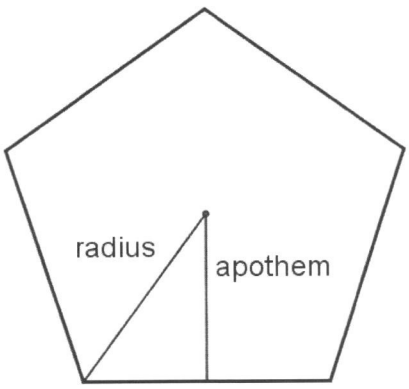

Names for shapes

3 sides: triangle
4 sides: quadrilateral
5 sides: pentagon
6 sides: hexagon
7 sides: heptagon
8 sides: octagon
9 sides: nonagon
10 sides: decagon
12 sides: dodecagon
n sides: n-gon

Sum and measure of the interior angle(s) of a polygon

To find the sum of the interior angles of a polygon, use the formula: sum of interior angles $= (n-2)180°$, where n is the number of sides in the polygon. This formula works with all polygons, not just regular polygons. To find the measure of one interior angle of a regular polygon, use the formula $\frac{(n-2)180°}{n}$, where n is the number of sides in the polygon.

Diagonal, convex, concave, polygons

A diagonal is a line segment that joins two non-adjacent vertices of a polygon. A convex polygon is a polygon whose diagonals all lie within the interior of the polygon. A concave polygon is a polygon with a least one diagonal that lies outside the polygon. In the diagram below, quadrilateral *ABCD* is concave because diagonal $\overline{AC}$ lies outside the polygon.

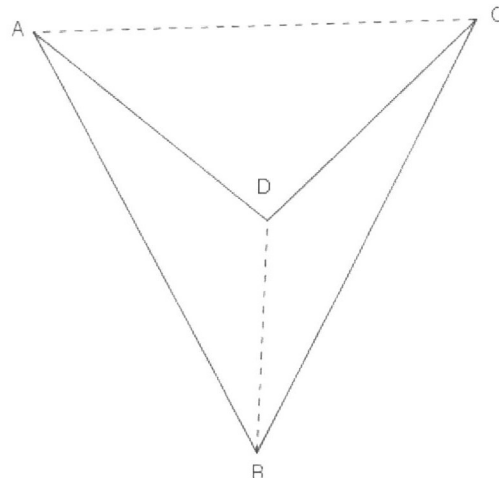

The number of diagonals a polygon has can be found by using the formula: number of diagonals $= \frac{n(n-3)}{2}$, where *n* is the number of sides in the polygon. This formula works for all polygons, not just regular polygons.

Equilateral, isosceles, scalene

An equilateral triangle is a triangle with three congruent sides. An equilateral triangle will also have three congruent angles. An isosceles triangle is a triangle with two congruent sides. An isosceles triangle will also have two congruent angles opposite the two congruent sides. A scalene triangle is a triangle with no congruent sides. A scalene triangle will also have three angles of different measures. The angle with the largest measure is opposite the longest side, and the angle with the smallest measure is opposite the shortest side.

Equilateral   Isosceles   Scalene

Acute, right, and obtuse

An acute triangle is a triangle whose three angles are all less than 90º. If two of the angles are equal, the acute triangle is also an isosceles triangle. If the three angles are all equal, the acute triangle is also an equilateral triangle. A right triangle is a triangle with exactly one angle equal to 90º. All right triangles follow the Pythagorean Theorem. A right triangle can never be acute or obtuse. An obtuse triangle is a triangle with exactly one angle greater than 90º. The other two angles may or may not be equal. If the two remaining angles are equal, the obtuse triangle is also an isosceles triangle. The sum of the measures of the interior angles of a triangle is always 180º. Therefore, a triangle can never have more than one angle greater than or equal to 90º.

Triangle Inequality Theorem

The Triangle Inequality Theorem states that the sum of the measures of any two sides of a triangle is always greater than the measure of the third side. If the sum of the measures of two sides were equal to the third side, a triangle would be impossible because the two sides would lie flat across the third side and there would be no vertex. If the sum of the measures of two of the sides was less than the third side, a closed figure would be impossible because the two shortest sides would never meet.

Similar triangles

In any triangle, the angles opposite congruent sides are congruent, and the sides opposite congruent angles are congruent. The largest angle is always opposite the longest side, and the smallest angle is always opposite the shortest side. The line segment that joins the midpoints of any two sides of a triangle is always parallel to the third side and exactly half the length of the third side. Similar triangles are triangles whose corresponding angles are equal and whose corresponding sides are proportional. Represented by AA. Similar triangles whose corresponding sides are congruent are also congruent triangles.

Types of congruent triangles

Three sides of one triangle are congruent to the three corresponding sides of the second triangle. Represented as SSS.

Two sides and the included angle (the angle formed by those two sides) of one triangle are congruent to the corresponding two sides and included angle of the second triangle. Represented by SAS.

Two angles and the included side (the side that joins the two angles) of one triangle are congruent to the corresponding two angles and included side of the second triangle. Represented by ASA.

Two angles and a non-included side of one triangle are congruent to the corresponding two angles and non-included side of the second triangle. Represented by AAS.

Note that AAA is not a form for congruent triangles. This would say that the three angles are congruent, but says nothing about the sides. This meets the requirements for similar triangles, but not congruent triangles.

Properties of quadrilaterals

A quadrilateral whose diagonals bisect each other is a parallelogram. A quadrilateral whose opposite sides are parallel (2 pairs of parallel sides) is a parallelogram. A quadrilateral whose diagonals are perpendicular bisectors of each other is a rhombus. A quadrilateral whose opposite sides (both pairs) are parallel and congruent is a rhombus. A parallelogram that has a right angle is a rectangle. (Consecutive angles of a parallelogram are supplementary. Therefore if there is one right angle in a parallelogram, there are four right angles in that parallelogram.) A rhombus with one right angle is a square. Because the rhombus is a special form of a parallelogram, the rules about the angles of a parallelogram also apply to the rhombus.

Center, radius, and diameter

Center: A single point that is equidistant from every point on a circle. (Point O in the diagram below.)

Radius: A line segment that joins the center of the circle and any one point on the circle. All radii of a circle are equal. (Segments OX, OY, and OZ in the diagram below.)

Diameter: A line segment that passes through the center of the circle and has both endpoints on the circle. The length of the diameter is exactly twice the length of the radius. (Segment XZ in the diagram below.)

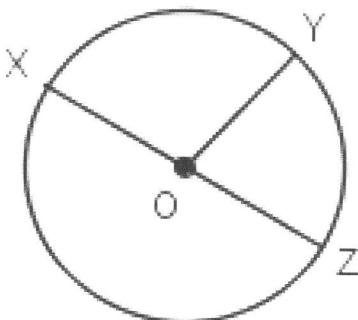

Concentric, arc, and semicircle

Concentric circles are circles that have the same center, but not the same length of radii. A bulls-eye target is an example of concentric circles. An arc is a portion of a circle. Specifically, an arc is the set of points between and including two points on a circle. An arc does not contain any points inside the circle. When a segment is drawn from the endpoints of an arc to the center of the circle, a sector is formed. A semicircle is an arc whose endpoints are the endpoints of the diameter of a circle. A semicircle is exactly half of a circle.

Chord, secant, tangent, and point of tangency

Chord: A line segment that has both endpoints on a circle. In the diagram below, $\overline{EB}$ is a chord.

Secant: A line that passes through a circle and contains a chord of that circle. In the diagram below, $\overleftrightarrow{EB}$ is a secant and contains chord $\overline{EB}$.

Tangent: A line in the same plane as a circle that touches the circle in exactly one point. While a line segment can be tangent to a circle as part of a line that is tangent, it is improper to say a tangent can be a line segment by itself that touches the circle in exactly one point. In the diagram below, $\overleftrightarrow{CD}$ is tangent to circle A. Notice that $\overline{FB}$ is not tangent to the circle. $\overline{FB}$ is a line segment that touches the circle in exactly one point, but if the segment were extended, it would touch the circle in a second point.

Point of Tangency: The point at which a tangent touches a circle. In the diagram below, point B is the point of tangency.

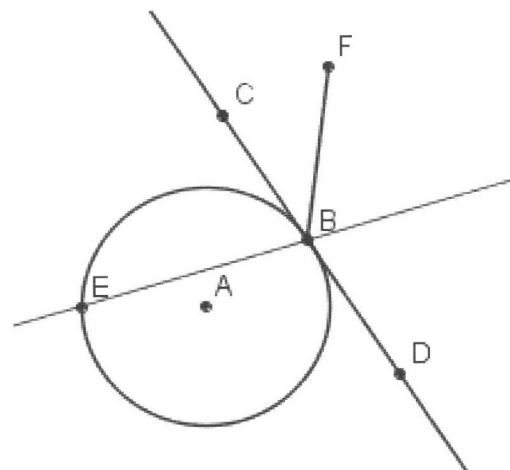

Central angles, major and minor arcs

Central Angle: An angle whose vertex is the center of a circle and whose legs intercept an arc of the circle.

Major Arc: An arc of a circle, having a measure of at least 180º. The measure of the major arc can be found by subtracting the measure of the central angle from 360º.

Minor Arc: An arc of a circle, having a measure less than 180º. The measure of the central angle is equal to the measure of the arc.

Semicircle: An arc having a measure of exactly 180º.

Inscribed angles and intercepted arcs

An inscribed angle is an angle whose vertex lies on a circle and whose legs contain chords of that circle. The portion of the circle intercepted by the legs of the angle is called the intercepted arc. The measure of the intercepted arc is exactly twice the measure of the inscribed angle. In the diagram below, angle ABC is an inscribed angle. arc $AC = 2(m\angle ABC)$

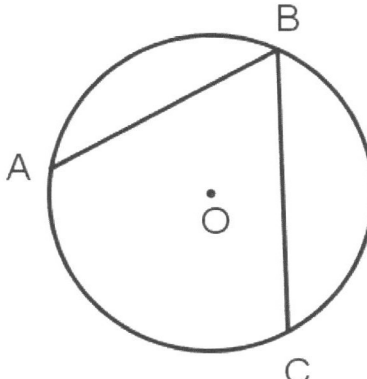

Any angle inscribed in a semicircle is a right angle. The intercepted arc is 180° making the inscribed angle half that, or 90°. In the diagram below, angle ABC is inscribed in semicircle ABC, making angle B equal to 90°.

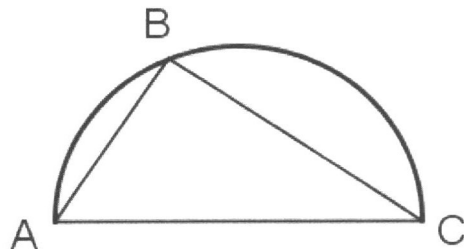

Secants

A secant is a line that intersects a curve in two points. Two secants may intersect inside the circle, on the circle, or outside the circle. When the two secants intersect on the circle, an inscribed angle is formed.

When two secants intersect inside a circle, the measure of each of two vertical angles is equal to half the sum of the two intercepted arcs. In the diagram below, $m\angle AEB = \frac{1}{2}(\text{arc}AB + \text{arc}CD)$ and $m\angle BEC = \frac{1}{2}(\text{arc}BC + \text{arc}AD)$.

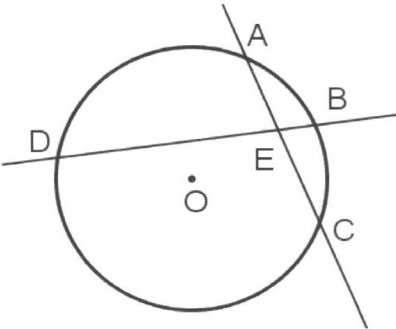

When two secants intersect outside a circle, the measure of the angle formed is equal to half the difference of the two arcs that lie between the two secants. In the diagram below, $m\angle E = \frac{1}{2}(\text{arc}AB - \text{arc}CD)$.

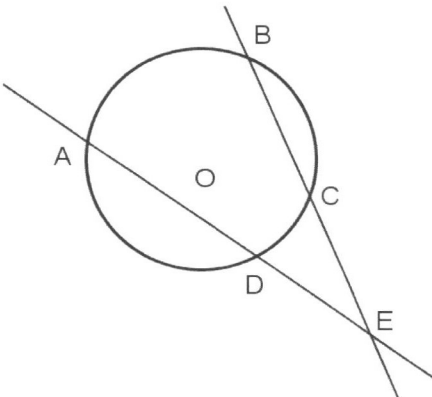

Arc length and sector

The arc length of a circle is the length of a portion of the circumference between two points on the circle. When the arc is defined by two radii forming a central angle, the formula for arc length is $s = r\theta$, where s is the arc length, r is the length of the radius, and θ is the measure of the central angle in radians.

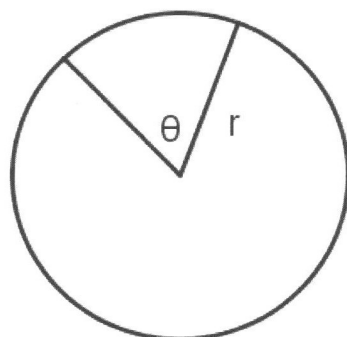

A sector is the portion of a circle formed by two radii and their intercepted arc. While the arc length is exclusively the points that are also on the circumference of the circle, the sector is the entire area bounded by the arc and the two radii.

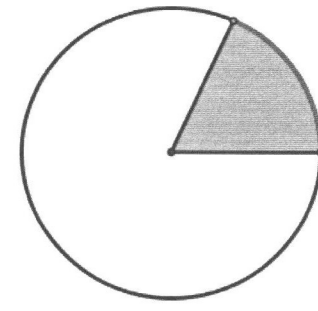

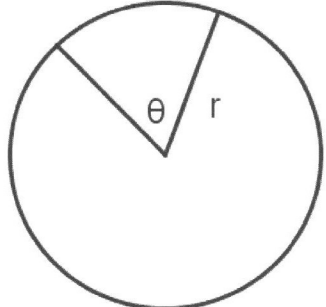

Inscribed and circumscribed

A circle is inscribed in a polygon if each of the sides of the polygon is tangent to the circle. A polygon is inscribed in a circle if each of the vertices of the polygon lies on the circle.
A circle is circumscribed about a polygon if each of the vertices of the polygon lies on the circle. A polygon is circumscribed about the circle if each of the sides of the polygon is tangent to the circle. If one figure is inscribed in another, then the other figure is circumscribed about the first figure.

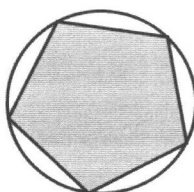

Circle circumscribed about a pentagon
Pentagon inscribed in a circle

Pythagorean Theorem

A right triangle has exactly one right angle. (If a figure has more than one right angle, it must have more than three sides, since the sum of the three angles of a triangle must equal 180º.) The side opposite the right angle is called the hypotenuse. The other two sides are called the legs. The Pythagorean Theorem states a unique relationship among the legs and hypotenuse of a right triangle: $a^2 + b^2 = c^2$, where a and b are the lengths of the legs of a right triangle, and c is the length of the hypotenuse. Note that this formula will only work with right triangles. Do not attempt to use it with
triangles that are not right triangles.

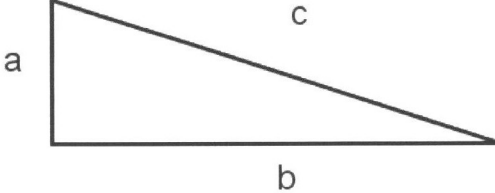

Area and perimeter (triangle)

The area of a triangle is given by the formula $A = \frac{1}{2}bh$, where A is the area of the triangle, b is the length of the base, and h is the height of the triangle perpendicular to the base. If you know the three sides of a scalene triangle, you can use the formula $A = \sqrt{s(s-a)(s-b)(s-c)}$, where A is the area, s is the semiperimeter $s = \frac{a+b+c}{2}$, and a, b, and c are the lengths of the three sides. The perimeter of a triangle is given by the formula $P = a + b + c$, where P is the perimeter, and a, b, and c are the lengths of the three sides. In this case, the triangle may be any shape. The variables a, b, and c are not exclusive to right triangles in the perimeter formula.

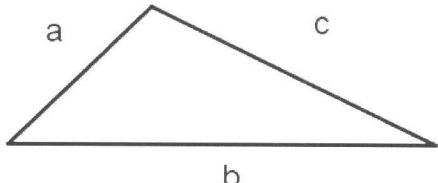

Area and perimeter (square)

The area of a square is found by using the formula $A = s^2$, where A is the area of the square, and s is the length of one side. The perimeter of a square is found by using the formula $P = 4s$, where P is the perimeter of the square, and s is the length of one side. Because all four sides are equal in a square, it is faster to multiply the length of one side by 4 than to add the same number four times. You could use the formulas for rectangles and get the same answer.

Area and perimeter (rectangle)

The area of a rectangle is found by the formula $A = lw$, where A is the area of the rectangle, l is the length (usually considered to be the longer side) and w is the width (usually considered to be the shorter side). The numbers for l and w are interchangeable. The perimeter of a rectangle is found by the formula $P = 2l + 2w$ or $P = 2(l + w)$, where P is the perimeter of the rectangle, l is the length, and w is the width. It may be easier to add the length and width first and then double the result, as in the second formula.

Area and perimeter (parallelogram)

The area of a parallelogram is found by the formula $A = bh$, where A is the area, b is the length of the base, and h is the height. Note that the base and height correspond to the length and width in a rectangle, so this formula would apply to rectangles as well. The perimeter of a parallelogram is found by the formula $P = 2a + 2b$ or $P = 2(a + b)$, where P is the perimeter, and a and b are the lengths of the two sides. Do not confuse the height of a parallelogram with the length of the second side. The two are only the same measure in the case of a rectangle.

Area and perimeter (trapezoid)

The area of a trapezoid is found by the formula $A = \frac{1}{2}h(b_1 + b_2)$, where A is the area, h is the height (segment joining and perpendicular to the parallel bases), and b_1 and b_2 are the two parallel sides (bases). Do not use one of the other two sides as the height unless that side is also perpendicular to the parallel bases. The perimeter of a trapezoid is found by the formula $P = a + b_1 + c + b_2$, where P is the perimeter, and a, b_1, c, and b_2 are the four sides of the trapezoid. Notice that the height does not appear in this formula.

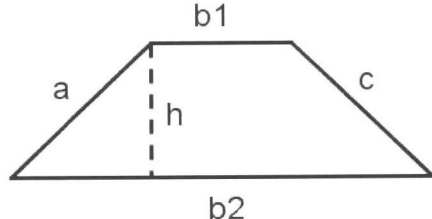

Area, circumference, and diameter (circle)

The area of a circle is found by the formula $A = \pi r^2$, where A is the area and r is the length of the radius. If the diameter of the circle is given, remember to divide it in half to get the length of the radius before proceeding. The circumference of a circle is found by the formula $C = 2\pi r$, where C is the circumference and r is the radius. Again, remember to convert the diameter if you are given that measure rather than the radius. To find the diameter when you are given the radius, double the length of the radius.

Area and arc length (sector of a circle)

The area of a sector of a circle is found by the formula $= \frac{\theta r^2}{2}$, where A is the area, θ is the measure of the central angle in radians, and r is the radius. To find the area when the central angle is in degrees, use the formula $= \frac{\theta \pi r^2}{360}$, where θ is the measure of the central angle in degrees and r is the radius. The arc length of a sector of a circle is found by the formula: arc length $= r\theta$, where r is the radius and θ is the measure of the central angle in radians. To find the arc length when the central angle is given in degrees, use the formula: arc length $= \frac{\theta(2\pi r)}{360}$, where θ is the measure of the central angle in degrees and r is the radius.

Lateral surface area and volume (sphere)

The lateral surface area is the area around the outside of the sphere. The lateral surface area is given by the formula $A = 4\pi r^2$, where r is the radius. The answer is generally given in terms of pi. A sphere does not have separate formulas for lateral surface area and total surface area as other solid figures do. Often, a problem may ask for the surface area of a sphere. Use the above formula for all problems involving the surface area of a sphere. The volume is given by the formula $V = \frac{4}{3}\pi r^3$, where r is the radius.

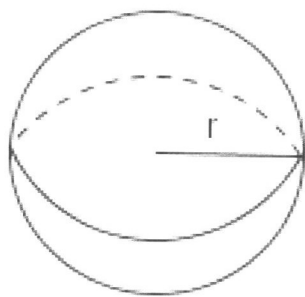

Volume and total surface area (right prism)

The volume of a right prism is found by the formula $V = Bh$, where V is the volume, B is the area of the base, and h is the height (perpendicular distance between the bases). The total surface area is the area of the entire outside surface of a solid. The total surface area of a right prism is found by the formula $TA = 2B + $ (sum of the areas of the sides), where TA is the total surface area and B is the area of one base. To use this formula, you must remember the formulas for the planar figures. If the problem asks for the lateral surface area (the area around the sides, not including the bases), use the formula $LA = $ sum of the areas of the sides. Again, you will need to remember the formulas for the various planar figures.

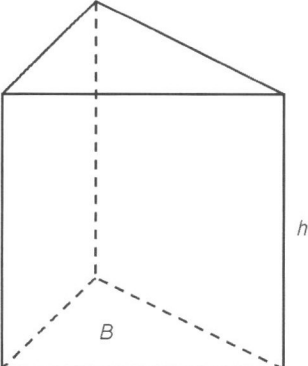

Volume and total surface area (rectangular prism)

The volume of a rectangular prism is found by the formula $V = lwh$, where V is the volume, l is the length, w is the width, and h is the height. Total surface area is the area of the entire outside surface of the solid. The total surface area of a rectangular prism is found by the formula $TA = 2lw + 2lh + 2wh$ or $TA = 2(lw + lh + wh)$, where TA is the total surface area, l is the length, w is the width, and h is the height. If the problem asks for lateral surface area, find the total area of the sides, but not the bases. Use the formula $LA = 2lh + 2wh$ or $LA = 2(lh + wh)$, where l is the length, w is the width, and h is the height.

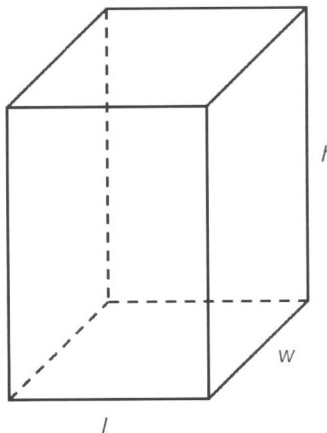

Volume and total surface area (cube)

The volume of a cube is found by the formula $V = s^3$, where V is the volume and s is the length of a side. This is the same as the formula for the volume of a rectangular prism, except the length, width, and height are all equal. The total surface area of a cube is found by the formula $TA = 6s^2$, where TA is the total surface area and s is the length of a side. You could use the formula for the total surface area of a rectangular prism, but if you remember that all six sides of a cube are equal, this formula is much faster.

Volume, lateral surface area, and total surface area (right circular cylinder)

The volume of a right circular cylinder is found by the formula $V = \pi r^2 h$, where V is the volume, r is the radius, and h is the height. The lateral surface area is the surface area without the bases. The formula is $LA = 2\pi rh$, where LA is the lateral surface area, r is the radius, and h is the height. Remember that if you unroll a cylinder, the piece around the middle is a rectangle. The length of a side of the rectangle is equal to the circumference of the circular base, or $2\pi r$. Substitute this formula for the length, and substitute the height of the cylinder for the width in the formula for the area of a rectangle. The total surface area of a cylinder is the lateral surface area plus the area of the two bases. The bases of a cylinder are circles, making the formula for the total surface area of a right circular cylinder $TA = 2\pi rh + 2\pi r^2$, where TA is the total area, r is the radius, and h is the height.

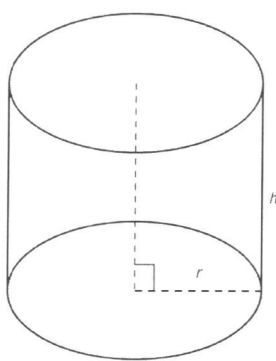

Pyramid volume

The volume of a pyramid is found by the formula $V = \frac{1}{3}Bh$, where V is the volume, B is the area of the base, and h is the height (segment from the vertex perpendicular to the base). Notice this formula is the same as $\frac{1}{3}$ the volume of a right prism. In this formula, B represents the *area* of the base, not the length or width of the base. The base can be different shapes, so you must remember the various formulas for the areas of plane figures. In determining the height of the pyramid, use the perpendicular distance from the vertex to the base, not the slant height of one of the sides.

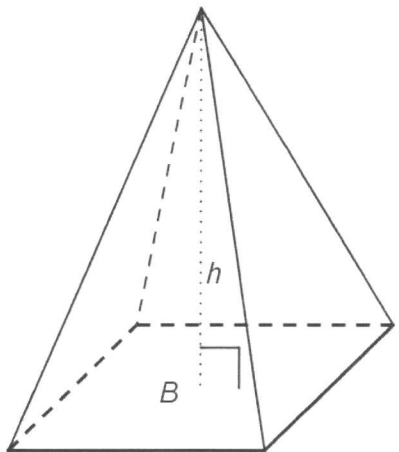

Volume, lateral surface area, and total surface area (right circular cone)

The volume of a right circular cone is found by the formula $V = \frac{1}{3}\pi r^2 h$, where V is the volume, r is the radius, and h is the height. Notice this is the same as $\frac{1}{3}$ the volume of a right circular cylinder. The lateral surface area of a right circular cone is found by the formula $LA = \pi r\sqrt{r^2 + h^2}$ or $LA = \pi rs$, where LA is the lateral surface area, r is the radius, h is the height, and s is the slant height (distance from the vertex to the edge of the circular base). $s = \sqrt{r^2 + h^2}$. The total surface area of a right circular cone is the same as the lateral surface area plus the area of the circular base. The formula for total surface area is $TA = \pi r\sqrt{r^2 + h^2} + \pi r^2$ or $TA = \pi rs + \pi r^2$, where TA is the total surface area, r is the radius, h is the height, and s is the slant height.

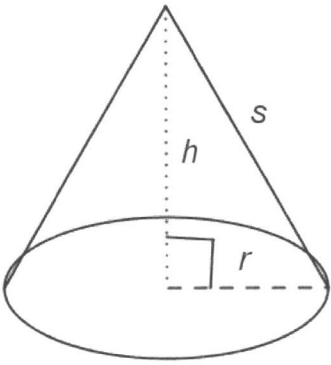

Area and perimeter (equilateral triangle)

The area of an equilateral triangle is found by the formula $A = \frac{\sqrt{3}}{4}s^2$, where A is the area and s is the length of a side. You could use the $30° - 60° - 90°$ ratios to find the height of the triangle and then use the standard triangle area formula, but this is faster. The perimeter of an equilateral triangle is found by the formula $P = 3s$, where P is the perimeter and s is the length of a side. If you know the length of the apothem (distance from the center of the triangle perpendicular to the base) and the length of a side, you can use the formula $A = \frac{1}{2}ap$, where a is the length of the apothem and p is the perimeter.

Area and perimeter (isosceles triangle)

The area of an isosceles triangle is found by the formula $= \frac{1}{2}b\sqrt{a^2 - \frac{b^2}{4}}$, where A is the area, b is the base (the unique side), and a is the length of one of the two congruent sides.
If you do not remember this formula, you can use the Pythagorean Theorem to find the height so you can use the standard formula for the area of a triangle. The perimeter of an isosceles triangle is found by the formula $A = 2a + b$, where P is the perimeter, a is the length of one of the congruent sides, and b is the base (the unique side).

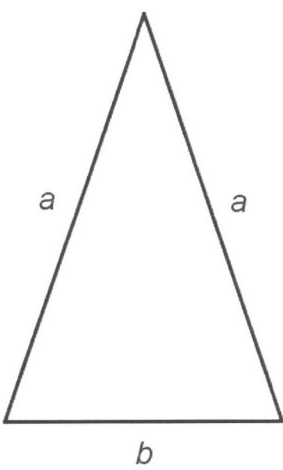

Preimage, image, translation, reflection, rotation, and dilation

Preimage: The original unchanged image in its original position.

Image: A unique set of points

Translation: A case where a geometric image is slid, usually horizontally or vertically. The resulting image is congruent to the original image, but has been moved in a straight line.

Reflection: A case where a geometric image is flipped across a line of reflection. The resulting image is congruent to and a mirror image of the original image.

Rotation: A case where a geometric image is rotated around the center of rotation to a new position. The new image is congruent to the original image, but has been turned to a new position.

Dilation: A case where a geometric image has been expanded or contracted by a scale factor. The resulting image is similar to the original image, but not congruent.

Projection of a point and segment on a line

The projection of a point on a line is the point at which a perpendicular line drawn from the given point to the given line intersects the line. This is also the shortest distance from the given point to the line. The projection of a segment on a line is a segment whose endpoints are the points formed when perpendicular lines are drawn from the endpoints of the given segment to the given line. This is similar to the length a diagonal line *appears* to be when viewed from above.

Ellipse that is taller than it is wide

An ellipse is the set of all points in a plane, whose total distance from two fixed points called the foci (singular: focus) is constant, and whose center is the midpoint between the foci. The standard equation of an ellipse that is taller than it is wide is $\frac{(y-k)^2}{a^2} + \frac{(x-h)^2}{b^2} = 1$, where a and b are coefficients. The center is the point (h, k) and the foci are the points $(h, k + c)$ and $(h, k - c)$, where $c^2 = a^2 - b^2$ and $a^2 > b^2$. The major axis has length $2a$, and the minor axis has length $2b$. Eccentricity (e) is a measure of how elongated an ellipse is, and is the ratio of the distance between the foci to the length of the major axis. Eccentricity will have a value between 0 and 1. The closer to 1 the eccentricity is, the closer the ellipse is to being a circle. The formula for eccentricity is $= \frac{c}{a}$.

Ellipse that is wider than it is tall.

The standard equation of an ellipse that is wider than it is tall is $\frac{(x-h)^2}{a^2} + \frac{(y-k)^2}{b^2} = 1$, where a and b are coefficients. The center is the point (h, k) and the foci are the points $(h + c, k)$ and $(h - c, k)$, where $c^2 = a^2 - b^2$ and $a^2 > b^2$. The major axis has length $2a$, and the minor axis has length $2b$. Eccentricity (e) is a measure of how elongated an ellipse is, and is the ratio of the distance between the foci to the length of the major axis. Eccentricity will have a value between 0 and 1. The closer to 1 the eccentricity is, the closer the ellipse is to being a circle. The formula for eccentricity is $= \frac{c}{a}$.

Geometric description of parabola

Parabola: The set of all points in a plane that are equidistant from a fixed line, called the directrix, and a fixed point not on the line, called the focus.

Axis: The line perpendicular to the directrix that passes through the focus.

For parabolas that open up or down, the standard equation is $(x - h)^2 = 4c(y - k)$, where h, c, and k are coefficients. If c is positive, the parabola opens up. If c is negative, the parabola opens down. The vertex is the point (h, k). The directrix is the line having the equation $y = -c + k$, and the focus is the point $(h, c + k)$.

For parabolas that open left or right, the standard equation is $(y - k)^2 = 4c(x - h)$, where k, c, and h are coefficients. If c is positive, the parabola opens to the right. If c is negative, the parabola opens to the left. The vertex is the point (h, k). The directrix is the line having the equation $x = -c + h$, and the focus is the point $(c + h, k)$.

Geometric description of horizontal hyperbola

A hyperbola is the set of all points in a plane, whose distance from two fixed points, called foci, has a constant difference. The standard equation of a horizontal hyperbola is $\frac{(x-h)^2}{a^2} - \frac{(y-k)^2}{b^2} = 1$, where a, b, h, and k are real numbers. The center is the point (h, k), the vertices are the points $(h + a, k)$ and $(h - a, k)$, and the foci are the points that every point on one of the parabolic curves is equidistant from and are found using the formulas $(h + c, k)$ and $(h - c, k)$, where $c^2 = a^2 + b^2$.

The asymptotes are two lines the graph of the hyperbola approaches but never reaches, and are given by the equations $y = \left(\frac{b}{a}\right)(x - h) + k$ and $y = -\left(\frac{b}{a}\right)(x - h) + k$.

Geometric description of vertical hyperbola

A vertical hyperbola is formed when a plane makes a vertical cut through two cones that are stacked vertex-to-vertex.

The standard equation of a vertical hyperbola is $\frac{(y-k)^2}{a^2} - \frac{(x-h)^2}{b^2} = 1$, where a, b, k, and h are real numbers. The center is the point (h, k), the vertices are the points $(h, k + a)$ and $(h, k - a)$, and the foci are the points that every point on one of the parabolic curves is equidistant from and are found using the formulas $(h, k + c)$ and $(h, k - c)$ $(h, k + c)$, where $c^2 = a^2 + b^2$. The asymptotes are two lines the graph of the hyperbola approaches but never reach, and are given by the equations $y = \left(\frac{a}{b}\right)(x - h) + k$ and $y = -\left(\frac{a}{b}\right)(x - h) + k$.

Trigonometric ratios of right triangles

$$\sin A = \frac{\text{opposite side}}{\text{hypotenuse}} = \frac{a}{c}$$
$$\cos A = \frac{\text{adjacent side}}{\text{hypotenuse}} = \frac{b}{c}$$
$$\tan A = \frac{\text{opposite side}}{\text{adjacent side}} = \frac{a}{b}$$
$$\csc A = \frac{\text{hypotenuse}}{\text{opposite side}} = \frac{c}{a}$$
$$\sec A = \frac{\text{hypotenuse}}{\text{adjacent side}} = \frac{c}{b}$$
$$\cot A = \frac{\text{adjacent side}}{\text{opposite side}} = \frac{b}{a}$$

In the diagram below, angle C is the right angle, and side c is the hypotenuse. Side a is the side adjacent to angle B and side b is the side adjacent to angle A. These formulas will work for any acute angle in a right triangle. They will NOT work for any triangle that is not a right triangle. Also, they will not work for the right angle in a right triangle, since there is not a distinct adjacent side to differentiate from the hypotenuse.

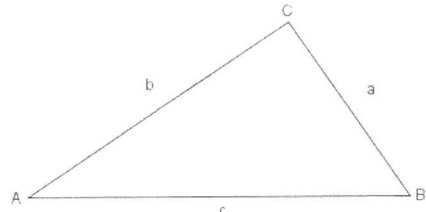

1 yard in feet and inches
1 yard = 3 feet
1 yard = 36 inches

1 mile in feet and yards
1 mile = 5280 feet
1 mile = 1760 yards

1 acre in square feet
1 acre = 43,560 square feet

1 quart in pints and cups
1 quart = 2 pints
1 quart = 4 cups

1 gallon in quarts, pints, and cups
1 gallon = 4 quarts
1 gallon = 8 pints
1 gallon = 16 cups
1 pound in ounces
1 pound = 16 ounces

Do not assume that because something weighs one pound that its volume is one pint. Ounces of weight are not equivalent to fluid ounces, which measure volume.

1 ton in pounds
1 ton = 2000 pounds

In the United States, the word "ton" by itself refers to a short ton or a net ton. Do not confuse this with a long ton (also called a gross ton) or a metric ton (also spelled *tonne*), which have different measurement equivalents.

Fluid measurements

1 cup in fluid ounces
1 cup = 8 fluid ounces

Note: This does NOT mean that one cup of something is the same as a half pound. Fluid ounces are measures of volume and have no correspondence with measures of weight.

1 pint in cups and fluid ounces
1 pint = 2 cups
1 pint = 16 ounces

Again, the phrase, "A pint's a pound the world round," does not apply. A pint of something does not necessarily weigh one pound, since one fluid ounce is not the same as one ounce in weight. The expression is valid only for helping you remember the number 16, since most people can remember there are 16 ounces in a pound.

Metric measurements

<u>1 liter in milliliters and cubic centimeters</u>
1 liter = 1000 milliliters
1 liter = 1000 cubic centimeters

Do not confuse *cubic centimeters* with *centiliters*. 1 liter = 1000 cubic centi*meters*, but 1 liter = 100 centi*liters*.
<u>1 meter in millimeters and centimeters</u>
1 meter = 1000 millimeters
1 meter = 100 centimeters

<u>1 gram in milligrams</u>
1 gram = 1000 milligrams

<u>1 kilogram in grams</u>
1 kilogram = 1000 grams

Kilo, centi, and milli

Kilo-: one thousand (1 *kilo*gram is one thousand grams.)
Centi-: one hundredth (1 *centi*meter is one hundredth of a meter.)
Milli-: one thousandth (1 *milli*liter is one thousandth of a liter.)

Converting unit measurements

When going from a larger unit to a smaller unit, multiply the numerical value of the known amount by the equivalent amount. When going from a smaller unit to a larger unit, divide the numerical value of the known amount by the equivalent amount. Also, you can set up conversion fractions where one fraction is the conversion fact, with the unit of the unknown amount in the numerator and the unit of the known value in the denominator. The second fraction has the known value from the problem in the numerator, and the unknown in the denominator. Multiply the two fractions to get the converted measurement.

Precision and accuracy

Precision: How reliable and repeatable a measurement is. The more consistent the data is with repeated testing, the more precise it is. For example, hitting a target consistently in the same spot, which may or may not be the center of the target, is precision.

Accuracy: How close the data is to the correct data. For example, hitting a target consistently in the center area of the target, whether or not the hits are all in the same spot, is accuracy.

Note that it is possible for data to be precise without being accurate. If a scale is off balance, the data will be precise, but will not be accurate. For data to have precision and accuracy, it must be repeatable and correct.

Approximate and maximum possible error

Approximate Error: The amount of error in a physical measurement. Approximate error is often reported as the measurement, followed by the ± symbol and the amount of the approximate error.

Maximum Possible Error: Half the magnitude of the smallest unit used in the measurement. For example, if the unit of measurement is 1 centimeter, the maximum possible error is $\frac{1}{2}$ cm, written as ±0.5 cm following the measurement. It is important to apply significant figures in reporting maximum possible error. Do not make the answer appear more accurate than the least accurate of your measurements.

Data Analysis, Statistics, and Probability

Charts and tables

Charts and tables are ways of organizing information in separate rows and columns that are each labeled to identify and explain the data contained in them. Some charts and tables are organized horizontally, with row lengths giving the details about the labeled information. Other charts and tables are organized vertically, with column heights giving the details about the labeled information.

Frequency tables show how frequently each unique value appears in the set. A relative frequency table is one that shows the proportions of each unique value compared to the entire set. Relative frequencies are given as percents; however, the total percent for a relative frequency table will not necessarily equal 100 percent due to rounding.

Pictograph

A pictograph is a graph, generally in the horizontal orientation, that uses pictures or symbols to represent the data. Each pictograph must have a key that defines the picture or symbol and gives the quantity each picture or symbol represents. Pictures or symbols on a pictograph are not always shown as whole elements. In this case, the fraction of the picture or symbol shown represents the same fraction of the quantity a whole picture or symbol stands for. For example, a row with $3\frac{1}{2}$ ears of corn, where each ear of corn represents 100   stalks of corn in a field, would equal $3\frac{1}{2} \cdot 100 = 350$ stalks of corn in the field.

Circle graphs

Circle graphs, also known as pie charts, provide a visual depiction of the relationship of each type of data compared to the whole set of data. The circle graph is divided into sections by drawing radii to create central angles whose percentage of the circle is equal to the individual data's percentage of the whole set. Each 1% of data is equal to $3.6º$ in the circle graph. Therefore, data represented by a $90º$ section of the circle graph makes up 25% of the whole. When complete, a circle graph often looks like a pie cut into uneven wedges.

Line graph

Line graphs have one or more lines of varying styles (solid or broken) to show the different values for a set of data. The individual data are represented as ordered pairs, much like on a Cartesian plane. In this case, the x- and y-axes are defined in terms of their units, such as dollars or time. The individual plotted points are joined by line segments to show whether the value of the data is increasing (line slanting upward), decreasing (line slanting downward) or staying the same (horizontal line). Multiple sets of data can be graphed on the same line graph to give an easy visual comparison. An example of this would be graphing achievement test scores for different groups of students over the same time period to see which group had the greatest increase or decrease in performance from year-to-year.

Line plot

A line plot, also known as a dot plot, has plotted points that are NOT connected by line segments. In this graph, the horizontal axis lists the different possible values for the data, and the vertical axis lists the number of times the individual value occurs. A single dot is graphed for each value to show the number of times it occurs. This graph is more closely related to a bar graph than a line graph. Do not connect the dots in a line plot or it will misrepresent the data.

Stem and leaf plot

A stem and leaf plot is useful for depicting groups of data that fall into a range of values. Each piece of data is separated into two parts: the first, or left, part is called the stem; the second, or right, part is called the leaf. Each stem is listed in a column from smallest to largest. Each leaf that has the common stem is listed in that stem's row from smallest to largest. For example, in a set of two-digit numbers, the digit in the tens place is the stem, and the digit in the ones place is the leaf. With a stem and leaf plot, you can easily see which subset of numbers (10s, 20s, 30s, etc.) is the largest. This information is also readily available by looking at a histogram, but a stem and leaf plot also allows you to look closer and see exactly which values fall in that range.

Bar graph

A bar graph is one of the few graphs that can be drawn correctly in two different configurations – both horizontally and vertically. A bar graph is similar to a line plot in the way the data is organized on the graph. Both axes must have their categories defined for the graph to be useful. Rather than placing a single dot to mark the point of the data's value, a bar, or thick line, is drawn from zero to the exact value of the data, whether it is a number, percentage, or other numerical value. Longer bar lengths correspond to greater data values. To read a bar graph, read the labels for the axes to determine the units being reported. Then look where the bars end in relation to the scale given on the corresponding axis and read the number.

Histogram

At first glance, a histogram looks like a vertical bar graph. The difference is that a bar graph has a separate bar for each piece of data and a histogram has one continuous bar for each *range* of data. For example, a histogram may have one bar for the range 0–9, one bar for 10–19, etc. While a bar graph has numerical values on one axis, a histogram has numerical values on both axes. Each range is of equal size, and they are ordered left to right from lowest to highest. The height of each column on a histogram represents the number of data values within that range. Like a stem and leaf plot, a histogram makes it easy to glance at the graph and quickly determine which range has the greatest quantity of values.

Scatter plot

Bivariate data is simply data from two different variables. (The prefix *bi-* means *two*.) In a scatter plot, each value in the set of data is plotted on a grid similar to a Cartesian plane, where each axis represents one of the two variables. By looking at the pattern formed by the points on the grid, you can easily determine whether or not there is a relationship between the two variables, and what that relationship is, if it exists. The variables may be directly proportionate, inversely proportionate, or show no proportion at all. It will also be easy to determine if the data is linear, and if so, to find an equation to relate the two variables.

Central tendency

The measure of central tendency is a statistical value that gives a general tendency for the center of a group of data. There are several different ways of describing the measure of central tendency. Each one has a unique way it is calculated, and each one gives a slightly different perspective on the data set. Whenever you give a measure of central tendency, always make sure the units are the same. If the data has different units, such as hours, minutes, and seconds, convert all the data to the same unit, and use the same unit in the measure of central tendency. If no units are given in the data, do not give units for the measure of central tendency.

Statistical mean

The statistical mean of a group of data is the same as the arithmetic average of that group. To find the mean of a set of data, first convert each value to the same units, if necessary. Then find the sum of all the values, and count the total number of data values, making sure you take into consideration each individual value. If a value appears more than once, count it more than once. Divide the sum of the values by the total number of values and apply the units, if any. Note that the mean does not have to be one of the data values in the set, and may not divide evenly.

$$\text{mean} = \frac{\text{sum of the data values}}{\text{quantity of data values}}$$

Central tendency

While the mean is relatively easy to calculate and averages are understood by most people, the mean can be very misleading if used as the sole measure of central tendency. If the data set has outliers (data values that are unusually high or unusually low compared to the rest of the data values), the mean can be very distorted, especially if the data set has a small number of values. If unusually high values are countered with unusually low values, the mean is not affected as much. For example, if five of the twenty students in a class get a 100 on a test, but the other 15 students have an average of 60 on the same test, the class average would appear as 70. Whenever the mean is skewed by outliers, it is always a good idea to include the median as an alternate measure of central tendency. The big disadvantage of using the median as a measure of central tendency is that is relies solely on a value's relative size as compared to the other values in the set. When the individual values in a set of data are evenly dispersed, the median can be an accurate tool. However, if there is a group of rather large values or a group of rather small values that are not offset by a different group of values, the information that can be inferred from the median may not be accurate. The main disadvantage of the mode is that the values of the other data in the set have no bearing on the mode. The mode may be the largest value, the smallest value, or a value anywhere in between in the set. The mode only tells which value or values, if any, occurred the most number of times. It does not give any suggestions about the remaining values in the set.

Statistical median

The statistical median value is the value in the middle of the set of data. To find the median, list all data values in order from smallest to largest or from largest to smallest. Any value that is repeated in the set must be listed the same number of times. If there are an odd number of data values, the median is the value in the middle of the list. If there is an even number of data values, the median is the arithmetic mean of the two middle values.

Statistical mode

The statistical mode is the data value that occurs the most number of times in the data set. It is possible to have exactly one mode, more than one mode, or no mode. To find the mode of a set of data, arrange the data like you do to find the median (all values in order, listing all multiples of data values). Count the number of times each value appears in the data set. If all values appear an equal number of times, there is no mode. If one value appears more than any other value, that value is the mode. If two or more values appear the same number of times, but there are other values that appear fewer times and no values that appear more times, all of those values are the modes.

Measure of dispersion

The measure of dispersion is a single value that helps to "interpret" the measure of central tendency by providing more information about how the data values in the set are distributed about the measure of central tendency. The measure of dispersion helps to eliminate or reduce the disadvantages of using the mean, median, or mode as a single measure of central tendency, and give a more accurate picture of the data set as a whole. To have a measure of dispersion, you must know or calculate the range, standard deviation, or variance of the data set.

Range

The range of a set of data is the difference between the greatest and lowest values of the data in the set. To calculate the range, you must first make sure the units for all data values are the same, and then identify the highest and lowest values. Using the values with the same units, use the formula range = highest value – lowest value. If there are multiple data values that are equal for the highest or lowest, just use one of the values in the formula. Write the answer with the same units as the data values you used to do the calculations.

Standard deviation

Standard deviation is a measure of dispersion that compares all the data values in the set to the mean of the set to give a more accurate picture. To find the standard deviation of a population, use the formula $= \sqrt{\frac{\sum_{i=1}^{n}(x_i - \bar{x})^2}{n}}$, where σ is the standard deviation of a population, x represents the individual values in the data set, $\bar{x}$ is the mean of the data values in the set, and n is the number of data values in the set. The higher the value of the standard deviation is, the greater the variance of the data values from the mean.

Variance

The variance of a population, or just variance, is the square of the standard deviation of that population. While the mean of a set of data gives the average of the set and gives information about where a specific data value lies in relation to the average, the variance of the population gives information about the degree to which the data values are spread out and tell you how close an individual value is to the average compared to the other values. The units associated with variance are the same as the units of the data values. If there are different units used among the data values, you must first convert all the values to the same unit.

Percentiles and quartiles

Percentiles and quartiles are other methods of describing data within a set. Percentiles tell what percentage of the data in the set fall below a specific point. For example, achievement test scores are often given in percentiles. A score at the 80th percentile is one which is equal to or higher than 80 percent of the scores in the set. In other words, 80 percent of the scores were lower than that score. Quartiles are percentile groups that make up quarter sections of the data set. The first quartile is the 25th percentile. The second quartile is the 50th percentile. This is also the median of the data set. The third quartile is the 75th percentile.

Five number summary

The 5-number summary of a set of data gives a very informative picture of the set. The five numbers in the summary include the minimum value, maximum value, and the three quartiles. This information gives the reader the range and median of the set, as well as an indication of how the data is spread about the median. A box-and-whiskers plot is a graphical representation of the 5-number summary. To draw a box-and-whiskers plot, plot the points of the 5-number summary on a number line. Draw a box whose ends are through the points for the first and third quartiles. Draw a vertical line in the box through the median to divide the box in half. Draw a line segment from the first quartile point to the minimum value, and from the third quartile point to the maximum value.

Skewness

Skewness is a way to describe the symmetry or asymmetry of the distribution of values in a data set. If the distribution of values is symmetrical, there is no skew. In general the closer the mean of a data set is to the median of the data set, the less skew there is. Generally, if the mean is to the right of the median, the data set is positively skewed, or right-skewed, and if the mean is to the left of the median, the data set is negatively skewed, or left-skewed. However, this rule of thumb is not infallible. When the data values are graphed on a curve, a set with no skew will be a perfect bell curve. To estimate skew, use the formula $skew = \frac{\sqrt{n(n-1)}}{n-2}\left(\frac{\frac{1}{n}\sum_{i=1}^{n}(x_i-\bar{x})^3}{\left(\frac{1}{n}\sum_{i=1}^{n}(x_i-\bar{x})^2\right)^{\frac{3}{2}}}\right)$ where n is the number of values is the set, x_i is the ith value in the set, and $\bar{x}$ is the mean of the set.

Simple regression

In statistics, simple regression is using an equation to represent a relation between independent and dependent variables in the data. The independent variable is also referred to as the explanatory variable or the predictor, and is generally represented by the variable x in the equation. The dependent variable, usually represented by the variable y, is also referred to as the response variable. The equation may be any type of function – linear, quadratic, exponential, etc. The best way to handle this task is to use the regression feature of your graphing calculator. This will easily give you the curve of best fit and provide you with the coefficients and other information you need to derive an equation.

Scatter plots

Scatter plots are useful in determining the type of function represented by the data and finding the simple regression. Linear scatter plots may be positive or negative. Nonlinear scatter plots are generally exponential or quadratic. You must be able to identify the following types of scatter plots on the test:

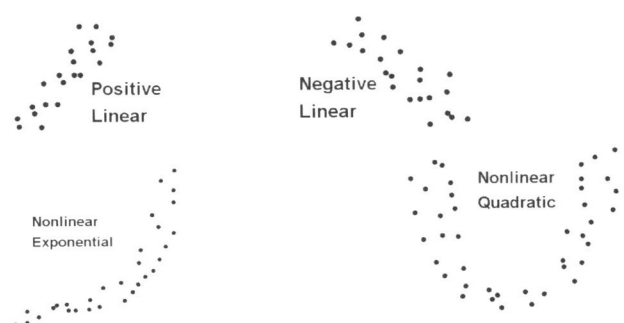

Line of best fit, regression coefficients, residuals, and least-squares regression line

In a scatter plot, the line of best fit is the line that best shows the trends of the data. The line of best fit is given by the equation $\hat{y} = ax + b$, where a and b are the regression coefficients. The regression coefficient a is also the slope of the line of best fit, and b is also the y-coordinate of the point at which the line of best fit crosses the x-axis. Not every point on the scatter plot will be on the line of best fit. The differences between the y-values of the points in the scatter plot and the corresponding y-values according to the equation of the line of best fit are the residuals. The line of best fit is also called the least-squares regression line because it is also the line that has the lowest sum of the squares of the residuals.

Correlation coefficient

The correlation coefficient is a numerical value that indicates how strong the relationship is between the two variables of a linear regression equation. A correlation coefficient of –1 is a perfect negative correlation. A correlation coefficient of +1 is a perfect positive correlation. Correlation coefficients close to –1 or +1 are very strong correlations. A correlation coefficient equal to zero indicates there is no correlation between the two variables. This test is a good indicator of whether or not the equation for the line of best fit is accurate. The formula for the correlation coefficient is $r = \dfrac{\sum_{i=1}^{n}(x_i - \bar{x})(y_i - \bar{y})}{\sqrt{\sum_{i=1}^{n}(x_i - \bar{x})^2}\sqrt{\sum_{i=1}^{n}(y_i - \bar{y})^2}}$ where r is the correlation coefficient, n is the number of data values in the set, (x_i, y_i) is a point in the set, and $\bar{x}$ and $\bar{y}$ are the means.

68-95-99.7 rule

The 69–95–99.7 rule describes how a normal distribution of data should appear when compared to the mean. This is also a description of a normal bell curve. According to this rule, 68 percent of the data values in a normally distributed set should fall within one standard deviation of the mean (34 percent above and 34 percent below the mean), 95 percent of the data values should fall within two standard deviations of the mean (47.5 percent above and 47.5 percent below the mean), and 99.7 percent of the data values should fall within three standard deviations of the mean, again, equally distributed on either side of the mean. This means that only 0.3 percent of all data values should fall more than three standard deviations from the mean.

Z-scores

A z-score is an indication of how many standard deviations a given value falls from the mean. To calculate a z-score, use the formula $= \frac{x-\mu}{\sigma}$, where x is the data value, μ is the mean of the data set, and σ is the standard deviation of the population. If the z-score is positive, the data value lies above the mean. If the z-score is negative, the data value falls below the mean. These scores are useful in interpreting data such as standardized test scores, where every piece of data in the set has been counted, rather than just a small random sample. In cases where standard deviations are calculated from a random sample of the set, the z-scores will not be as accurate.

Population and parameter

In statistics, the population is the entire set of data to be included in the study, rather than just a random sample. For example, a study to determine how well students in the area schools perform on a standardized test would have a population of all the students enrolled in those schools, although a study may include a random sample of students from each school. A parameter is a numerical value that gives information about the population, such as the mean, median, mode, or standard deviation. Remember that the symbol for the mean of a population is μ and the symbol for the standard deviation of a population is σ.

Sample and statistic

A sample is a portion of the entire population. A statistic is a numerical value that gives information about the sample, such as mean, median, mode, or standard deviation. Keep in mind that the symbols for mean and standard deviation are different when they are referring to a sample rather than the entire population. For a sample, the symbol for mean is $\bar{x}$ and the symbol for standard deviation is s. The mean and standard deviation of a sample may or may not be accurate when compared to the mean and standard deviation of the population. However, if the sample is random and large enough, an accurate enough value can be obtained. Samples are generally used when the population is too large to justify including every element.

Inferential statistics and sampling distribution

Inferential statistics is the branch of statistics that uses samples to make predictions about an entire population. This type of statistics is often seen in political polls, where a sample of the population is questioned about a particular topic or politician to gain an understanding about the attitudes of the entire population of the country. Often, exit polls are conducted on election days using this method. Inferential statistics can have a large margin of error if you do not have a valid sample. The statistical values calculated from the various samples of the same size make up the sampling distribution. For example, if several samples of identical size are randomly selected from a large population and then the mean of each sample is calculated, the values of the means would be a sampling distribution.

Sampling distribution of the mean

Represented by the symbol $\bar{x}$, the sampling distribution of the mean has three important characteristics. First, the mean of the sampling distribution of $\bar{x}$ equals the mean of the sampled population. The sampled population includes all of the samples in the distribution combined. Second, assuming the standard deviation is positive, the standard deviation of the sampling distribution of $\bar{x}$ equals the standard deviation of the sampled population divided by the square root of the sample size. Finally, as the sample size gets larger and closer to the actual population number, the sampling distribution of $\bar{x}$ gets closer to a normal distribution.

Central Limit Theorem

According to the central limit theorem, no matter what the original distribution of a sample is, the distribution of the means tends to get closer and closer to a normal distribution as the sample size gets larger and larger. In other words, if you have a large population that does not represent a normal distribution, and then take random samples of two elements from that population, the means of the groups of two will form a more normal distribution. Increase the sample size to three elements for each calculation of the mean, and the distribution gets more normal than with a sample size of two. This pattern will continue to form a more normal distribution of the means as the sample size increases.

Survey studies

A survey study is a method of gathering information from a small group in an attempt to gain enough information to make accurate general assumptions about the population. Once a survey study is completed, the results are then put into a summary report. Survey studies are generally in the format of surveys, interviews, or questionnaires as part of an effort to find opinions of a particular group or to find facts about a group. It is important to note that the findings from a survey study are only as accurate as the sample chosen from the population. Inappropriate samples, such as ones that are too small for the population size, or ones that are not chosen purely at random, will not yield accurate results for the population. Generalizations concerning the population cannot be made in these cases.

Correlational studies

Correlational studies seek to determine how much one variable is affected by changes in a second variable. For example, correlational studies may look for a relationship between the amount of time a student spends studying for a test and the grade that student earned on the test, between student scores on college admissions tests and student grades in college, or between employment status and degrees earned. It is important to note that correlational studies cannot show a cause and effect, but rather can show only that two variables are or are not potentially related.

Experimental studies

Experimental studies take correlational studies one step farther, in that they attempt to prove or disprove a cause-and-effect relationship. These studies are performed by conducting a series of experiments to test the hypothesis. For a study to be scientifically accurate, it must have both an experimental group that receives the specified treatment and a control group that does not get the treatment. This is the type of study pharmaceutical companies do as part of drug trials for new medications. Experimental studies are only valid when proper scientific method has been followed. In other words, the experiment must be well-planned and executed without bias in the testing process. All subjects must be selected at random, and the process of determining which subject is in which of the two groups must also be completely random.

Observational studies

Observational studies are the opposite of experimental studies. In observational studies, the tester cannot change or in any way control all of the variables in the test. For example, a study to determine which gender does better in math classes in school is strictly observational. You cannot change a person's gender, and you cannot change the subject being studied. The big downfall of the observational study is that you have no way of proving a cause-and-effect relationship because you cannot control outside influences. Events outside of school can influence a student's performance in school, and observational studies would not take that into consideration

Type of samples

A sample is a piece of the entire population that is selected for a particular study in an effort to gain knowledge or information about the entire population. For most studies, a random sample is necessary to produce valid results. Random samples should not have any particular influence to cause someone to select that element over another. The goal is for the random sample to be a representative sample, or a sample whose characteristics give an accurate picture of the characteristics of the entire population. To accomplish this, you must make sure you have a proper sample size, or an appropriate number of elements in the sample.

Bias and extraneous variables

In statistical studies, try to avoid bias at all costs. Bias is an error that causes the study to favor one set of results over another. For example, if a survey to determine how the country views the president's job performance only speaks to registered voters in the president's party, the results will be skewed because a disproportionately large number of responders would tend to show approval, while a disproportionately large number of people in the opposite party would tend to express disapproval. Extraneous variables are outside influences that can affect the outcome of a study. They are not always avoidable, but could trigger bias in the result.

Frequency curves

The five general shapes of frequency curves are symmetrical, U-shaped, skewed, J-shaped, and multimodal. Symmetrical curves are also known as bell curves or normal curves. Values equidistant from the median have equal frequencies. U-shaped curves have two maxima – one at each end. Skewed curves have the maximum point off-center. Curves that are negative skewed, or left skewed, have the maximum on the right side of the graph so there is longer tail and lower slope on the left side. The opposite is true for curves that are positive skewed, or right skewed. J-shaped curves have a maximum at one end and a minimum at the other end. Multimodal curves have multiple maxima. If the curve has exactly two maxima, it is called a bimodal curve.

Sample space and outcome

The total number of all possible results of a random test or experiment is called a sample space, or sometimes a universal sample space. The sample space, represented by one of the variables S, Ω, or U (for universal sample space) has individual elements called outcomes. Other terms for outcome that may be used interchangeably include elementary outcome, simple event, or sample point. The number of outcomes in a given sample space could be infinite or finite, and some tests may yield multiple unique sample sets. For example, tests conducted by drawing playing cards from a standard deck would have one sample space of the card values, another sample space of the card suits, and a third sample space of suit-denomination combinations. Note that on this test, all sample spaces are considered finite.

Event

An event, represented by the variable E, is a portion of a sample space. It may be one outcome or a group of outcomes from the same sample space. If an event occurs, then the test or experiment will generate an outcome that satisfies the requirement of that event. For example, given a standard deck of 52 playing cards as the sample space, and defining the event as the collection of face cards, then the event will occur if the card drawn is a J, Q, or K. If any other card is drawn, the event is said to have not occurred.

Probability measure and probability

For every sample space, each possible outcome has a specific likelihood, or probability, that it will occur. The probability measure, also called the distribution, is a function that assigns a real number probability, from zero to one, to each outcome. For a probability measure to be accurate, every outcome must have a real number probability measure that is greater than or equal to zero and less than or equal to one. Also, the probability measure of the sample space must equal one, and the probability measure of the union of multiple outcomes must equal the sum of the individual probability measures.

Probability of an event

Probabilities of events are expressed as real numbers from zero to one. They give a numerical value to the chance that a particular event will occur. The probability of an event occurring is the sum of the probabilities of the individual elements of that event. For example, in a standard deck of 52 playing cards as the sample space and the collection of face cards as the event, the probability of drawing a specific face card is $\frac{1}{52} = 0.019$, but the probability of drawing any one of the twelve face cards is $12(0.019) = 0.228$. Note that rounding of numbers can generate different results. If you multiplied 12 by the fraction $\frac{1}{52}$ before converting to a decimal, you would get the answer $\frac{12}{52} = 0.231$. If, when taking the exam, you get an answer that is not a choice, try the other method.

Likelihood of outcomes

The likelihood of a outcome occurring, or the probability of an outcome occurring, is given by the formula $P(E) = \frac{\text{Number of possible events}}{\text{Total number of possible outcomes in the sample space}}$ where $P(E)$ is the probability of an event E occurring, and each outcome is just as likely to occur as any other outcome. If each outcome has the same probability of occurring as every other possible outcome, the outcomes are said to be equally likely to occur. The total number of possible outcomes in the event must be less than or equal to the total number of possible outcomes in the sample space. If the two are equal, then the event is certain to occur and the probability is 1. If the number of outcomes that satisfy the event is zero, then the event is impossible and the probability is 0.

Simple sample space outcome

For a simple sample space, possible outcomes may be determined by using a tree diagram or an organized chart. In either case, you can easily draw or list out the possible outcomes. For example, to determine all the possible ways three objects can be ordered, you can draw a tree diagram:

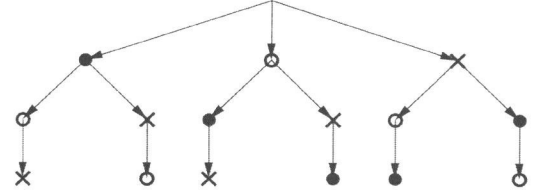

You can also make a chart to list all the possibilities:

First object	Second object	Third object
●	X	O
●	O	X
O	●	X
O	X	●
X	●	O
X	O	●

Either way, you can easily see there are six possible ways the three objects can be ordered.

Less straightforward sample space outcome

When the test on a given sample space does not lend itself to a tree diagram or organized chart, you can use other methods, such as the multiplication principle, permutations, or combinations, to determine the total number of possible outcomes. Each of these may also be used for simple sample spaces as well, although tree diagrams or charts may be faster in those situations. The multiplication rule states that the probability of two outcomes occurring simultaneously is the product of their individual probabilities. Permutations are outcomes in which each element must occur in a specific order. Combinations are outcomes in which the elements may be arranged in any order.

Permutations and combinations

A permutation is an arrangement of a specific number of a set of objects in a specific order. No unique combination of elements from the set may be rearranged and used a second time. To find the number of possible outcomes from a group of items, use the formula $_nP_r = \frac{n!}{(n-r)!}$, where n is the total number of items in the set, r is the number of distinct objects taken together from the set, and $_nP_r$ is the number of permutations of those objects taken together. Combinations are similar to permutations, except there are no restrictions regarding the order of the elements. While ABC is considered a different permutation than BCA, ABC and BCA are considered the same combination. To calculate the number of unique combinations possible from a given set, use the formula $_nC_r = \binom{n}{r} = \frac{n!}{r!(n-r)!}$, where n is the total number of items in the set, r is the number of distinct objects taken together from the set, and $_nC_r$ is the number of combinations of those objects.

Note that a combination lock should be called a permutation lock because the order of the numbers is important when unlocking the lock.

Random variable and probability distribution

In probability, the random variable is not really a variable, but rather a function that generates a variable with a real number value that is determined purely by chance and assigned to each possible outcome of a sample space. Once the values of the random variable have been determined, a probability distribution is set up. The probability distribution can be a chart, graph, formula, or table that gives the individual probabilities of all the values of the random variable. It described the range of possibilities for the random variable, and gives the probability of the random variable falling somewhere within that range.

Event complement

The complement of an event is the opposite of the probability of an event occurring. Represented by the symbol $\bar{A}$, it is the probability that event A does not happen. When you know the probability of event A occurring, you can use the formula $(\bar{A}) = 1 - P(A)$, where $P(\bar{A})$ is the probability of event A not occurring, and $P(A)$ is the probability of event A occurring, to find the complement of the event. Compound events are events that combine two or more events into a single desired outcome. (Think of it like compound words combining two words into a single new word.) For compound events, the notation $P(A \text{ or } B)$ means the probability that event A occurs, or event B occurs, or events A and B occur at the same time during the same test of an experiment.

Addition Rule for probability

The addition rule for probability is used for finding the probability of a compound event. Use the formula $P(A \text{ or } B) = P(A) + P(B) - P(A \text{ and } B \text{ occurring at the same time})$, where $P(A)$ is the probability of the event A occurring exclusively, $P(B)$ is the probability of event B occurring exclusively, and $P(A \text{ and } B \text{ occurring at the same time})$ is the probability of both events occurring to find the probability of a compound event. The probability of both events occurring at the same time must be subtracted to eliminate any overlap in the first two probabilities.

Multiplication Rule for probability

The multiplication rule can be used to find the probability of two independent events occurring using the formula $P(A \text{ and } B) = P(A)\,P(B)$, where $P(A \text{ and } B)$ is the probability of two independent events occurring, $P(A)$ is the probability of the first event occurring, and $P(B)$ is the probability of the second event occurring. The multiplication rule can also be used to find the probability of two dependent events occurring using the formula $P(A \text{ and } B) = P(A) \cdot P(B|A)$, where $P(A \text{ and } B)$ is the probability of two dependent events occurring, $P(A)$ is the probability of the first event occurring, and $P(B|A)$ is the probability of the second event occurring after the first event has already occurred. Before using the multiplication rule, you MUST first determine whether the two events are dependent or independent.

Mutually exclusive, independent, and dependent

If two events have no outcomes in common, they are said to be mutually exclusive. For example, in a standard deck of 52 playing cards, the event of all card suits is mutually exclusive to the event of all card values. If two events have no bearing on each other so that one event occurring has no influence on the probability of another event occurring, the two events are said to be independent. For example, rolling a standard six-sided die multiple times does not change that probability that a particular number will be rolled from one roll to the next. If the outcome of one event does affect the probability of the second event, the two events are said to be dependent. For example, if cards are drawn from a deck, the probability of drawing an ace after an ace has been drawn is different than the probability of drawing an ace if no ace (or no other card, for that matter) has been drawn.

Conditional probability

Conditional probability is the probability of a dependent event occurring once the original event has already occurred. Given event A and dependent event B, the probability of event B occurring when event A has already occurred is represented by the notation $P(A|B)$. To find the probability of event B occurring, take into account the fact that event A has already occurred and adjust the total number of possible outcomes. For example, suppose you have ten balls numbered 1–10 and you want ball number 7 to be pulled in two pulls. On the first pull, the probability of getting the 7 is $\frac{1}{10}$ because there is one ball with a 7 on it and 10 balls to choose from. Assuming the first pull did not yield a 7, the probability of pulling a 7 on the second pull is now $\frac{1}{9}$ because there are only 9 balls remaining for the second pull.

Probability that at least one of something will occur

Use a combination of the multiplication rule and the rule of complements to find the probability that at least one outcome of the element will occur. This given by the general formula $P(\text{at least one event occurring}) = 1 - P(\text{no outcomes occurring})$. For example, to find the probability that at least one even number will show when a pair of dice is rolled, find the probability that two odd numbers will be rolled (no even numbers) and subtract from one. You can always use a tree diagram or make a chart to list the possible outcomes when the sample space is small, such as in the dice-rolling example, but in most cases it will be much faster to use the multiplication and complement formulas.

Odds in favor

In probability, the odds in favor of an event are the number of times the event will occur compared to the number of times the event will not occur. To calculate the odds in favor of an event, use the formula $\frac{P(A)}{1-P(A)}$, where $P(A)$ is the probability that the event will occur. Many times, odds in favor is given as a ratio in the form $\frac{a}{b}$ or $a{:}b$, where a is the probability of the event occurring and b is the complement of the event, the probability of the event not occurring. If the odds in favor are given as 2:5, that means that you can expect the event to occur two times for every 5 times that it does not occur. In other words, the probability that the event will occur is $\frac{2}{2+5} = \frac{2}{7}$.

Odds against

In probability, the odds against an event are the number of times the event will not occur compared to the number of times the event will occur. To calculate the odds against an event, use the formula $\frac{1-P(A)}{P(A)}$, where $P(A)$ is the probability that the event will occur. Many times, odds against is given as a ratio in the form $\frac{b}{a}$ or $b{:}a$, where b is the probability the event will not occur (the complement of the event) and a is the probability the event will occur. If the odds against an event are given as 3:1, that means that you can expect the event to not occur 3 times for every one time it does occur. In other words, 3 out of every 4 trials will fail.

Expected value

Expected value is a method of determining expected outcome in a random situation. It is really a sum of the weighted probabilities of the possible outcomes. Multiply the probability of an event occurring by the weight assigned to that probability (such as the amount of money won or lost). A practical application of the expected value is to determine whether a game of chance is really fair. If the sum of the weighted probabilities is greater than or equal to zero, the game is generally considered fair because the player has a fair chance to win, or at least to break even. If the expected value is less than one, then players lose more than they win. For example, a lottery drawing allows the player to choose any three-digit number, 000–999. The probability of choosing the winning number is 1:1000. If it costs $1 to play, and a winning number receives $500, the expected value is $\left(-\$1 \cdot \frac{999}{1,000}\right) + \left(\$500 \cdot \frac{1}{1,000}\right) = -0.499$ or $-\$0.50$. You can expect to lose on average 50 cents for every dollar you spend.

Empirical probability

Empirical probability is based on conducting numerous repeated experiments and observations rather than by applying pre-defined formulas to determine the probability of an event occurring. To find the empirical probability of an event, conduct repeated trials (repetitions of the same experiment) and record your results. The empirical probability of an event occurring is the number of times the event occurred in the experiment divided by the total number of trials you conducted to get the number of events. Notice that the total number of trials is used, not the number of unsuccessful trials. A practical application of empirical probability is the insurance industry. There are no set functions that define life span, health, or safety. Insurance companies look at factors from hundreds of thousands of individuals to find patterns that they then use to set the formulas for insurance premiums.

Objective and subjective probability

Objective probability is based on mathematical formulas and documented evidence. Examples of objective probability include raffles or lottery drawings where there is a pre-determined number of possible outcomes and a predetermined number of outcomes that correspond to an event. Other cases of objective probability include probabilities of rolling dice, flipping coins, or drawing cards. Most gambling is based on objective probability. Subjective probability is based on personal or professional feelings and judgments. Often, there is a lot of guesswork following extensive research. Areas where subjective probability is applicable include sales trends and business expenses. Attractions set admission prices based on subjective probabilities of attendance based on varying admission rates in an effort to maximize their profit.

Trigonometry, Calculus, and Discrete Mathematics

Unit circles and standard position

A unit circle is a circle with a radius of 1 that has its center at the origin. The equation of the unit circle is $x^2 + y^2 = 1$. Notice that this is an abbreviated version of the standard equation of a circle. Because the center is the point $(0, 0)$, the values of h and k in the general equation are equal to zero and the equation simplifies to this form.

Standard Position: The position of an angle of measure θ whose vertex is at the origin, the initial side crosses the unit circle at the point $(1, 0)$, and the terminal side crosses the unit circle at some other point (a, b). In the standard position, $\sin \theta = b$, $\cos \theta = a$, and $\tan \theta = \frac{b}{a}$.

Positive trigonometric functions

In the first quadrant, all six trigonometric functions are positive (sin, cos, tan, csc, sec, cot). In the second quadrant, sin and csc are positive. In the third quadrant, tan and cot are positive. In the fourth quadrant, cos and sec are positive. If you remember the phrase, "ALL Students Take Classes," you will be able to remember the sign of each trigonometric function in each quadrant. ALL represents all the signs in the first quadrant. The "S" in "Students" represents the sine function and its reciprocal in the second quadrant. The "T" in "Take" represents the tangent function and its reciprocal in the third quadrant. The "C" in "Classes" represents the cosine function and its reciprocal.

Converting rectangular and polar coordinates

Rectangular coordinates are those that lie on the square grids of the Cartesian plane. Polar coordinates are those that lie on the circular polar graph. To convert a point from rectangular (x, y) format to polar (r, θ) format, use the formula (x, y) to $(r, \theta) \Rightarrow r = \sqrt{x^2 + y^2}$; $\tan \theta = \frac{y}{x}$ when $x \neq 0$. If x is positive, use the positive square root value for r. If x is negative, use the negative square root value for r. If x = 0, use the following rules:

If x = 0 and y = 0, then $\theta = 0$

If x = 0 and y > 0, then $\theta = \frac{\pi}{2}$

If x = 0 and y < 0, then $\theta = \frac{3\pi}{2}$

To convert a point from polar (r, θ) format to rectangular (x, y) format, use the formula (r, θ) to $(x, y) \Rightarrow x = r \cos \theta$; $y = r \sin \theta$

Domain, range, and asymptotes

The domain is the set of all possible real number values of x on the graph of a trigonometric function. Some graphs will impose limits on the values of x. The range is the set of all possible real number values of y on the graph of a trigonometric function. Some graphs will impose limits on the values of y. Asymptotes are lines which the graph of a trigonometric function approaches but never reaches. Asymptotes exist for values of x in the graphs of the tangent, cotangent, secant, and cosecant. The sine and cosine graphs do not have any asymptotes. The domain, range, and asymptotes for each of the trigonometric functions are as follows:

- In the sine function, the domain is all real numbers, the range is $-1 \leq y \leq 1$, and there are no asymptotes.
- In the cosine function, the domain is all real numbers; the range is $-1 \leq y \leq 1$, and there are no asymptotes.
- In the tangent function, the domain is $x \in$ all real numbers; $x \neq \frac{\pi}{2} + k\pi$, the range is all real numbers; and the asymptotes are the lines $x = \frac{\pi}{2} + k\pi$.
- In the cosecant function, the domain is $x \in$ all real numbers; $x \neq k\pi$, the range is $(-\infty, -1] \cup [1, \infty)$, and the asymptotes are the lines $x = k\pi$.
- In the secant function, the domain is $x \in$ all real numbers; $x \neq \frac{\pi}{2} + k\pi$, the range is $(-\infty, 1] \cup [1, \infty)$, and the asymptotes are the lines $x = \frac{\pi}{2} + k\pi$.
- In the cotangent function, the domain is $x \in$ all real numbers; $x \neq k\pi$, the range is all real numbers, and the asymptotes are the lines $x = k\pi$.

In each of the above cases, k represents any integer.

Radian measurements of angles

$0°, 30°, 45°, 60°,$ and $90°$.

$0° = 0$ radians, $30° = \frac{\pi}{6}$ radians, $45° = \frac{\pi}{4}$ radians, $60° = \frac{\pi}{3}$ radians, and $90° = \frac{\pi}{2}$ radians

Sine, cosine, tangent, cosecant, secant, and cotangent of angles

$\sin 0° = 0$	$\cos 0° = 1$	$\tan 0° = 0$
$\sin 30° = \dfrac{1}{2}$	$\cos 30° = \dfrac{\sqrt{3}}{2}$	$\tan 30° = \dfrac{\sqrt{3}}{3}$
$\sin 45° = \dfrac{\sqrt{2}}{2}$	$\cos 45° = \dfrac{\sqrt{2}}{2}$	$\tan 45° = 1$
$\sin 60° = \dfrac{\sqrt{3}}{2}$	$\cos 60° = \dfrac{1}{2}$	$\tan 60° = \sqrt{3}$
$\sin 90° = 1$	$\cos 90° = 0$	$\tan 90° =$ undefined
$\csc 0° =$ undefined	$\sec 0° = 1$	$\cot 0° =$ undefined
$\csc 30° = 2$	$\sec 30° = \dfrac{2\sqrt{3}}{3}$	$\cot 30° = \sqrt{3}$
$\csc 45° = \sqrt{2}$	$\sec 45° = \sqrt{2}$	$\cot 45° = 1$
$\csc 60° = \dfrac{2\sqrt{3}}{3}$	$\sec 60° = 2$	$\cot 60° = \dfrac{\sqrt{3}}{3}$
$\csc 90° = 1$	$\sec 90° =$ undefined	$\cot 90° = 0$

These are all values you should have memorized or be able to find quickly.

Graph of the sine function with a period of $360°$ or 2π

A period of 360º or 2π means that the graph makes one complete cycle every 360º. Because $\sin 0° = 0$, the graph of $y = \sin x$ begins at the origin or pole (point (0, 0) in either graphing system), with the x-axis representing the angle measure, and the y-axis representing the sine of the angle. The graph of the sine function is a smooth curve that begins at the origin, peaks at the point $(90°, 1)$, crosses the x-axis at $(180°, 0)$, has its lowest point at $(270°, -1)$, and returns to the x-axis to complete one cycle at $(360°, 0)$.

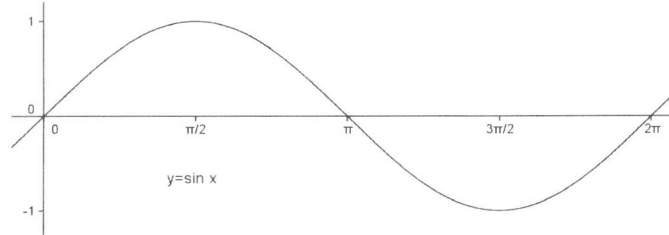

On a polar graph, the sine function graphs as a circle along the y-axis with a diameter bounded by the points $(0, 0)$ and $\left(1, \dfrac{\pi}{2}\right)$.

Graph of the cosine function with $\text{period} = 360° = 2\pi$

A period of 360º means that the graph makes one complete cycle every 360º. Because $\cos 0° = 1$, the graph of $y = \cos x$ begins at the point $(0, 1)$, with the x-axis representing the angle measure, and the y-axis representing the cosine of the angle. The graph of the cosine function is a smooth curve that begins at the point $(0, 1)$, crosses the x-axis at the point $(90°, 0)$, has its lowest point at $(180°, -1)$, crosses the x-axis again at the point $(270°, 0)$, and returns to a peak at the point $(360°, 1)$ to complete one cycle.

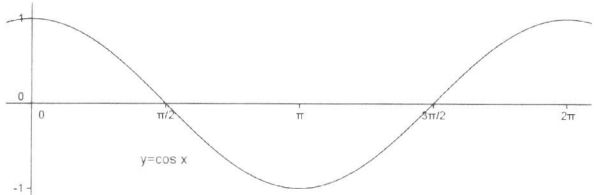

On the polar graph, the graph of the cosine function is a circle on the x-axis with a diameter bounded by the points $(0, 0)$ and $(1, 0)$.

Graph of the tangent function with $\text{period} = 180° = \pi$

A period of 180º means that the graph makes one complete cycle every 180º. The x-axis represents the angle measure, and the y-axis represents the tangent of the angle. The graph of the tangent function is a series of smooth curves that cross the x-axis every 180º or π radians and have an asymptote every $(k \cdot 180°) + 90°$ or $k\pi + \frac{\pi}{2}$ radians. The polar graph of the tangent function is two parabolas with vertices at the pole. One parabola open upward and the other parabola opens downward. The asymptotes are vertical lines that cross the x-axis at $\frac{\pi}{2}$ and $-\frac{\pi}{2}$.

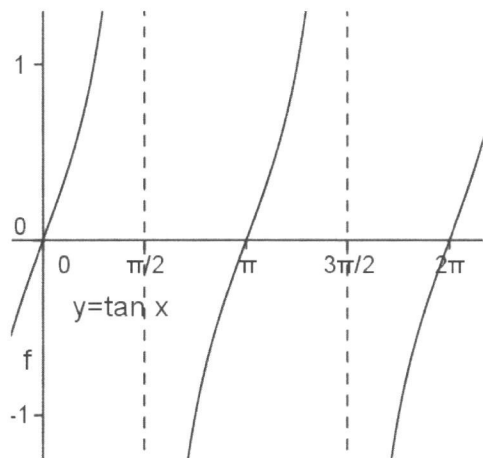

Law of Sines and the Law of Cosines

Oblique triangles are any triangles that do not have a right angle. The Law of Sines states that $\frac{\sin A}{a} = \frac{\sin B}{b} = \frac{\sin C}{c}$, where A, B, and C are the angles of a triangle, and a, b, and c are the sides opposite their respective angles. This formula will work with all triangles, including right triangles.

Remember that the sine of a right angle is equal to 1. The Law of Cosines is given by the formula $c^2 = a^2 + b^2 - 2ab(\cos C)$, where a, b, and c are the sides of a triangle, and C is the angle opposite side c. Notice that this formula is similar to the Pythagorean Theorem. While the Pythagorean Theorem is limited to right triangles, this formula will work with any triangle, including right triangles. (Because $\cos 90° = 0$, the last term of the formula is equal to zero, leaving $c^2 = a^2 + b^2$.)

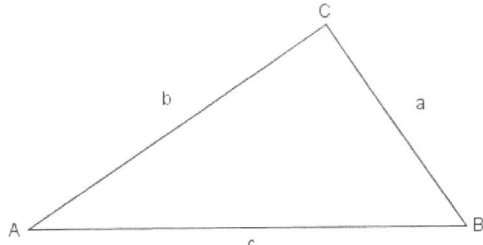

Trigonometric reciprocal, ratio, trigonometric, and cofunction identities

To take the reciprocal of a number means to place that number as the denominator of a fraction with a numerator of 1.

The trigonometric reciprocal identities are $\csc \theta = \frac{1}{\sin \theta}$; $\sec \theta = \frac{1}{\cos \theta}$; and $\cot \theta = \frac{1}{\tan \theta}$.

The trigonometric ratio identities are: $\tan \theta = \frac{\sin \theta}{\cos \theta}$ and $\cot \theta = \frac{\cos \theta}{\sin \theta}$.

The Pythagorean Theorem states that $a^2 + b^2 = c^2$. The trigonometric identities that have this same format are: $\sin^2 \theta + \cos^2 \theta = 1$, $\tan^2 \theta + 1 = \sec^2 \theta$, and $\cot^2 \theta + 1 = \csc^2 \theta$.

The trigonometric cofunction identities use the trigonometric relationships of complementary angles (angles whose sum is 90º). These are: $\sin x = \cos(90° - x)$, $\sec x = \csc(90° - x)$, $\tan x = \cot(90° - x)$, $\cos x = \sin(90° - x)$, $\csc x = \sec(90° - x)$, and $\cot x = \tan(90° - x)$.

Sine cosine, or tangent of the sum or difference of two angles

To find the sine of the sum or difference of two angles, use the formula: $\sin(\alpha \pm \beta) = \sin \alpha \cos \beta \pm \cos \alpha \sin \beta$, where α and β are two angles with known sine values.

To find the cosine of the sum or difference of two angles, use the formula: $\cos(\alpha \pm \beta) = \cos \alpha \cos \beta \mp \sin \alpha \sin \beta$, where α and β are two angles with known cosine values.

To find the tangent of the sum or difference of two angles, use the formula: $\tan(\alpha \pm \beta) = \frac{\tan \alpha \pm \tan \beta}{1 \mp \tan \alpha \tan \beta}$, where α and β are two angles with known tangent values.

These formulas will be provided on the formula sheet during the exam, but you must know how to use them and that α and β represent two angles that have known exact sine and cosine, and tangent values.

Sine and cosine of half of a known angle

To find the sine or cosine of half of a known angle, use the following formulas:

$$\sin\frac{\theta}{2} = \pm\sqrt{\frac{1-\cos\theta}{2}}$$

$$\cos\frac{\theta}{2} = \pm\sqrt{\frac{1+\cos\theta}{2}}$$

where θ is an angle with a known exact cosine value. To determine the sign of the answer, you must notice the quadrant the given angle is in and apply the correct sign for the trigonometric function you are using. These formulas will be provided on the formula sheet during the exam, but you must know how to use them and that θ represents an angle that has a known exact value. If you are asked to find the exact sine or cosine of an angle that you do not know, such as $\sin 22.5°$, you can rewrite the given angle as a half angle, such as $\sin\frac{45°}{2}$, and use this formula.

Tangent and cotangent of half of a known angle

To find the tangent or cotangent of half of a known angle, use the following formulas:

$$\tan\frac{\theta}{2} = \frac{\sin\theta}{1+\cos\theta}$$
$$\cot\frac{\theta}{2} = \frac{\sin\theta}{1-\cos\theta}$$

where θ is an angle with known exact sine and cosine values. These formulas will work for finding the tangent or cotangent of half of any angle with known sine and cosine values because no sine or cosine values are undefined. While these formulas are not necessarily provided on the formula page in the test booklet, you are expected to know them and how to use them. You are allowed (and encouraged!) to save the formulas in your graphing calculator prior to the test day. Make sure you know how to access stored formulas, and that you can determine when to use each formula.

Sine, cosine, tangent, and cotangent of twice a known angle

In each case, use one of the Double Angle Formulas. To find the sine or cosine of twice a known angle, use one of the following formulas:
$$\sin(2\theta) = 2\sin\theta\cos\theta$$
$$\cos(2\theta) = \cos^2\theta - \sin^2\theta \text{ or}$$
$$\cos(2\theta) = 2\cos^2\theta - 1 \text{ or}$$
$$\cos(2\theta) = 1 - 2\sin^2\theta$$

To find the tangent or cotangent of twice a known angle, use the formulas:
$$\tan(2\theta) = \frac{2\tan\theta}{1-\tan^2\theta}$$
$$\cot(2\theta) = \frac{\cot\theta - \tan\theta}{2}$$

In each case, θ is an angle with known exact sine, cosine, tangent, and cotangent values.

While these formulas are not necessarily provided on the formula page in the test booklet, you are expected to know them and how to use them. You are allowed (and encouraged!) to save the formulas in your graphing calculator prior to the test day. Make sure you know how to access stored formulas, and that you can determine when to use each formula.

Range of the inverse of the sine, cosine, and tangent functions

The inverse of the sine function, for example, is written $y = \arcsin x$ or $y = \sin^{-1} x$. Both notations represent the same thing. The value of y is the angle whose sine is x. In the second notation, the -1 is not an exponent, but rather an indication that it is the inverse, or arc, of the trigonometric function.

The range of the inverse of the sine function is $\left[-\frac{\pi}{2}, \frac{\pi}{2}\right]$ or $[-90º, 90º]$.

The range of the inverse of the cosine function is $[0, \pi]$ or $[0º, 180º]$.

The range of the inverse of the tangent function is $\left[-\frac{\pi}{2}, \frac{\pi}{2}\right]$ or $[-90º, 90º]$.

In each case, the range is the minimum and maximum values, inclusive, for the angle measurement of the inverses of the three trigonometric functions. All angle measurements are given in radians first, followed by degrees.

Product of the sines and cosines of two angles

To find the product of the sines and cosines of two different angles, use one of the following formulas:

$$\sin \alpha \sin \beta = \frac{1}{2}[\cos(\alpha - \beta) - \cos(\alpha + \beta)]$$
$$\cos \alpha \cos \beta = \frac{1}{2}[\cos(\alpha + \beta) + \cos(\alpha - \beta)]$$
$$\sin \alpha \cos \beta = \frac{1}{2}[\sin(\alpha + \beta) + \sin(\alpha - \beta)]$$
$$\cos \alpha \sin \beta = \frac{1}{2}[\sin(\alpha + \beta) - \sin(\alpha - \beta)]$$

where α and β are two unique angles. While these formulas may not necessarily be provided on the formula page in the test booklet, you are expected to know them and how to use them. You are allowed (and encouraged!) to save the formulas in your graphing calculator prior to the test day. Make sure you know how to access stored formulas, and that you can determine when to use each formula.

Solving trigonometric equations and algebraic equations

Trigonometric and algebraic equations are solved following the same rules, but while algebraic expressions have one unique solution, trigonometric equations could have multiple solutions, and you must find them all. When solving for an angle with a known trigonometric value, you must

- 74 -

consider the sign and include all angles with that value. Your calculator may only give one value as an answer. It is your responsibility to find the other quadrant that has the same sign for that trigonometric function and find the angle that has the same reference angle.

Inverse trigonometric functions

The inverse of $\sin x$ is written $\sin^{-1} x$ and means the angle whose sine is x. The inverse can also be written as $y = \arcsin x$. The inverse of $\cos x$ is written $\cos^{-1} x$ and means the angle whose cosine is x. The inverse can also be written as $y = \arccos x$. The inverse of $\tan x$ is written $\tan^{-1} x$ and means the angle whose tangent is x. The inverse can also be written as $y = \arctan x$. The inverse of $\csc x$ is written $\csc^{-1} x$ and means the angle whose cosecant is x. The inverse can also be written as $y = \operatorname{arccsc} x$. The inverse of $\sec x$ is written $\sec^{-1} x$ and means the angle whose secant is x. The inverse of can also be written as $y = \operatorname{arcsec} x$. The inverse of $\cot x$ is written $\cot^{-1} x$ and means the angle whose cotangent is x. The inverse of can also be written as $y = \operatorname{arccot} x$.

De Moivre's Theorem

De Moivre's Theorem is used to find the powers of complex numbers (numbers that contain the imaginary number i) written in polar form. Given a trigonometric expression that contains i, such as $z = r \cos x + ir \sin x$, where r is a real number and x is an angle measurement in polar form, use the formula $z^n = r^n(\cos nx + i \sin nx)$, where r and n are real numbers, x is the angle measure in polar form, and i is the imaginary number $i = \sqrt{-1}$. The expression $\cos x + i \sin x$ can be written cis x, making the formula appear in the format $z^n = r^n$ cis nx. Note that De Moivre's Theorem is only for angles in polar form. If you are given an angle in degrees, you must convert to polar form before using the formula.

Polar coordinate system

The polar coordinate system is based on a circular graph, rather than the square graph of the Cartesian graph. Points in the polar coordinate system are in the format (r, θ), where r is the distance from the origin (think radius of the circle) and θ is the smallest positive angle (moving counterclockwise around the circle) made with the positive horizontal axis. The rings of the polar graph correspond to the x-axis of the Cartesian plane, and the spokes of the polar graph correspond to the y-axis of the Cartesian plane. Graphs that would normally stretch out across the x-axis in the Cartesian coordinate system will wrap around to form loops in the polar coordinate system.

Limits of functions

The limit of a function is represented by the notation $\lim_{x \to a} f(x) = L$, where a is the value x approaches as it increases or decreases in value moving toward a, and L is the limit, or the value of the function at the point it reaches a. Technically, the limit only exists if the limit is the same when approached from the right (represented as $\lim_{x \to a^+} f(x)$) and from the left (represented as $\lim_{x \to a^-} f(x)$). Notice the symbol by the a in each case. When x approaches a from the right, it approaches from the positive end of the number line. When x approaches a from the left, it approaches from the negative end of the number line.

When limit does not exist

If the limit as x approaches a differs depending on the direction from which it approaches, then the limit does not exist at a. In other words, if $\lim_{x \to a^+} f(x)$ does not equal $\lim_{x \to a^-} f(x)$, then the limit does not exist at a. The limit also does not exist if either of the one-sided limits does not exist. Situations in which the limit does not exist include a function that jumps from one value to another at a, one that oscillates between two different values as x approaches a, or functions that increase or decrease without bounds as they approach a. Note that it is possible for two functions that do not have limits to be multiplied to get a new function that does have a limit. Just because two functions do not have limits, do not assume that the product will not have a limit.

Finding limits by direct substitution

To find the limit of a function ($\lim_{x \to a} f(x)$) by direct substitution, substitute the value of a for x in the function and solve. The following patterns apply to finding the limit of a function by direct substitution:

$\lim_{x \to a} b = b$, where b is any real number

$\lim_{x \to a} x = a$

$\lim_{x \to a} x^n = a^n$, where n is any positive integer

$\lim_{x \to a} \sqrt{x} = \sqrt{a}; a > 0$

$\qquad \lim_{x \to a} \sqrt[n]{x} = \sqrt[n]{a}$, where n is a positive integer and $a > 0$ for all even values of n

$\lim_{x \to a} \dfrac{1}{x} = \dfrac{1}{a}; a \neq 0$

You can also use substitution for finding the limit of a trigonometric function, a polynomial function, or a rational function. Be sure that you do not allow the denominator of a rational expression to equal zero in any of your substitutions.

Limit of a composite function

In finding the limit of a composite function, begin by finding the limit of the innermost function. For example, to find $\lim_{x \to a} f(g(x))$, first find the value of $\lim_{x \to a} g(x)$ by substitution. Then substitute this value for x in $f(x)$ and solve. The result is the limit of the original problem. Sometimes solving $\lim_{x \to a} \dfrac{f(x)}{g(x)}$ by the direct substitution method will result in the numerator and denominator both being equal to zero. This outcome is called an indeterminate form. To find the limit in this situation, factor both the numerator and denominator by the binomial $x - a$ and reduce the fraction. Then find the limit by substitution.

L'Hôpital's rule

L'Hôpital's rule is a useful method for finding the limit of a problem in the indeterminate form. Rather than factoring and reducing the fraction to find the limit by substitution, L'Hôpital's rule allows you to find the limit using derivatives. Assuming both the numerator and denominator are differentiable, and that both are equal to zero when the direct substitution method is used, take the derivative of both the numerator and the denominator and then use the direct substitution method. For example, if $\lim_{x \to a} \frac{f(x)}{g(x)} = \frac{0}{0}$, take the derivatives of $f(x)$ and $g(x)$ and then find $\lim_{x \to a} \frac{f'(x)}{g'(x)}$. Note that this method will only work if $g'(x) \neq 0$. You can also use L'Hôpital's rule when the limits of the numerator and denominator are both $\pm\infty$.

Properties of limits

When finding the limit of the sum or difference of two functions, find the limit of each individual function and then add or subtract the results. For example, $\lim_{x \to a}[f(x) \pm g(x)] = \lim_{x \to a} f(x) \pm \lim_{x \to a} g(x)$. To find the limit of the product or quotient of two functions, find the limit of each individual function and the multiply or divide the results. For example, $\lim_{x \to a}[f(x) \cdot g(x)] = \lim_{x \to a} f(x) \cdot \lim_{x \to a} g(x)$ and $\lim_{x \to a} \frac{f(x)}{g(x)} = \frac{\lim_{x \to a} f(x)}{\lim_{x \to a} g(x)}$, where $g(x) \neq 0$ and $\lim_{x \to a} g(x) \neq 0$. When finding the quotient of the limits of two functions, make sure the denominator is not equal to zero. If it is, use differentiation or L'Hôpital's rule to find the limit. To find the limit of a power of a function or a root of a function, find the limit of the function and then raise the limit to the original power or take the root of the limit. For example, $\lim_{x \to a}[f(x)]^n = [\lim_{x \to a} f(x)]^n$ and $\lim_{x \to a} \sqrt[n]{f(x)} = \sqrt[n]{\lim_{x \to a} f(x)}$, where n is a positive integer and $\lim_{x \to a} f(x) > 0$ for all even values of n. To find the limit of a function multiplied by a scalar, find the limit of the function and multiply the result by the scalar. For example, $\lim_{x \to a} kf(x) = k \lim_{x \to a} f(x)$, where k is a real number.

Derivative

The derivative is a measure of how much something is changing at a specific point, and is the slope of a line tangent to a curve at the specific point. The derivative of a function $f(x)$ is written $f'(x)$, and read, "f prime of x." Other notations for the derivative include $D_x f(x)$, y', $D_x y$, $\frac{dy}{dx}$, and $\frac{d}{dx} f(x)$. The exact formula for finding the derivative of a function is $f'(x) = \lim_{h \to 0} \frac{f(z+h) - f(x)}{h}$, where h is a real number. However, there is a simpler method you can use to find the derivative of a polynomial. Given a function $f(x) = a_n x^n + a_{n-1} x^{n-1} + a_{n-2} x^{n-2} + \cdots + a_1 x + a_0$, multiply each exponent by its corresponding coefficient to get the new coefficient and reduce the value of the exponent by one. Coefficients with no variable are dropped. This gives $f'(x) = n a_n x^{n-1} + (n-1) a_{n-1} x^{n-2} + \cdots + a_1$, a pattern that can be repeated for each successive derivative.

Differentiable functions

Differentiable functions are functions that have a derivative. Some basic rules for finding derivatives of functions are:

$f(x) = c \Rightarrow f'(x) = 0$; where c is a constant

$f(x) = x \Rightarrow f'(x) = 1$

$(cf(x))' = cf'(x)$; where c is a constant

$f(x) = x^n \Rightarrow f'(x) = nx^{n-1}$; where n is a real number

- 77 -

$$(f + g)'(x) = f'(x) + g'(x)$$

$$(fg)'(x) = f(x)g'(x) + f'(x)g(x)$$

$$\left(\frac{f}{g}\right)'(x) = \frac{f'(x)g(x) - f(x)g'(x)}{[g(x)]^2}$$

$$(f \circ g)'(x) = f'\big(g(x)\big) \cdot g'(x)$$

This last formula is also known as the Chain Rule.

One problem may require the use of several of these rules. If you are finding the derivative of a polynomial that is raised to a power, let the polynomial be represented by $g(x)$ and use the Chain Rule.

These rules may also be used to take multiple derivatives of the same function. The derivative of the derivative is called the second derivative and is represented by the notation $f''(x)$. Taking one more derivative, if possible, gives the third derivative and is represented by the notation $f'''(x)$ or $f^{(3)}(x)$.

Implicit differentiation

An implicit function is one where it is impossible, or very difficult, to express one variable in terms of another by normal algebraic methods. This would include functions that have both variables raised to a power greater than 1, functions that have two variables multiplied by each other, or a combination of the two. In this situation, differentiate each individual term as normal, following the differentiation rules, including the Chain Rule. If a term contains the variable y, include $\frac{dy}{dx}$ at the end of the term. Once the derivative of each individual term has been found, use the rules of algebra to solve for $\frac{dy}{dx}$ to get the final answer. For example, to determine the value of $\frac{dy}{dx}$ in the equation $xy^2 = 3y + 2x$, take the derivative of each term with respect to x: $y^2 + 2xy\frac{dy}{dx} = 3\frac{dy}{dx} + 2$. Note that the first term in the original equation required the use of the chain rule. Using algebra, isolate $\frac{dy}{dx}$ on one side of the equation to yield $\frac{dy}{dx} = \frac{y^2-2}{3-2xy}$.

Trigonometric differentiation

Trigonometric functions are any functions that include one of the six trigonometric expressions. The following rules for derivatives apply for all trigonometric differentiation:

$$\frac{d}{dx}(\sin x) = \cos x$$

$$\frac{d}{dx}(\cos x) = -\sin x$$

$$\frac{d}{dx}(\tan x) = \sec^2 x$$

For functions that are a combination of trigonometric and algebraic expressions, use the following formulas:

$$\frac{d}{dx}(\sin u) = \cos u \ D_x u \qquad\qquad \frac{d}{dx}(\cos u) = -\sin u \ D_x u$$

$$\frac{d}{dx}(\tan u) = \sec^2 u \ D_x u \qquad\qquad \frac{d}{dx}(\sec u) = \tan u \sec u \ D_x u$$

$$\frac{d}{dx}(\csc u) = -\csc u \cot u \ D_x u \qquad\qquad \frac{d}{dx}(\cot u) = -\csc^2 u \ D_x u$$

Functions involving the inverses of the trigonometric functions can also be differentiated using the following formulas, provided the algebraic expression contained in the function is differentiable.

$$\frac{d}{dx}(\sin^{-1} u) = \frac{1}{\sqrt{1-u^2}}\frac{du}{dx} \qquad\qquad \frac{d}{dx}(\cos^{-1} u) = \frac{-1}{\sqrt{1-u^2}}\frac{du}{dx}$$

$$\frac{d}{dx}(\tan^{-1} u) = \frac{1}{1+u^2}\frac{du}{dx} \qquad\qquad \frac{d}{dx}(\csc^{-1} u) = \frac{-1}{u\sqrt{u^2-1}}\frac{du}{dx}$$

$$\frac{d}{dx}(\sec^{-1} u) = \frac{1}{u\sqrt{u^2-1}}\frac{du}{dx} \qquad\qquad \frac{d}{dx}(\cot^{-1} u) = \frac{-1}{1+u^2}\frac{du}{dx}$$

In each of the above expressions, u represents a differentiable function. Also, the value of u must be such that the radicand, if applicable, is a positive number. Remember the expression $\frac{du}{dx}$ means to take the derivative of the function u with respect to the variable x.

Exponential and logarithmic differentiation

Exponential functions are in the form e^x, which has itself as its derivative: $\frac{d}{dx} e^x = e^x$. For functions that have a function as the exponent rather than just an x, use the formula $\frac{d}{dx} e^u = e^u \frac{du}{dx}$. The inverse of the exponential function is the natural logarithm. To find the derivative of the natural logarithm, use the formula $\frac{d}{dx}\ln u = \frac{1}{u}\frac{du}{dx}$. If you are trying to solve an expression with a variable in the exponent, use the formula $a^x = e^{x\ln a}$, where a is a positive real number and x is any real number. To find the derivative of a function in this format, use the formula $\frac{d}{dx}a^x = a^x \ln a$. If the exponent is a function rather than a single variable x, use the formula $\frac{d}{dx}a^u = a^u \ln a \frac{du}{dx}$. If you are trying to solve an expression involving a logarithm, use the formula $\frac{d}{dx}(\log_a x) = \frac{1}{x\ln a}$ or $\frac{d}{dx}(\log_a |u|) = \frac{1}{u\ln a}\frac{du}{dx}; u \neq 0$.

In cases where differentiation seems difficult, try taking the logs of the functions first and then taking the derivative.

High-order derivatives

High-order derivatives are any derivative beyond the first derivative. The derivative of any function is also a function that has a derivative. To determine the number of nontrivial derivatives a function has, look at the order of the function and add one. For example, a function whose term of highest order has an order of 5, the function will have six possible derivatives, including the final one that yields zero as the derivative. When you have a function with each term in the format kx^n, where k and n are real numbers, use the following formula to find the pth derivative of the function:

$f^{(p)}(x) = \frac{k \cdot n!}{(n-p)!} x^{n-p}$. Anytime p is greater than the order of the function, the answer is zero. Remember that $0! = 1$, so when $n = p$, do not think you have the null set.

Rolle's Theorem

Rolle's Theorem states that if a differentiable function has two different values in the domain that correspond to a single value in the range, then the function must have a point between them where the slope of the tangent to the graph is zero. This point will be a maximum or a minimum value of the function between those two points. The maximum or minimum point is the point at which $f'(c) = 0$, where c is within the appropriate interval of the function's domain. The following graph shows a function with one maximum in the second quadrant and one minimum in the fourth quadrant.

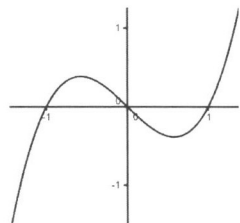

Mean Value Theorem

According to the Mean Value Theorem, between any two points on a curve, there exists a tangent to the curve whose slope is parallel to the chord formed by joining those two points. Remember the formula for slope: $m = \frac{\Delta x}{\Delta y}$. In a function, $f(x)$ represents the value for y. Therefore, if you have two points on a curve, m and n, the corresponding points are $(m, f(m))$ and $(n, f(n))$. Assuming $m < n$, the formula for the slope of the chord joining those two points is $\frac{f(n)-f(m)}{n-m}$. This must also be the slope of a line parallel to the chord, since parallel lines have equal slopes. Therefore, there must be a value p between m and n such that $f'(p) = \frac{f(n)-f(m)}{n-m}$.

Continuity of functions

For a function to have continuity, its graph must be an unbroken curve. That is, it is a function that can be graphed without having to lift the pencil to move it to a different point. To say a function is continuous at point p, you must show the function satisfies three requirements. First, $f(p)$ must exist. If you evaluate the function at p, it must yield a real number. Second, there must exist a relationship such that
$\lim_{x \to p} f(x) = f(p)$.

Finally, the following relationship must be true:

$$\lim_{x \to p^+} F(x) = \lim_{x \to p^-} F(x) = F(p)$$

If all three of these requirements are met, a function is considered continuous at p. If any one of them is not true, the function is not continuous at p.

Tangents and normals

Tangents are lines that touch a curve in exactly one point and have the same slope as the curve at that point. To find the slope of a curve at a given point and the slope of its tangent line at that point, find the derivative of the function of the curve. If the slope is undefined, the tangent is a vertical line. If the slope is zero, the tangent is a horizontal line. A line that is normal to a curve at a given point is perpendicular to the tangent at that point. Assuming $f'(x) \neq 0$, the equation for the normal line at point (a, b) is: $y - b = -\frac{1}{f'(a)}(x - a)$. The easiest way to find the slope of the normal is to take the negative reciprocal of the slope of the tangent. If the slope of the tangent is zero, the slope of the normal is undefined. If the slope of the tangent is undefined, the slope of the normal is zero.

Rate of change, velocity, and acceleration

The first derivative is used to find the instantaneous rate of change at a particular point in time. For example, as a roller coaster travels along its track, the speed changes with the variations in the track. If the position of the rollercoaster with respect to time is the function $p(t)$, then the velocity, or rate of change in position, of the rollercoaster at a given point in time is $p'(t)$. The second derivative is used to find the acceleration of an object at a particular point in time. Again, if the function $p(t)$ represents the position of the rollercoaster with respect to time, then $p''(t)$ is the acceleration, or instantaneous change in velocity, of the rollercoaster at a given point in time.

Relative minimum, relative maximum, and relative extremum

Remember Rolle's Theorem, which stated that if two points have the same value in the range that there must be a point between them where the slope of the graph is zero. This point is located at a peak or valley on the graph. A peak is a maximum point, and a valley is a minimum point. The relative minimum is the lowest point on a graph for a given section of the graph. It may or may not be the same as the absolute minimum, which is the lowest point on the entire graph. The relative maximum is the highest point on one section of the graph. Again, it may or may not be the same as the absolute maximum. A relative extremum (plural extrema) is a relative minimum or relative maximum point on a graph.

Critical point and sign diagram

A critical point is a point $(n, f(n))$ that is part of the domain of a function, such that either $f'(n) = 0$ or $f'(n)$ does not exist. If either of these conditions is true, then n is either an inflection point or a point at which the slope of the curve changes sign. If the slope changes sign, then a relative minimum or maximum occurs. In graphing an equation with relative extrema, use a sign diagram to approximate the shape of the graph. Once you have determined the relative extrema, calculate the sign of a point on either side of each critical point. This will give a general shape of the graph, and you will know whether each critical point is a relative minimum, a relative maximum, or a point of inflection.

First Derivative Test

Remember that critical points occur where the slope of the curve is 0. Also remember that the first derivative of a function gives the slope of the curve at a particular point on the curve. Because of this property of the first derivative, the first derivative test can be used to determine if a critical point is a minimum or maximum. If $f'(x)$ is negative at a point to the left of a critical number and

$f'(x)$ is positive at a point to the right of a critical number, then the critical number is a relative minimum. If $f'(x)$ is positive to the left of a critical number and $f'(x)$ is negative to the right of a critical number, then the critical number is a relative maximum. If $f'(x)$ has the same sign on both sides, then the critical number is a point of inflection.

Second derivative

The second derivative, designated by $f''(x)$, is helpful in determining whether the relative extrema of a function are relative maximums or relative minimums. If the second derivative at the critical point is greater than zero, the critical point is a relative minimum. If the second derivative at the critical point is less than zero, the critical point is a relative maximum. If the second derivative at the critical point is equal to zero, you must use the first derivative test to determine whether the point is a relative minimum or a relative maximum.

Determining concavity

There are a couple of ways to determine the concavity of the graph of a function. To test a portion of the graph that contains a point with domain p, find the second derivative of the function and evaluate it for p. If $f''(p) > 0$, then the graph is concave upward at that point. If $f''(p) < 0$, then the graph is concave downward at that point. The second way to determine the concavity of the graph of a function is to use a sign diagram.

Point of inflection

The point of inflection on the graph of a function is the point at which the concavity changes from concave downward to concave upward or from concave upward to concave downward. The easiest way to find the points of inflection is to find the second derivative of the function and then solve the equation $f''(x) = 0$. Remember that if $f''(p) > 0$, the graph is concave upward, and if $f''(p) < 0$, the graph is concave downward. Logically, the concavity changes at the point when $f''(p) = 0$.

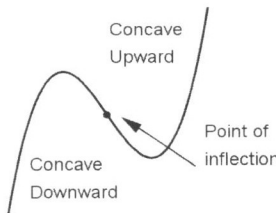

Derivative tests to graph a function

Begin by solving the equation $f(x) = 0$ to find all the zeros of the function, if they exist. Plot these points on the graph. Then, find the first derivative of the function and solve the equation $f'(x) = 0$ to find the critical points. Remember the numbers obtained here are the x portions of the coordinates. Substitute these values for x in the original function and solve for y to get the full coordinates of the points. Plot these points on the graph. Take the second derivative of the function and solve the equation $f''(x) = 0$ to find the points of inflection. Substitute in the original function to get the coordinates and graph these points. Test points on both sides of the critical points to test for concavity and draw the curve.

Rectilinear motion

Rectilinear motion is motion along a straight line rather than a curved path. This concept is generally used in problems involving distance, velocity, and acceleration. Average velocity over a period of time is found using the formula average velocity $= \frac{s(t_2)-s(t_1)}{t_2-t_1}$, where t_1 and t_2 are specific points in time and $s(t_1)$ and $s(t_2)$ are the distances traveled at those points in time.

Instantaneous velocity at a specific time is found using the formula $= \lim_{h \to 0} \frac{s(t+h)-s(t)}{h}$, or $v = s'(t)$.

Remember that velocity at a given point is found using the first derivative, and acceleration at a given point is found using the second derivative. Therefore, the formula for acceleration at a given point in time is found using the formula $a(t) = v'(t) = s''(t)$, where a is acceleration, t is time, v is velocity, and s is distance (the spot at that point in time).

Antiderivative

The antiderivative of a function is the function whose first derivative is the original function. Antiderivatives are represented by capital letters, while their first derivatives are represented by lower case letters. For example, if $F' = f$, then F is the antiderivative of f. Antiderivatives are also known as indefinite integrals. When taking the derivative of a function, the constant term at the end of the function has a zero value in the first derivative. Because there is no way to know what the value of the original constant was when looking at the first derivative, the antiderivative is indefinite.

$$\int \cos x \ dx = \sin x + C \qquad \int \sec x \tan x \ dx = \sec x + C$$

$$\int \sin x \ dx = -\cos x + C \qquad \int \csc x \cot x \ dx = -\csc x + C$$

$$\int \sec^2 x \ dx = \tan x + C \qquad \int \csc^2 x \ dx = -\cot x + C$$

$$\int \frac{1}{x} \ dx = \ln |x| + C \qquad \int e^x \ dx = e^x + C$$

Indefinite integral

To find the indefinite integral, reverse the process of differentiation. In differentiation, you multiplied the coefficient of the term by the exponent of the variable and then reduced the exponent by one. In integration, add one to the value of the exponent, and then divide the coefficient of the term by this number to get the original function. Because you do not know the value of the constant term at the end, add C to the end of the function once you have completed this process for each term. Use the following formulas:

$\int 0 \ dx = C$

$\int k \ dx = kx + C$

$\int x^n \ dx = \frac{x^{n+1}}{n+1} + C$, where $n \neq -1$

- 83 -

Finding the integral of a function is the exact opposite of finding the derivative of the function. Use the trigonometric or logarithmic differentiation formulas in reverse, and add C to the end to compensate for the unknown term. In instances where a negative sign appears in the differentiation formula, move the negative sign to the opposite side (multiply both sides by -1) to reverse for the integration formula. You should end up with the following formulas:

$$\int \cos x \ dx = \sin x + C \qquad \int \sec x \tan x \ dx = \sec x + C$$

$$\int \sin x \ dx = -\cos x + C \qquad \int \csc x \cot x \ dx = -\csc x + C$$

$$\int \sec^2 x \ dx = \tan x + C \qquad \int \csc^2 x \ dx = -\cot x + C$$

$$\int \frac{1}{x} \ dx = \ln |x| + C \qquad \int e^x \ dx = e^x + C$$

Integration by substitution

The formula for integration by substitution is given by the equation
$$f\big(g(x)\big)g'(x)dx = \int_{g(a)}^{g(b)} f(u) \ du \, ; u = g(x) \text{ and } du = g'(x)dx.$$

This is the integration version of the chain rule for differentiation. When a function is in a format that is difficult or impossible to integrate using traditional integration methods and formulas due to multiple functions being combined, use the change of variable formula to convert the function to a simpler format that is much easier to integrate.

Integration by parts

Whenever you are asked to find the integral of the product of two different functions or parts, use integration by parts to make the process simpler. Integration by parts is, in effect, the opposite of applying the product rule in differentiation. Recall that
$(fg)'(x) = f(x)g'(x) + g(x)f'(x).$ This can also be written $\frac{d}{dx}(u \cdot v) = u\frac{dv}{dx} + v\frac{du}{dx}$
$\frac{d}{dx}(u \cdot v) = u\frac{dv}{dx} + v\frac{du}{dx}$, where $u = f(x)$, $v = g(x)$, $du = f'(x)$, and $dv = g'(x)$.

Rearranging to integral form gives the formula $\int u \ dv = uv - \int v \ du$, which can also be written as $\int f(x)g'(x) \ dx = f(x)g(x) - \int f'(x)g(x) \ dx.$

Fundamental Theorems of Calculus

The Fundamental Theorem of Calculus shows that the process of indefinite integration can be reversed by finding the first derivative of the resulting function. It also gives the relationship between differentiation and integration over a closed interval of the function. For example, assuming a function is continuous over the interval $[m, n]$, you can find the definite integral by using the formula $\int_m^n f(x) \ dx = F(n) - F(m)$. Many times the notation $\int_m^n f(x) \ dx = F(x)\big|_m^n = F(n) - F(m)$ is also used to represent the Fundamental Theorem of Calculus. To find the average value of the function over the given interval, use the formula $\frac{1}{n-m}\int_m^n f(x) \ dx$. The Second Fundamental Theorem of Calculus is related to the first. This theorem states that, assuming the function is continuous over the interval you are considering, taking the derivative of the integral of

- 84 -

a function will yield the original function. The general format for this theorem is $\frac{d}{dx}\int_c^x f(x)\,dx = f(x)$ for any point having a domain value equal to c in the given interval.

Properties of integrals

For each of the following properties of integrals of function f, the variables m, n, and p represent values in the domain of the given interval of f. If f exists at $x = n$, then $\int_n^n f(x)\,dx = 0$.

If f is integrable over the interval from m to n, then $\int_m^n f(x)\,dx = -\int_n^m f(x)\,dx$.

If f is integrable over the interval from m to n and k is a real-number constant, then the function kf is integrable over the interval from m to n and $\int_m^n kf(x)\,dx = k\int_m^n f(x)\,dx$.

If f is integrable over the interval from m to n, m to p, and p to n, then $\int_m^n f(x)\,dx = \int_m^p f(x)\,dx + \int_p^n f(x)\,dx$.

If f is integrable over the interval from $-m$ to m and f is an even function, then $\int_{-m}^m f(x)\,dx = 2\int_0^m f(x)\,dx$.

If f is integrable over the interval from $-m$ to m and f is an odd function, then $\int_{-m}^m f(x)\,dx = 0$.

Integrals and Riemann Sums

While the indefinite integral has an undefined constant added at the end, the definite integral has an exact real number added to the end of the resulting function, known as a limiting sum. To find the definite integral of a function over a closed interval, use the formula $\int_n^m f(x)\,dx = \lim_{max\,\Delta x_i - 0} \sum_{i=1}^p f(c_i)\Delta x_i$, where the interval from m to n is divided into p different parts that may or may not be all the same size, c_i is a point in the ith part of the interval from x_{i-1} to x_i, and $\Delta x_i = x_i - x_{i-1}$. This formula assumes the limit at this point exists. A Riemann sum is the limiting sum from the definite integral. The Riemann sum is useful for calculating the area of a region bounded by a curve, the x-axis, and two points on the curve.

Trapezoidal Rule

The trapezoidal rule, also called the trapezoid rule or the trapezium rule, is another way to approximate the area under a curve. In this case, a trapezoid is drawn such that one side of the trapezoid is on the x-axis and the parallel sides terminate on points of the curve so that part of the curve is above the trapezoid and part of the curve is below the trapezoid. While this does not give an exact area for the region under the curve, it does provide a close approximation.

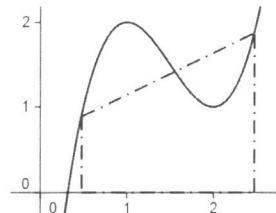

Sequence and element

A function with a domain comprised of the set of positive integers is a sequence. Each member of the sequence is an element, or individual term. Each element of a sequence is identified by the notation a_n, where a is the term of the sequence, and n is the integer identifying which term in the sequence a is. There are two different ways to represent a sequence that contains the element a_n. The first is the simple notation $\{a_n\}$. The expanded notation of a sequence is $a_1, a_2, a_3, \dots a_n, \dots$. Notice that the expanded form does not end with the nth term. There is no indication that the nth term is the last term in the sequence, only that the nth term is an element of the sequence.

Limit, converge, and diverge

Some sequences will have a limit, or a value the sequence approaches but never passes. A sequence that has a limit is known as a convergent sequence because all the values of the sequence seemingly converge at that point. Sequences that do not converge at a particular limit are divergent sequences. The easiest way to determine whether a sequence converges or diverges is to find the limit of the sequence. If the limit is a real number, the sequence is a convergent sequence. If the limit is infinity, the sequence is a divergent sequence. Remember the following rules for finding limits:

$\lim_{n \to \infty} k = k$ for all real numbers k

$\lim_{n \to \infty} \frac{1}{n} = 0$

$\lim_{n \to \infty} \frac{k}{n^p} = 0$ for all real numbers k and positive rational numbers p.

Various properties

The limit of the sums of two sequences is equal to the sum of the limits of the two sequences: $\lim_{n \to \infty}(a_n + b_n) = \lim_{n \to \infty} a_n + \lim_{n \to \infty} b_n$.

The limit of the difference between two sequences is equal to the difference between the limits of the two sequences $\lim_{n \to \infty}(a_n - b_n) = \lim_{n \to \infty} a_n - \lim_{n \to \infty} b_n$.
The limit of the product of two sequences is equal to the product of the limits of the two sequences: $\lim_{n \to \infty}(a_n \cdot b_n) = \lim_{n \to \infty} a_n \cdot \lim_{n \to \infty} b_n$.

The limit of the quotient of two sequences is equal to the quotient of the limits of the two sequences, with some exceptions: $\lim_{n \to \infty}\left(\frac{a_n}{b_n}\right) = \frac{\lim_{n \to \infty} a_n}{\lim_{n \to \infty} b_n}$. In the quotient formula, it is important to consider that $b_n \neq 0$ and $\lim_{n \to \infty} b_n \neq 0$.

The limit of a sequence multiplied by a scalar is equal to the scalar multiplied by the limit of the sequence: $\lim_{n \to \infty} k a_n = k \lim_{n \to \infty} a_n$, where k is any real number.

Squeeze Theorem

The squeeze theorem is known by many names, including the sandwich theorem, the sandwich rule, the squeeze lemma, the squeezing theorem, and the pinching theorem. No matter what you

- 86 -

call it, the principle is the same. To prove the limit of a difficult function exists, find the limits of two functions, one on either side of the unknown, that are easy to compute. If the limits of these functions are equal, then that is also the limit of the unknown function. In mathematical terms, the theorem is:

If $g(x) \leq f(x) \leq h(x)$ for all values of x where $f(x)$ is the function with the unknown limit, and if $\lim_{x \to a} g(x) = \lim_{x \to a} h(x)$, then this limit is also equal to $\lim_{x \to a} f(x)$.

Absolute values of limits

To find the limit of an expression containing an absolute value sign, take the absolute value of the limit. If $\lim_{n \to \infty} a_n = L$, where L is the numerical value for the limit, then $\lim_{n \to \infty} |a_n| = |L|$. Also, if $\lim_{n \to \infty} |a_n| = 0$, then $\lim_{n \to \infty} a_n = 0$. The trick comes when you are asked to find the limit as n approaches from the left. Whenever the limit is being approached from the left, it is being approached from the negative end of the domain. The absolute value sign makes everything in the equation positive, essentially eliminating the negative side of the domain. In this case, rewrite the equation without the absolute value signs and add a negative sign in front of the expression. For example, $\lim_{n \to 0^-} |x|$ becomes $\lim_{n \to 0^-} (-x)$.

Monotonic, nonincreasing, and nondecreasing

A monotonic sequence is a sequence that is either nonincreasing or nondecreasing. The term *nonincreasing* is used to describe a sequence whose terms either get progressively smaller in value or remain the same. The term *nondecreasing* is used to describe a sequence whose terms either get progressively larger in value or remain the same. A nonincreasing sequence is bounded above. This means that all elements of the sequence must be less than a given real number. A nondecreasing sequence is bounded below. This means that all elements of the sequence must be greater than a given real number. Any monotonic sequence that has either an upper bound or a lower bound is a converging sequence.

Infinite series

An infinite series, also referred to as just a series, is a series that has no limit. Each infinite sequence represents an infinite series according to the equation $\sum_{n=1}^{\infty} a_n = a_1 + a_2 + a_3 + \cdots + a_n + \cdots$. This notation can be shortened to $\sum_{n=1}^{\infty} a_n$ or $\sum a_n$. Every infinite series has a sequence of partial sums, where the first partial sum is equal to the first element of the series, the second partial sum is equal to the first two elements of the series, and the nth partial sum is equal to the sum of the first n elements of the series.

Sequence of partial sums

Every infinite series has a sequence of partial sums that either converges or diverges. Like the test for convergence in a sequence, finding the limit of the sequence of partial sums will indicate whether it is a converging sequence or a diverging sequence. If there exists a real number S such that $\lim_{n \to \infty} S_n = S$, where S_n is the sequence of partial sums, then the sequence converges. If the limit equals infinity, then the sequence diverges. If $\lim_{n \to \infty} S_n = S$ and S is a real number, then S is also equal to the sum of the series.

Convergent series

To find the sum as n approaches infinity for the sum of two convergent series, find the sum as n approaches infinity for each individual series and add the results.

$$\sum_{n=1}^{\infty} (a_n + b_n) = \sum_{n=1}^{\infty} a_n + \sum_{n=1}^{\infty} b_n$$

To find the sum as n approaches infinity for the difference between two convergent series, find the sum as n approaches infinity for each individual series and subtract the results.

$$\sum_{n=1}^{\infty} (a_n - b_n) = \sum_{n=1}^{\infty} a_n - \sum_{n=1}^{\infty} b_n$$

To find the sum as n approaches infinity for the product of a scalar and a convergent series, find the sum as n approaches infinity for the series and multiply the result by the scalar.

$$\sum_{n=1}^{\infty} k a_n = k \sum_{n=1}^{\infty} a_n$$

Geometric series

A geometric series is an infinite series in which each term is multiplied by a constant real number r, called the ratio. This is represented by the equation

$$\sum_{n=1}^{\infty} ar^{n-1} = a_1 + a_2 r + a_3 r^2 + \cdots + a_n r^{n-1} + \cdots.$$

If the absolute value of r is greater than or equal to one, then the geometric series is a diverging series. If the absolute value of r is less than one but greater than zero, the geometric series is a converging series. To find the sum of a converging geometric series, use the formula $\sum_{n=1}^{\infty} ar^{n-1} = \frac{a}{1-r}$, where $0 < |r| < 1$. If the series converges, it converges to zero. Otherwise, it diverges.

Nth term test for divergence

The nth term test for divergence involves taking the limit of the nth term of a series and determining whether or not the limit is equal to zero. If the limit of the nth term is not equal to zero, then the series is a diverging series. Do not make the assumption that if the limit of the nth term is equal to zero that the series is automatically a converging series. This information alone is not enough to make a definitive determination of convergence or divergence. This test only works to prove divergence, and only when the limit of the nth term is anything except zero.

Matrix

A matrix is an array of number arranged in columns and rows. A matrix that has exactly one column or exactly one row is a vector. A matrix with an equal number of columns and rows is called a square matrix. A matrix (plural matrices) is used to represent the coefficients of a system of linear equations and is useful in solving those systems. Each element of a matrix is a real or complex number, or may be an expression representing a real or complex number. A matrix is generally represented by a capital letter, with its elements represented by the corresponding lowercase letter with two subscripts indicating the row and column of the element. For example, n_{ab} represents the element n in row a column b of matrix N.

Matrix order

A matrix is described in terms of the number of rows and columns it contains in the format $a \times b$, where a is the number of rows and b is the number of columns. A matrix of order $1 \times b$ has 1 row with multiple elements. It is called a row vector of order b. A matrix of order $a \times 1$ has 1 column with multiple elements. It is called a column vector of order a. Any matrix of order $a \times b$ where $a = b$ is a square matrix. It is important to note that graphing calculators (required for the test) have the capability of solving matrices. If you have enough memory in your calculator, you can enter a matrix of order up to 99×99, depending on the calculator.

Main diagonal

The main diagonal only applies to a square matrix. In this case, it is the elements found in a line from the top left corner to the bottom right corner of the square matrix. For example, a square matrix N of order 4 would have the elements n_{11}, n_{22}, n_{33}, and n_{44} as the main diagonal

$$\begin{bmatrix} n_{11} & n_{12} & n_{13} & n_{14} \\ n_{21} & n_{22} & n_{23} & n_{24} \\ n_{31} & n_{32} & n_{33} & n_{34} \\ n_{41} & n_{42} & n_{43} & n_{44} \end{bmatrix}$$

A matrix of order 5×4 would not have a main diagonal because no straight line between the top left corner and the bottom right corner that joins the elements.

$$\begin{bmatrix} n_{11} & n_{12} & n_{13} & n_{14} \\ n_{21} & n_{22} & n_{23} & n_{24} \\ n_{31} & n_{32} & n_{33} & n_{34} \\ n_{41} & n_{42} & n_{43} & n_{44} \\ n_{51} & n_{52} & n_{53} & n_{54} \end{bmatrix}$$

Diagonal, identity and zero matrix

A diagonal matrix is a square matrix that has a zero for every element in the matrix except the elements on the main diagonal. All the elements on the main diagonal must be nonzero numbers.

$$\begin{bmatrix} 2 & 0 & 0 & 0 \\ 0 & 3 & 0 & 0 \\ 0 & 0 & 4 & 0 \\ 0 & 0 & 0 & 5 \end{bmatrix}$$

If every element on the main diagonal of a diagonal matrix is equal to one, the matrix is also called an identity matrix.

$$\begin{bmatrix} 1 & 0 & 0 & 0 \\ 0 & 1 & 0 & 0 \\ 0 & 0 & 1 & 0 \\ 0 & 0 & 0 & 1 \end{bmatrix}$$

A zero matrix is a matrix that has zero as the value for every element in the matrix.

$$\begin{bmatrix} 0 & 0 & 0 & 0 \\ 0 & 0 & 0 & 0 \\ 0 & 0 & 0 & 0 \\ 0 & 0 & 0 & 0 \end{bmatrix}$$

The zero matrix is the *identity for matrix addition*. Do not confuse the zero matrix with the identity matrix.

Negative and equal matrix

The negative of a matrix is also known as the additive inverse of a matrix. If matrix N is the given matrix, then matrix $-N$ is its negative. This means that every element n_{ab} is equal to $-n_{ab}$ in the negative. To find the negative of a given matrix, change the sign of every element in the matrix and keep all elements in their original corresponding positions in the matrix. If two matrices have the same order and all corresponding elements in the two matrices are the same, then the two matrices are equal matrices.

Transposing a matrix

A matrix N may be transposed to matrix N^T by changing all rows into columns and changing all columns into rows. The easiest way to accomplish this is to swap the positions of the row and column notations for each element. For example, suppose the element in the second row of the third column of matrix N is $n_{23} = 4$. In the transposed matrix N^T, the transposed element would be $n_{32} = 4$, and it would be placed in the third row of the second column. To quickly transpose a matrix by hand, begin with the first column and rewrite a new matrix with those same elements in the same order in the first row. Write the elements from the second column of the original matrix in the second row of the transposed matrix. Continue this process until all columns have been completed. If the original matrix is identical to the transposed matrix, the matrices are symmetric.

Scalar and scalar product

Like any other situation in mathematics, a scalar is simply a number or a numerical amount. To find the scalar product of a matrix of any order, multiply each element of the original matrix by the scalar to get the element of the new matrix. The new matrix is of the same order as the original matrix, and each element, multiplied by the scalar, is placed in its corresponding position in the matrix. Follow this pattern when finding the scalar product of a matrix:

$$k \begin{bmatrix} n_{11} & n_{12} & n_{13} & n_{14} \\ n_{21} & n_{22} & n_{23} & n_{24} \\ n_{31} & n_{32} & n_{33} & n_{34} \\ n_{41} & n_{42} & n_{43} & n_{44} \end{bmatrix} = \begin{bmatrix} kn_{11} & kn_{12} & kn_{13} & kn_{14} \\ kn_{21} & kn_{22} & kn_{23} & kn_{24} \\ kn_{31} & kn_{32} & kn_{33} & kn_{34} \\ kn_{41} & kn_{42} & kn_{43} & kn_{44} \end{bmatrix}$$

Adding matrices and additive identity element

When adding matrices, the matrices must all be of the same order. To find the sum of two matrices of the same order, add the values of the corresponding elements and place the sum in the corresponding position of the new matrix. For all matrices, the additive identity element is the zero matrix. Adding zero to any number will not change the value of the number, and adding a zero matrix to any matrix of the same order will not change the value of the matrix. Follow this pattern when finding the sum of two matrices of the same order:

$$\begin{bmatrix} m_{11} & m_{12} \\ m_{21} & m_{22} \end{bmatrix} + \begin{bmatrix} n_{11} & n_{12} \\ n_{21} & n_{22} \end{bmatrix} = \begin{bmatrix} m_{11} + n_{11} & m_{12} + n_{12} \\ m_{21} + n_{21} & m_{22} + n_{22} \end{bmatrix}$$

Subtracting matrices and additive inverse

To find the difference between two matrices of the same order, find the negative of the second matrix and add it to the first matrix, following the rules of addition for matrices. Alternately, you can subtract each element of the second matrix from its corresponding element in the first matrix and write the difference in the corresponding position of the resulting matrix. For all matrices of the same order, the additive inverse is the negative of the original matrix. Follow this pattern when finding the difference between two matrices of the same order:

$$\begin{bmatrix} m_{11} & m_{12} \\ m_{21} & m_{22} \end{bmatrix} - \begin{bmatrix} n_{11} & n_{12} \\ n_{21} & n_{22} \end{bmatrix} = \begin{bmatrix} m_{11} - n_{11} & m_{12} - n_{12} \\ m_{21} - n_{21} & m_{22} - n_{22} \end{bmatrix}$$

Conformable matrices

Matrices that have the same order are called conformable matrices for matrix addition or matrix subtraction. For all addition and subtraction of matrices, the matrices involved must be conformable. There is no definition of addition or subtraction of matrices in any situation involving non-conformable matrices. For all conformable matrices, you can complete the addition of matrices on your graphing calculator with the addition key. To complete the subtraction of conformable matrices on your graphing calculator, you may have to first find the additive inverse of the second matrix and then use the addition feature to solve it as the sum of two conformable matrices.

Unlike conformable matrices for addition or subtraction, conformable matrices for multiplication must have the number of columns in the first matrix equal to the number of rows in the second matrix. The second matrix is considered to be premultiplied by the first matrix, and the first matrix is said to be postmultiplied by the second matrix. If the number of columns in the first matrix does not equal the number of rows in the second matrix, then the matrices are not conformable and the multiplication process is not defined. It is important to note that the commutative principle of multiplication does not apply to the multiplication of matrices.

Linear product vectors

The linear product, also referred to as the dot product, of two vectors is the sum of the products of the corresponding elements of the two vectors. To find the linear product, the first vector MUST be a row vector, and the second vector MUST be a column vector with an equal number of elements. Find the product of the first element in each vector, as well as the product of each subsequent pair of elements until each corresponding pair has been multiplied. Finally, find the sum of the products. Follow this pattern to find the linear product of two vectors:

$$[m_{11} \quad m_{12} \quad m_{13}] \cdot \begin{bmatrix} n_{11} \\ n_{21} \\ n_{31} \end{bmatrix} = m_{11}n_{11} + m_{12}n_{21} + m_{13}n_{31}$$

Linear product of matrices

To find the linear product of two matrices, the number of columns in the first matrix must equal the number of rows in the second matrix. The two matrices do not have to be of the same order as long as this condition is met. The resulting matrix will be a matrix of order equal to the number of rows in the first matrix and the number of columns in the second matrix. To multiply matrices, treat each row and column as individual vectors and follow the pattern for multiplying vectors. In the new matrix, the answer from multiplying the first row vector by the first column vector is the element positioned at the intersection of the first row, first column of the new matrix. The answer from multiplying the second row vector by the first column vector is the element positioned at the intersection of the second row, first column of the new matrix. Continue this pattern until each row of the first matrix has been multiplied by each column of the second vector.

$$\begin{bmatrix} m_{11} & m_{12} \\ m_{21} & m_{22} \\ m_{31} & m_{32} \end{bmatrix} \times \begin{bmatrix} n_{11} & n_{12} & n_{13} \\ n_{21} & n_{22} & n_{23} \end{bmatrix} = \begin{bmatrix} m_{11}n_{11} + m_{12}n_{21} & m_{11}n_{12} + m_{12}n_{22} & m_{11}n_{13} + m_{12}n_{23} \\ m_{21}n_{11} + m_{22}n_{21} & m_{21}n_{12} + m_{22}n_{22} & m_{21}n_{13} + m_{22}n_{23} \\ m_{31}n_{11} + m_{32}n_{21} & m_{31}n_{12} + m_{32}n_{22} & m_{31}n_{13} + m_{32}n_{23} \end{bmatrix}$$

Inverse of a 2x2 matrix

The inverse of matrix M is matrix N, such that $MN = NM$. In this case, matrix M and matrix N must both be square matrices of equal order. It is important to note that just because a matrix is a square matrix does not mean that matrix will have an inverse. If a square matrix does have an inverse, the inverse is unique to that square matrix, and the matrix is considered to be nonsingular. For any matrix M that has an inverse, the inverse is represented by the symbol M^{-1}. To calculate the inverse of a 2×2 square matrix, use the following pattern:

$$\begin{bmatrix} m_{11} & m_{12} \\ m_{21} & m_{22} \end{bmatrix}^{-1} = \begin{bmatrix} \dfrac{m_{22}}{\Delta} & \dfrac{-m_{12}}{\Delta} \\ \dfrac{-m_{21}}{\Delta} & \dfrac{m_{11}}{\Delta} \end{bmatrix}, \text{ where } \Delta = m_{11}m_{22} - m_{12}m_{21} \neq 0.$$

Determinant

A determinant is a scalar value that is determined by a function of a square matrix. The scalar value Δ obtained from a 2×2 square matrix $\begin{bmatrix} m_{11} & m_{12} \\ m_{21} & m_{22} \end{bmatrix}$ according to the formula $\Delta = m_{11}m_{22} - m_{12}m_{21} \neq 0$ is called the determinant of the matrix. The determinant of matrix N is denoted $\det(N)$ or $|N|$. To find the determinant of a 3×3 square matrix, follow the pattern below:

$$\det \begin{bmatrix} a & b & c \\ d & e & f \\ g & h & i \end{bmatrix} = aei + bfg + cdh - ceg - bdi - afh$$

Beyond a 3×3 matrix, the process for finding the determinant becomes cumbersome. Use your graphing calculator, converting decimals to fractions, if necessary.

Partitioned matrix

A partitioned matrix is matrix that has been divided, or partitioned, into square matrices. The individual square matrices may or may not be of the same order. Partitioned matrices can be used to find the inverses of nonsingular matrices. For example, given the 2×2 nonsingular matrix $N = \begin{bmatrix} a & b \\ c & d \end{bmatrix}$, you can find the inverse N^{-1} by creating a partitioned matrix, where the first partition is the original square matrix, and the second partition is the 2×2 identity matrix as follows: $\begin{bmatrix} a & b & | & 1 & 0 \\ c & d & | & 0 & 1 \end{bmatrix}$. To find the inverse of the original 2×2 matrix, perform elementary row operations, such as multiplying a row by a nonzero scalar, adding two rows, interchanging two rows, or a combination of these, to convert the partition on the left to an identity matrix. The result is that the partition on the right will be the inverse of the original matrix.

Transformation of an augmented matrix

The transformation of an augmented matrix is a process useful for solving systems of equations. When a system of equations is not easily solvable using normal algebraic procedures, use the transformation of an augmented matrix to find the solution, if it exists. If there is a solution, the system is consistent. If there is no solution, the system is inconsistent. Begin by arranging each equation of the system in the format $ax + by + cz = d$. Write the system of equations in the correct format, numbering the coefficients with subscripts as follows:

$$a_{11}x + b_{12}y + c_{13}z = d_1$$
$$a_{21}x + b_{22}y + c_{23}z = d_2$$
$$a_{31}x + b_{32}y + c_{33}z = d_3$$

Enter each coefficient into its corresponding position in the augmented matrix as follows:

$$\begin{matrix} a_{11} & b_{12} & c_{13} & d_1 \\ a_{21} & b_{22} & c_{23} & d_2 \\ a_{31} & b_{32} & c_{33} & d_3 \end{matrix}$$

To solve the augmented matrix and the system of equations, use the elementary row operations to form an identity matrix. If an identity matrix is not possible, get the augmented matrix as close as possible. If all but the last column forms an identity matrix, the values in the last column are the solutions to the system of equations, with $d_1 = x$, $d_2 = y$, and $d_3 = z$. If one or more rows of the identity matrix are incomplete, the solution is not a unique solution.

Reduced row-echelon forms

When a system of equations has a solution, finding the transformation of the augmented matrix will result in one of three reduced row-echelon forms. Only one of these forms will give a unique solution to the system of equations, however. Use the following formats and formulas to get the solutions to a system of equations:

$\begin{bmatrix} 1 & 0 & 0 & x_0 \\ 0 & 1 & 0 & y_0 \\ 0 & 0 & 1 & z_0 \end{bmatrix}$ gives the unique solution $x = x_0$; $y = y_0$; $z = z_0$

$\begin{bmatrix} 1 & 0 & k_1 & x_0 \\ 0 & 1 & k_2 & y_0 \\ 0 & 0 & 0 & 0 \end{bmatrix}$ gives a non-unique solution $x = x_0 - k_1 z$; $y = y_0 - k_2 z$

$\begin{bmatrix} 1 & j_1 & k_1 & x_0 \\ 0 & 0 & 0 & 0 \\ 0 & 0 & 0 & 0 \end{bmatrix}$ gives a non-unique solution $x = x_0 - j_1 y - k_1 z$

Reduced row-echelon forms can be used to solve systems of equations with more variables, but the process is extremely time-consuming. Use your graphing calculator to solve the system for you.

Determinant of a 3x3 matrix

Finding the determinant of a 3×3 matrix requires the use of multiple 2×2 determinants. Multiply the value in the first row, first column, by the value of the 2×2 determinant formed when the first row and first column are removed. Subtract the product of the value in the first row, second column, and the 2×2 determinant formed when the first row and second column are removed. Add the product of the value in the first row, third column, and the 2×2 determinant formed when the first row and third column are removed. The general pattern is as follows:

$$\begin{vmatrix} a_{11} & a_{12} & a_{13} \\ a_{21} & a_{22} & a_{23} \\ a_{31} & a_{32} & a_{33} \end{vmatrix} = a_{11} \begin{vmatrix} a_{22} & a_{23} \\ a_{32} & a_{33} \end{vmatrix} - a_{12} \begin{vmatrix} a_{21} & a_{23} \\ a_{31} & a_{33} \end{vmatrix} + a_{13} \begin{vmatrix} a_{21} & a_{22} \\ a_{31} & a_{32} \end{vmatrix}$$

Inverse matrix

To determine whether or not a matrix has an inverse, first consider the shape of the matrix. If the matrix is not a square matrix, it does not have an inverse. If the matrix is a square matrix of any order, find the determinant of the matrix. If the determinant is equal to zero, the matrix does not have an inverse. If the determinant is anything except zero, the matrix has an inverse. Keep in mind that if a square matrix has any row or column with all values in that row or column equal to zero, then the value of the matrix is equal to zero and there is no inverse.

Geometric transformations

The four geometric transformations are translations, reflections, rotations, and dilations. When geometric transformations are expressed as matrices, the process of performing the transformations is simplified. For calculations of the geometric transformations of a planar figure, make a $2 \times n$ matrix, where n is the number of vertices in the planar figure. Each column represents the rectangular coordinates of one vertex of the figure, with the top row containing the values of the x-coordinates and the bottom row containing the values of the y-coordinates. For example, given a planar triangular figure with coordinates (x_1, y_1), (x_2, y_2), and (x_3, y_3), the corresponding matrix is $\begin{bmatrix} x_1 & x_2 & x_3 \\ y_1 & y_2 & y_3 \end{bmatrix}$. You can then perform the necessary transformations on this matrix to determine the coordinates of the resulting figure.

Translation of a planar figure

A translation moves a figure along the x-axis, the y-axis, or both axes without changing the size or shape of the figure. To calculate the new coordinates of a planar figure following a translation, set up a matrix of the coordinates and a matrix of the translation values and add the two matrices.

$$\begin{bmatrix} h & h & h \\ v & v & v \end{bmatrix} + \begin{bmatrix} x_1 & x_2 & x_3 \\ y_1 & y_2 & y_3 \end{bmatrix} = \begin{bmatrix} h + x_1 & h + x_2 & h + x_3 \\ v + y_1 & v + y_2 & v + y_3 \end{bmatrix}$$

where h is the number of units the figure is moved along the x-axis (horizontally) and v is the number of units the figure is moved along the y-axis (vertically).

Reflection of a planar figure

$y = x$

To find the reflection of a planar figure over the x-axis, set up a matrix of the coordinates of the vertices and pre-multiply the matrix by the 2×2 matrix $\begin{bmatrix} 1 & 0 \\ 0 & -1 \end{bmatrix}$ so that $\begin{bmatrix} 1 & 0 \\ 0 & -1 \end{bmatrix}\begin{bmatrix} x_1 & x_2 & x_3 \\ y_1 & y_2 & y_3 \end{bmatrix} = \begin{bmatrix} x_1 & x_2 & x_3 \\ -y_1 & -y_2 & -y_3 \end{bmatrix}$. To find the reflection of a planar figure over the y-axis, set up a matrix of the coordinates of the vertices and pre-multiply the matrix by the 2×2 matrix $\begin{bmatrix} -1 & 0 \\ 0 & 1 \end{bmatrix}$ so that $\begin{bmatrix} -1 & 0 \\ 0 & 1 \end{bmatrix}\begin{bmatrix} x_1 & x_2 & x_3 \\ y_1 & y_2 & y_3 \end{bmatrix} = \begin{bmatrix} -x_1 & -x_2 & -x_3 \\ y_1 & y_2 & y_3 \end{bmatrix}$. To find the reflection of a planar figure over the line $y = x$, set up a matrix of the coordinates of the vertices and pre-multiply the matrix by the 2×2 matrix $\begin{bmatrix} 0 & 1 \\ 1 & 0 \end{bmatrix}$ so that $\begin{bmatrix} 0 & 1 \\ 1 & 0 \end{bmatrix}\begin{bmatrix} x_1 & x_2 & x_3 \\ y_1 & y_2 & y_3 \end{bmatrix} = \begin{bmatrix} y_1 & y_2 & y_3 \\ x_1 & x_2 & x_3 \end{bmatrix}$. Remember that the order of multiplication is important when multiplying matrices. The commutative property does not apply.

Rotation of a planar figure

To find the coordinates of the figure formed by rotating a planar figure about the origin θ degrees in a counterclockwise direction, set up a matrix of the coordinates of the vertices and pre-multiply the matrix by the 2×2 matrix $\begin{bmatrix} \cos\theta & \sin\theta \\ -\sin\theta & \cos\theta \end{bmatrix}$. For example, if you want to rotate a figure $90°$ clockwise around the origin, you would have to convert the degree measure to $270°$ counterclockwise and solve the 2×2 matrix you have set as the pre-multiplier: $\begin{bmatrix} \cos 270° & \sin 270° \\ -\sin 270° & \cos 270° \end{bmatrix} = \begin{bmatrix} 0 & -1 \\ 1 & 0 \end{bmatrix}$. Use this as the pre-multiplier for the matrix $\begin{bmatrix} x_1 & x_2 & x_3 \\ y_1 & y_2 & y_3 \end{bmatrix}$ and solve to find the new coordinates.

Dilation of a planar figure

To find the dilation of a planar figure by a scale factor of k, set up a matrix of the coordinates of the vertices of the planar figure and pre-multiply the matrix by the 2×2 matrix $\begin{bmatrix} k & 0 \\ 0 & k \end{bmatrix}$ so that $\begin{bmatrix} k & 0 \\ 0 & k \end{bmatrix} \begin{bmatrix} x_1 & x_2 & x_3 \\ y_1 & y_2 & y_3 \end{bmatrix} = \begin{bmatrix} kx_1 & kx_2 & kx_3 \\ ky_1 & ky_2 & ky_3 \end{bmatrix}$. In this case, k will be positive if the figure is being enlarged, and negative if the figure is being shrunk. Again, remember that when multiplying matrices, the order of the matrices is important. The commutative principle does not apply, and the matrix with the coordinates of the figure must be the second matrix.

Fundamental Counting Principle

The Fundamental Counting Principle deals specifically with situations in which the order that something happens affects the outcome. Specifically, the Fundamental Counting Principle states that if one event can have x possible different outcomes, and after the first outcome has been established the event can then have y possible outcomes, then there are $x \cdot y$ possible different ways the outcomes can happen in that order. For example, if two dice are rolled, one at a time, there are 6 possible outcomes for the first die, and 6 possible outcomes for the second die, for a total of $6 \cdot 6 = 36$ total possible outcomes. Also, suppose you have a bag containing one each of a penny, nickel, dime, quarter, and half dollar. There are 5 different possible outcomes the first time you pull a coin. Without replacing the first coin, there are 4 different possible outcomes for the second coin. This makes $5 \cdot 4 = 20$ different possible outcomes for the first two coins drawn when the order the coins are drawn makes a difference.

Addition Principle

The Addition Principle addresses situations in which two different tasks are completed at separate times with separate outcomes. The Addition Principle states that if one event can have x possible different outcomes, and a second unrelated event can have y possible different outcomes, and none of the outcomes are common to both events, then the total number of possible outcomes for the two separate events occurring at two separate times is $x + y$. If the two events can occur at the same time and some of the outcomes are common to both events, the total number of possible outcomes for the two events is $x + y -$ the number of outcomes common to both events.

Permutation

For each set of data, the individual elements may be arranged in different groups containing different numbers of elements arranged in different orders. For example, given the set of integers from one to three, inclusive, the elements of the set are 1, 2, and 3. They may be arranged as follows: 1, 2, 3, 12, 21, 13, 31, 23, 32, 123, 132, 231, 213, 312, and 321. These ordered sequences of elements from the given set of data are called permutations. It is important to note that in permutations, the order of the elements in the sequence is important. The sequence 123 is not the same as the sequence 213. Also, no element in the given set may be used more times as an element in a permutation than it appears as an element in the original set. For example, 223 is not a permutation in the above example because the number 2 only appears one time in the given set.

Factorial of a number

The factorial of a positive integer is represented by the ! sign. The factorial of a number is the product of the number and all positive integers less than the number. For example, 3! (read "3 factorial") means $3 \cdot 2 \cdot 1 = 6$. The exception to the rule is the case of zero factorial. In this case, $0! = 1$. This makes sense if you consider the pattern of factorials:

$$4! = 4 \cdot 3 \cdot 2 \cdot 1 = 24;$$
$$3! = 3 \cdot 2 \cdot 1 = \frac{4!}{4} = 6;$$
$$2! = 2 \cdot 1 = \frac{3!}{3} = 2;$$
$$1! = \frac{2!}{2} = 1;$$
$$0! = \frac{1!}{1} = 1$$

Number of permutations

The number of possible permutations of n items from a set of n items is $n!$, or $n(n-1)(n-2)(n-3)\ldots(3)(2)(1)$. To find the number of permutations of r items from a set of n items, use the formula $_nP_r = \frac{n!}{(n-r)!}$. When using this formula, each element of r must be unique. Also, this assumes that different arrangements of the same set of elements yields different outcomes. For example, 123 is not the same as 321; order is important! If the set contains duplicates of one or more elements, the formula changes slightly to accommodate the duplicates. Use the formula $= \frac{n!}{n_1!n_2!\ldots n_k!}$, where P is the number of permutations, n is the total number of elements in the set, and n_1, n_2, and n_3 are the number of duplicates of an individual element.

To find the total number of possible permutations of a set of unique items, you must apply the permutation formulas multiple times. For example, to find the total number of possible permutations of the set 1, 2, 3, first apply the formula $P = n!$ as follows: $P = n! = 3! = 6$. This gives the number of permutations of the three elements when all three elements are used. To find the number of permutations when two of the three elements are used, use the formula $_nP_r = \frac{n!}{(n-r)!}$, where n is 3 and r is 2.

$$_nP_r = \frac{n!}{(n-r)!} \Rightarrow {_3P_2} = \frac{3!}{(3-2)!} = \frac{6}{1} = 6$$

To find the number of permutations when one element is used, use the formula $_nP_r = \frac{n!}{(n-r)!}$, where n is 3 and r is 1.

$$_nP_r = \frac{n!}{(n-r)!} \Rightarrow {_3P_1} = \frac{3!}{(3-1)!} = \frac{3!}{2!} = \frac{6}{2} = 3$$

Find the sum of the three formulas: $6 + 6 + 3 = 15$ total possible permutations.

Combinations

For each set of data, the individual elements may be arranged in different groups containing different numbers of elements arranged in different orders. For example, given the set of integers from one to three, inclusive, the elements of the set are 1, 2, and 3. They may be arranged as follows: 1, 2, 3, 12, 21, 13, 31, 23, 32, 123, 132, 231, 213, 312, and 321. Some of the arrangements contain the exact same elements as other arrangements and must be discarded to avoid duplicates. This leaves 1, 2, 3, 12, 13, 23, and 123. These sequences of unique combinations of elements from the given set of data are called combinations. No element in the given set may be used more times as an element in a combination than it appears as an element in the original set. For example, 223 is not a combination in the above example because the number 2 only appears one time in the given set.

Difference between permutations and combinations

The biggest difference between permutations and combinations is the ordering of the sequences. In permutations, different sequences of the same group of elements create different permutations. In combinations, different sequences of the same group of elements create the same combination. It is easy to get the two terms confused, especially since the terms are misused in the English language. For example, combination locks do not require a combination, but a permutation. If you enter the correct numbers in the wrong order, you have entered a correct combination, but an incorrect permutation, and the lock will not open.

Number of combinations

In a set containing n elements, the number of combinations of r items from the set can be found using the formula $_nC_r = \frac{n!}{r!(n-r)!}$. Notice the similarity to the formula for permutations. In effect, you are dividing the number of permutations by $r!$ to get the number of combinations, and the formula may be written $_nC_r = \frac{_nP_r}{r!}$. When finding the number of combinations, it is important to remember that the elements in the set must be unique, that is, there must not be any duplicate items, and that no item is used more than once in any given sequence.

Recursive definition relative to a Fibonacci sequence

Whenever one element of a sequence is defined in terms of a previous element or elements of the sequence, the sequence has a recursive definition. For example, given the recursive definition $a_1 = 0; a_2 = 1; a_n = a_{n-1} + a_{(n-2)}$ for all $n \geq 2$, you get the sequence 0, 1, 1, 2, 3, 5, 8, ... This particular sequence is known as the Fibonacci sequence, and is defined as the numbers zero and one, and a continuing sequence of numbers, with each number in the sequence equal to the sum of the two previous numbers. It is important to note that the Fibonacci sequence can also be defined as the first two terms being equal to one, with the remaining terms equal to the sum of the previous two terms. Both definitions are considered correct in mathematics. Make sure you know which definition you are working with when dealing with Fibonacci numbers.

Recursive sequence closed form expression

Sometimes one term of a sequence with a recursive definition can be found without knowing the previous terms of the sequence. This case is known as a closed-form expression for a recursive definition. In this case, an alternate formula will apply to the sequence to generate the same sequence of numbers. However, not all sequences based on recursive definitions will have a closed-form expression. Some sequences will require the use of the recursive definition. For example, the Fibonacci sequence has a closed-form expression given by the formula $(n) = \frac{\phi^n - \left(\frac{-1}{\phi}\right)^n}{\sqrt{5}}$, where $f(n)$ is the nth term in the sequence, and φ is the golden ratio, which is equal to $\frac{1+\sqrt{5}}{2}$. In this case, $f(1) = 1$, so you know which definition of the Fibonacci sequence you have.

Cartesian product

A Cartesian product is the product of two sets of data, X and Y, such that all elements x are a member of set X, and all elements y are a member of set Y. The product of the two sets, $X \times Y$ is the set of all ordered pairs (x, y). For example, given a standard deck of 52 playing cards, there are four possible suits (hearts, diamonds, clubs, and spades) and thirteen possible card values (the numbers 2 through 10, ace, jack, queen, and king). If the card suits are set X and the card values are set Y, then there are $4 \times 13 = 52$ possible different (x, y) combinations, as seen in the 52 cards of a standard deck.

Binary relation

A binary relation, also referred to as a relation, dyadic relation, or 2-place relation, is a subset of a Cartesian product. It shows the relation between one set of objects and a second set of object, or between one set of objects and itself. The prefix *bi-* means *two*, so there are always two sets involved – either two different sets, or the same set used twice. The ordered pairs of the Cartesian product are used to indicate a binary relation. Relations are possible for situations involving more than two sets, but those are not called binary relations.

Types of relations

The five types of relations are reflexive, symmetric, transitive, antisymmetric, and equivalence. A reflexive relation has $x\Re x$ (x related to x) for all values of x in the set. A symmetric relation has $x\Re y \Rightarrow y\Re x$ for all values of x and y in the set. A transitive relation has $(x\Re y$ and $y\Re z) \Rightarrow x\Re z$ for all values of $x, y,$ and z in the set. An antisymmetric relation has $(x\Re y$ and $y\Re x) \Rightarrow x = y$ for all values of x and y in the set. A relation that is reflexive, symmetric, and transitive is called an equivalence relation. These definitions will be provided in the test booklet.

Sequence

Any function with the set of all natural numbers as the domain is also called a sequence. An element of a sequence is denoted by the symbol a_n, which represents the nth element of sequence a. Sequences may be arithmetic or geometric, and may be defined by a recursive definition, closed-form expression or both. Both arithmetic and geometric sequences have recursive definitions based on the first term of the sequence. Both arithmetic and geometric sequences also have formulas to find the sum of the first n terms in the sequence, assuming you know what the first term is. The sum of all the terms in a sequence is called a series.

Arithmetic sequence

An arithmetic sequence, or arithmetic progression, is a special kind of sequence in which each term has a specific quantity, called the common difference, that is added to the previous term. The common difference may be positive or negative. The general form of an arithmetic sequence containing n terms is $a_1, a_1 + d, a_1 + 2d, \ldots, a_1 + (n-1)d$, where d is the common difference. The formula for the general term of an arithmetic sequence is $a_n = a_1 + (n-1)d$, where a_n is the term you are looking for and d is the common difference. To find the sum of the first n terms of an arithmetic sequence, use the formula $s_n = \frac{n}{2}(a_1 + a_n)$.

Geometric sequence

A geometric sequence, or geometric progression, is a special kind of sequence in which each term has a specific quantity, called the common ratio, multiplied by the previous term. The common ratio may be positive or negative. The general form of a geometric sequence containing n terms is $a_1, a_1 r, a_1 r^2, \ldots, a_1 r^{n-1}$, where r is the common ratio. The formula for the general term of a geometric sequence is $a_n = a_1 r^{n-1}$, where a_n is the term you are looking for and r is the common ratio. To find the sum of the first n terms of a geometric sequence, use the formula $s_n = \frac{a_1(1-r^n)}{1-r}$.

Discrete math

Among mathematicians, there is not an agreed-upon definition of discrete math. What is agreed upon is the fact that discrete math deals with processes that use a finite, or countable, number of elements. In discrete math, the elements will be discontinuous, as this branch of mathematics does not involve the continuity that processes of calculus do. Generally, discrete math uses countable sets of rational numbers, although they do not use the set of all real numbers, as that would then make the math continuous and put it in the category of algebra or calculus. Discrete math has numerous applications in the fields of computer science and business.

Difference equation

Some systems or equations depend on the past values to determine future values. One example of this is the difference equation, which generates values recursively. The difference equation can generate recursive values in the form of a sequence of numbers, such as the Fibonacci sequence, where each element in the sequence depends on the value of previous elements in the sequence. The general form of a difference equation is $(n + 1) - f(n) = g(n)$, where n is a positive integer. Another form of the difference equation is a discrete dynamic system that has a specific equation to follow based on the input of a value to determine the output value. The third type of difference equation is an iterated map, which generates complex orbits of values.

First and second difference

The first difference of a difference equation is used to explain growth rate or decline within a sequence. The equation for the first difference is $\Delta a_n = a_{n+1} - a_n$, where Δa_n is the change, such as the growth or decline of a sequence. If Δa_n is positive, the elements of the sequence are increasing in value. If Δa_n is negative, the elements of the sequence are decreasing in value. If the value of Δa_n is constant, then the rate of increase or decrease is constant and the elements form a linear relationship. The second difference of a difference equation is $\Delta a_{n+1} = \Delta a_n$. When this value is constant, the elements form a quadratic relationship.

Vertex-edge graph

A vertex-edge graph is useful for solving problems involving schedules, relationships, networks, or paths among a set number of objects. The number of objects may be large, but it will never be infinite. The vertices or points on the graph represent the objects and are referred to as *nodes*. The nodes are joined by line segments called *edges* or links that show the specific paths that connect the various elements represented by the nodes. The number of nodes does not have to equal the number of edges. There may be more or less, depending on the number of allowable paths. An endpoint on a vertex-edge graph is a vertex on exactly one edge. In the case of a vertex that is an endpoint, the edge that the vertex is on is incident with the vertex. Two edges are considered to be adjacent if they share a vertex. Two vertices are considered to be adjacent if they share an edge.

Loop and degree sum formula

In a vertex-edge graph, a loop is an edge that has the same vertex as both endpoints. To calculate the degree of a vertex in a vertex-edge graph, count the number of edges that are incident with the vertex, counting loops twice since they meet the vertex at both ends. The degree sum formula states that the sum of the degrees of all vertices on a vertex-edge graph is always equal to twice the number of edges on the graph. Thus, the sum of the degrees will never be odd, even if there are an odd number of vertices.

Paths

In a vertex-edge graph, a path is a given sequence of vertices that follows one or more edges to get from vertex to vertex. There is no jumping over spaces to get from one vertex to the next, although doubling back over an edge already traveled is allowed. A simple path is a path that does not repeat an edge in traveling from beginning to end. Think of the vertex-edge graph as a map, with the vertices as cities on the map, and the edges as roads between the cities. To get from one city to another, you must drive on the roads. A simple path allows you to complete your trip without driving on the same road twice.

Circuits

In a vertex-edge graph, a circuit is a path that has the same starting and stopping point. Picturing the vertex-edge graph as a map with cities and roads, a circuit is like leaving home on vacation and then returning home after you have visited your intended destinations. You may go in one direction and then turn around, or you may go in a circle. A simple circuit on the graph completes the circuit without repeating an edge. This is like going on vacation without driving on the same road twice.

Euler and Hamiltonian path

On a vertex-edge graph, any path that uses each edge exactly one time is called an Euler path. One simple way to rule out the possibility of an Euler path is to calculate the degree of each vertex. If more than two vertices have an odd degree, an Euler path is impossible. A path that uses each vertex exactly one time is called a Hamiltonian path. If every pair of vertices is joined by an edge, the vertex-edge graph is said to be connected. If the vertex-edge graph has no simple circuits in it, then the graph is said to be a tree.

Practice Test

Practice Questions

Number Sense and Operations

1. In the base-5 number system, what is the sum of 303 and 2222?
   a. 2030
   b. 2525
   c. 3030
   d. 3530

2. Kim's current monthly rent is $800. She is moving to another apartment complex, where the monthly rent will be $1,100. What is the percent increase in her monthly rent amount?
   a. 25.5%
   b. 27%
   c. 35%
   d. 37.5%

3. Which of the following statements is true?
   a. The set of whole numbers is a subset of the set of natural numbers.
   b. The set of integers is a subset of the set of natural numbers.
   c. The set of integers is a subset of the set of rational numbers.
   d. The set of rational numbers is a subset of the set of integers.

4. Which of the following represents 55 in the base-2 system?
   a. 110
   b. 1101
   c. 101,111
   d. 110,111

5. Marlon pays $45 for a jacket that has been marked down 25%. What was the original cost of the jacket?
   a. $80
   b. $75
   c. $65
   d. $60

6. Which of the following statements is true?
   a. A number is divisible by 6 if the number is divisible by both 2 and 3.
   b. A number is divisible by 4 if the sum of all digits is divisible by 8.
   c. A number is divisible by 3 if the last digit is divisible by 3.
   d. A number is divisible by 7 if the sum of the last two digits is divisible by 7.

7. Which of the following is an irrational number?
   a. $4.\overline{2}$
   b. $\sqrt{2}$
   c. $\frac{4}{5}$
   d. $\frac{21}{5}$

8. Robert buys a car for $24,210. The price of the car has been marked down by 10%. What was the original price of the car?
   a. $25,900
   b. $26,300
   c. $26,900
   d. $27,300

9. Carlos spends $\frac{1}{8}$ of his monthly salary on utility bills. If his utility bills total $320, what is his monthly salary?
   a. $2,440
   b. $2,520
   c. $2,560
   d. $2,600

10. Which of the following is closed under the operation of division?
    a. whole numbers
    b. integers
    c. nonzero rational numbers
    d. irrational numbers

11. Which of the following accurately describes the set of integers?
    a. the set of counting numbers
    b. the set of counting numbers, plus zero
    c. the set of numbers that may be written as the ratio of $\frac{a}{b}$, where b ≠ 0
    d. the set of counting numbers, zero, and the negations of the counting numbers

12. Which of the following correctly compares the sets of rational and irrational numbers?
    a. The set of rational numbers is a subset of the set of irrational numbers.
    b. The set of irrational numbers is a subset of the set of rational numbers.
    c. The sets of irrational and rational numbers are disjoint.
    d. The sets of irrational and rational numbers are equal.

13. Which of the following illustrates the multiplicative inverse property?
    a. The product of a and 1 is a.
    b. The product of $\frac{1}{a}$ and a is 1.
    c. The variable a, raised to the negative 1 power, is equal to the ratio of 1 to a.
    d. The product of a and $-a$ is $-a^2$.

14. For any natural numbers, a, b, and c, assume $a|b$ and $a|c$. Which of the following statements is *not* necessarily true?
  a. $b|c$
  b. $a|(b-c)$
  c. $a|bc$
  d. $a|(b+c)$

15. Which of the following equations may be used to convert $0.\bar{4}$ to a fraction?
  a. $10x - x = 4.\bar{4} - 0.\bar{4}$
  b. $100x - x = 4.\bar{4} - 0.\bar{4}$
  c. $10x - x = 44.\bar{4} - 4.\bar{4}$
  d. $100x - 10x = 4.\bar{4} - 0.\bar{4}$

16. Jason decides to donate 1% of his annual salary to a local charity. If his annual salary is $45,000, how much will he donate?
  a. $4.50
  b. $45
  c. $450
  d. $4,500

17. Kendra uses the pie chart below to represent the allocation of her annual income. Her annual income is $40,000.

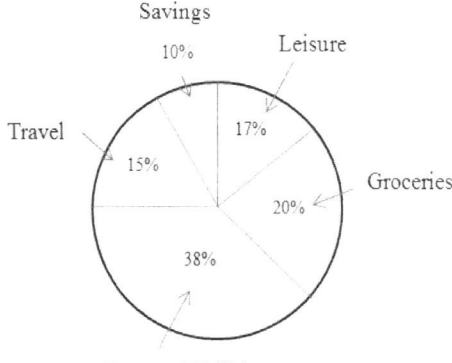

Which of the following statements is true?
  a. The amount of money she spends on travel and savings is more than $11,000.
  b. The amount of money she spends on rent and utilities is approximately $15,000.
  c. The amount of money she spends on groceries and savings is more than $13,000.
  d. The amount of money she spends on leisure is less than $5,000.

18. Which of the following correctly represents the expanded form of 0.867?

a. $8 \cdot \frac{1}{10^0} + 6 \cdot \frac{1}{10^1} + 7 \cdot \frac{1}{10^2}$

b. $8 \cdot \frac{1}{10^2} + 6 \cdot \frac{1}{10^3} + 7 \cdot \frac{1}{10^4}$

c. $8 \cdot \frac{1}{10^3} + 6 \cdot \frac{1}{10^2} + 7 \cdot \frac{1}{10^1}$

d. $8 \cdot \frac{1}{10^1} + 6 \cdot \frac{1}{10^2} + 7 \cdot \frac{1}{10^3}$

19. Which expression is represented by the diagram below?

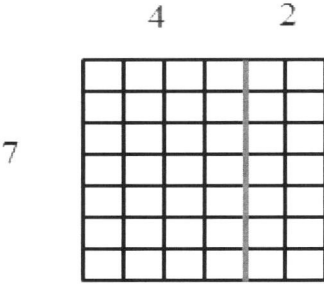

a. $7 + (4 + 2)$
b. $7 \cdot (4 \cdot 2)$
c. $7 + (4 \cdot 2)$
d. $7 \cdot (4 + 2)$

20. $b|a$ if
a. $a = b \cdot q$
b. $a = b + q$
c. $b = a \cdot q$
d. $b = a + q$

21. Which of the following sets is *not* closed under subtraction?
a. integers
b. real numbers
c. natural numbers
d. rational numbers

22. A dress is marked down 45%. The cost, after taxes, is $39.95. If the tax rate is 8.75%, what was the original price of the dress?
a. $45.74
b. $58.61
c. $66.79
d. $72.31

23. Amy saves $450 every 3 months. How much does she save after 3 years?
a. $4,800
b. $5,200
c. $5,400
d. $5,800

24. The table below shows the average amount of rainfall Houston receives during the summer and autumn months.

Month	Amount of Rainfall (in inches)
June	5.35
July	3.18
August	3.83
September	4.33
October	4.5
November	4.19

What percentage of rainfall received during this timeframe, is received during the month of October?
    a. 13.5%
    b. 15.1%
    c. 16.9%
    d. 17.7%

25. Which of the following represents 30,490?
    a. 3.049×10^{-4}
    b. 3.049×10^3
    c. 30.490×10^3
    d. 3.049×10^4

Algebra and Functions

26. Which of the following formulas may be used to represent the sequence 1, 2, 4, 8, 16, ...?
    a. $y = 2x$
    b. $y = x + 2$
    c. $y = 2^{x-1}$
    d. $y = x^2$

27. Which of the following formulas may be used to represent the sequence 8, 13, 18, 23, 28, ...?
    a. $a_n = 5n + 3$
    b. $a_n = n + 5$
    c. $a_n = n + 8$
    d. $a_n = 5n + 8$

28. Which of the following graphs does *not* represent a function?

a.

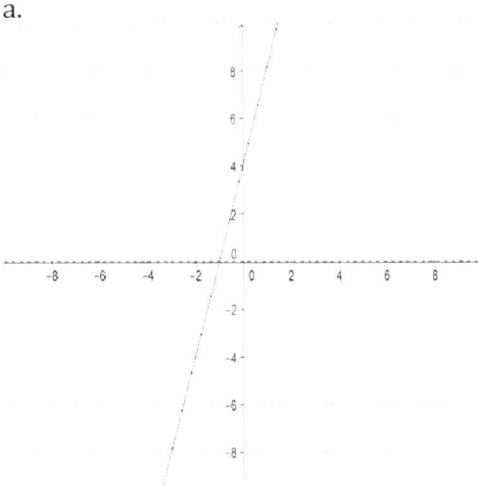

b.

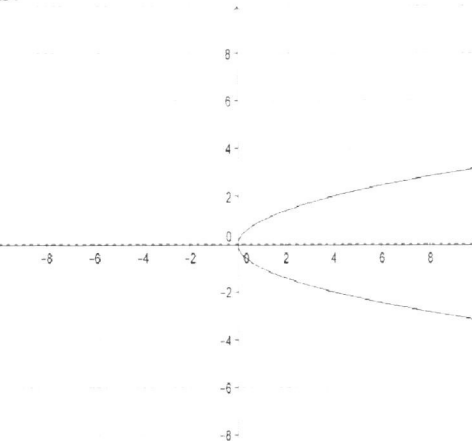

c.

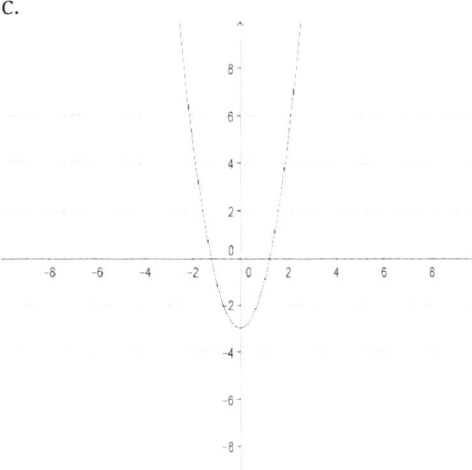

d.

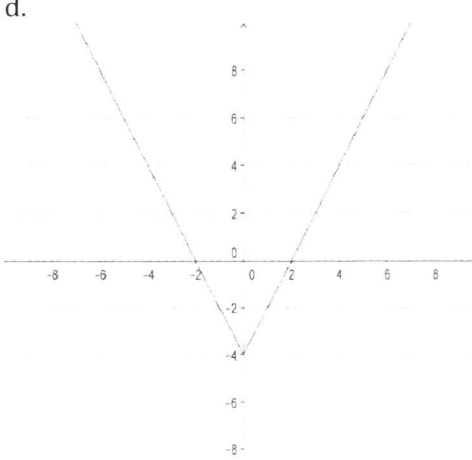

29. Which of the following represents a proportional relationship?

a.

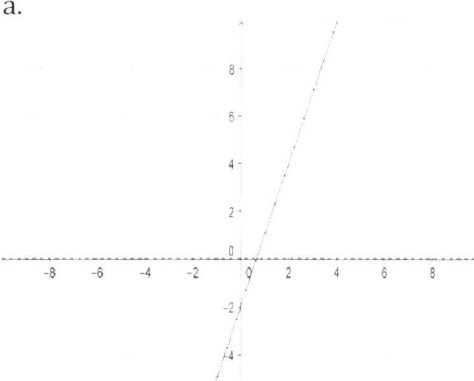

b.

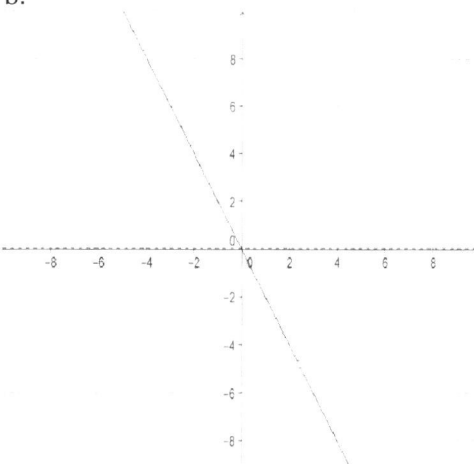

c.

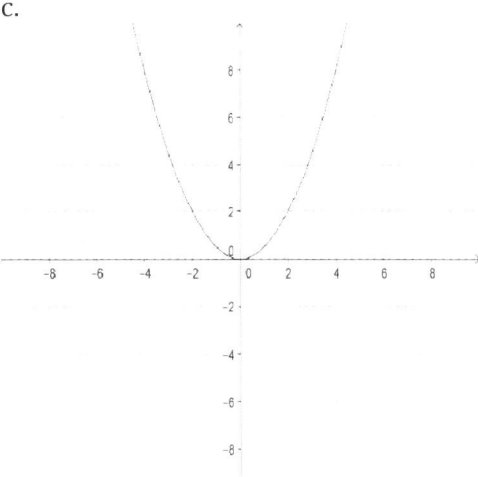

d.

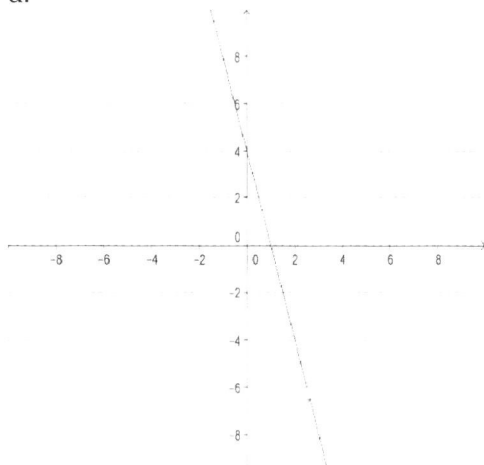

30. Which of the following represents the graph of $y = (x - 4)^2 + 3$?

a.

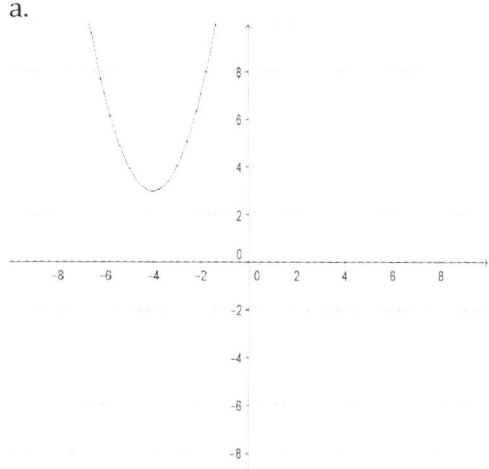

b.

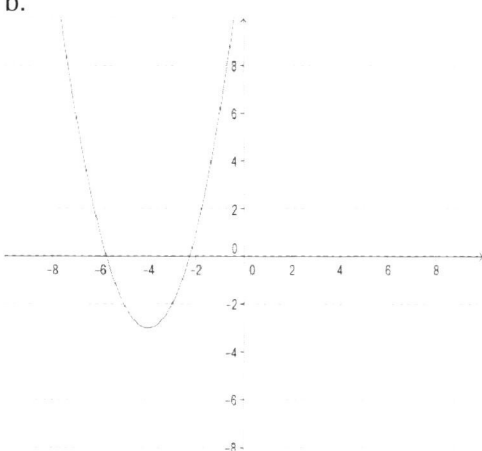

c.

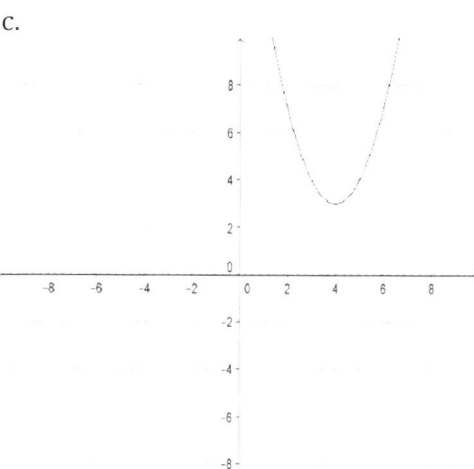

d.

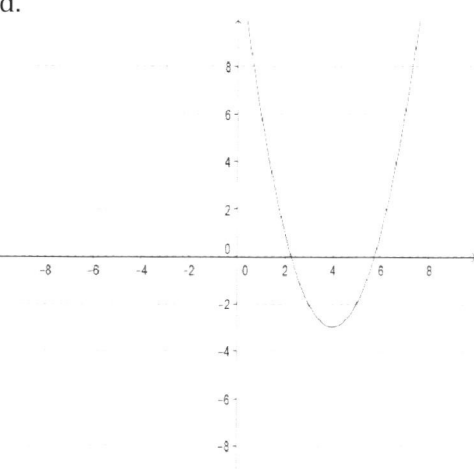

31. The expression $2x^2 - 4x - 30$ is equal to the product of $(x - 5)$ and which other factor?
    a. $(2x - 10)$
    b. $(2x + 25)$
    c. $(2x + 7)$
    d. $(2x + 6)$

32. What is the constant of proportionality represented by the table below?

x	y
2	−8
5	−20
7	−28
10	−40
11	−44

    a. −12
    b. −8
    c. −6
    d. −4

33. Which of the following represents an inverse proportional relationship?
    a. $y = 3x$
    b. $y = \dfrac{1}{3}x$
    c. $y = \dfrac{3}{x}$
    d. $y = 3x^2$

34. Which of the following expressions is equivalent to $-3x(x - 2)^2$?
    a. $-3x^3 + 6x^2 - 12x$
    b. $-3x^3 - 12x^2 + 12x$
    c. $-3x^2 + 6x$
    d. $-3x^3 + 12x^2 - 12x$

35. Which of the following graphs represents the solution to $y \geq 3x - 6$?

a.

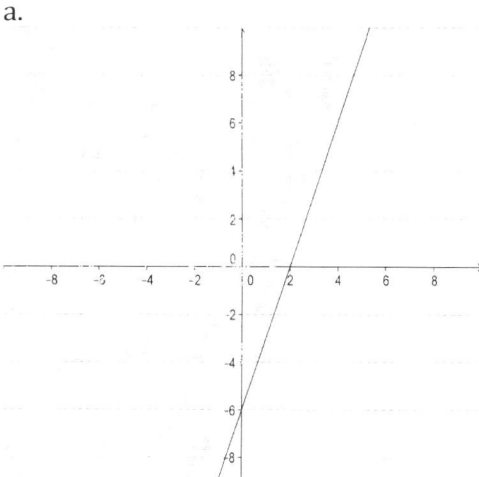

b.

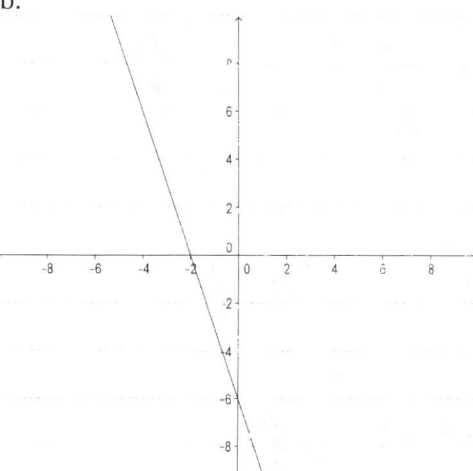

c.

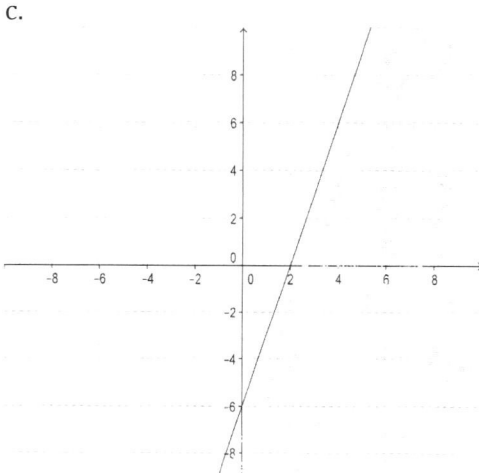

d.

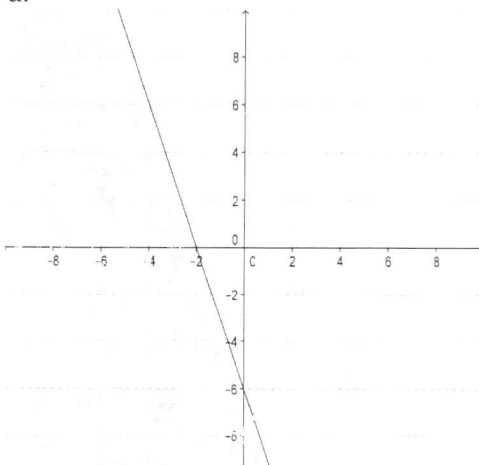

36. If $f(x) = \frac{x^3 - 2x + 1}{3x}$, what is $f(2)$?

a. $\frac{1}{3}$

b. $\frac{1}{2}$

c. $\frac{5}{6}$

d. $\frac{5}{2}$

37. The variables x and y are in a linear relationship. The table below shows a few sample values. Which of the following graphs correctly represents the linear equation relating x and y?

x	y
-2	-11
-1	-8
0	-5
1	-2
2	1

a.

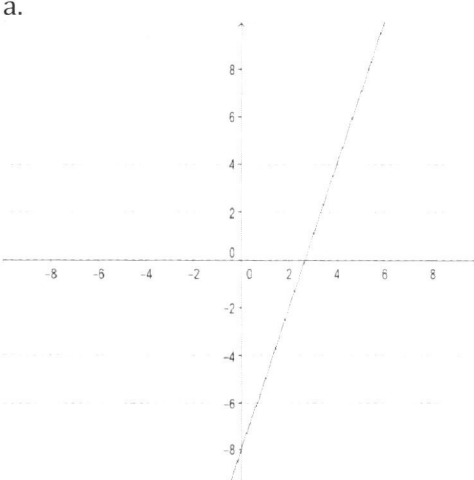

b.

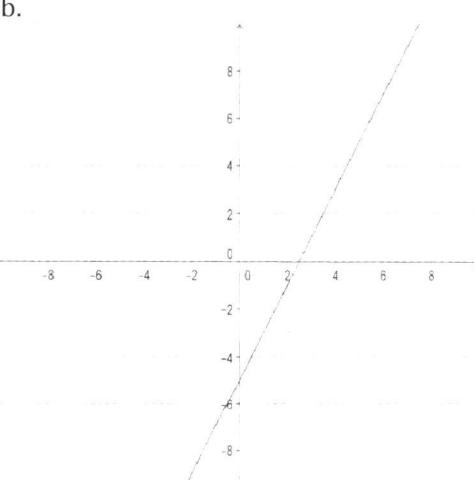

c.

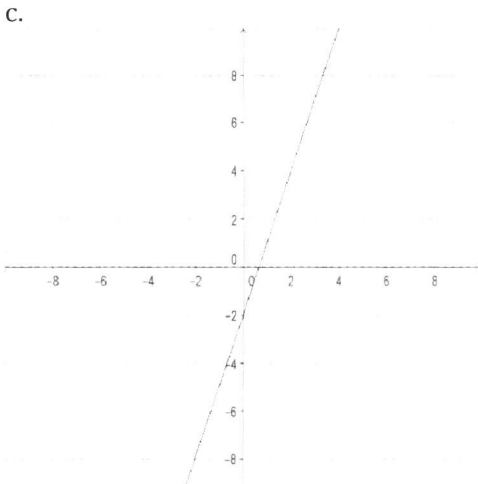

d.

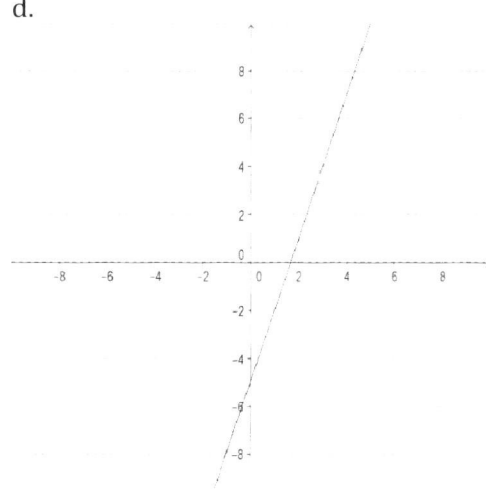

38. Which of the following is the graph of the equation $y = -4x - 6$?

a.

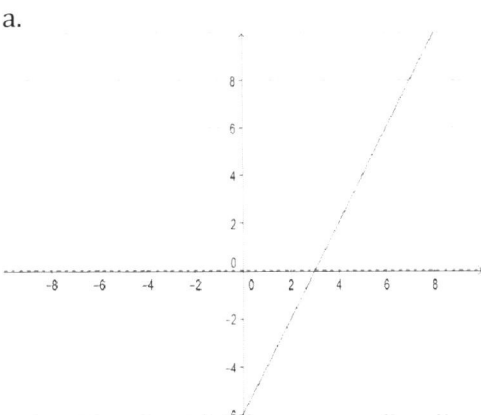

b.

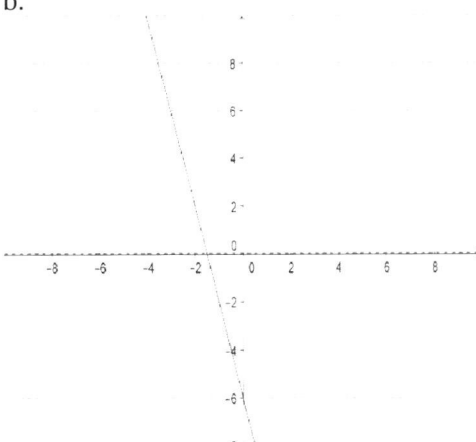

c.

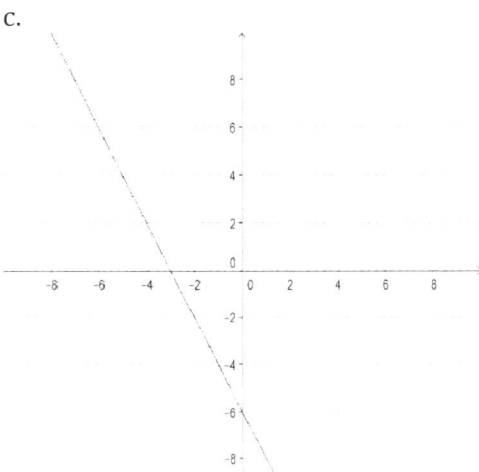

d.

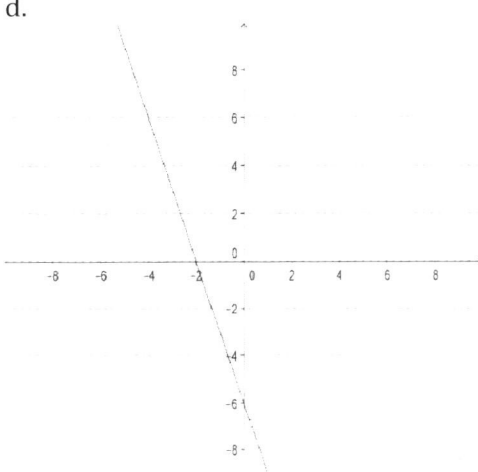

39. Given the graph below, what is the average rate of change from $f(2)$ to $f(5)$?

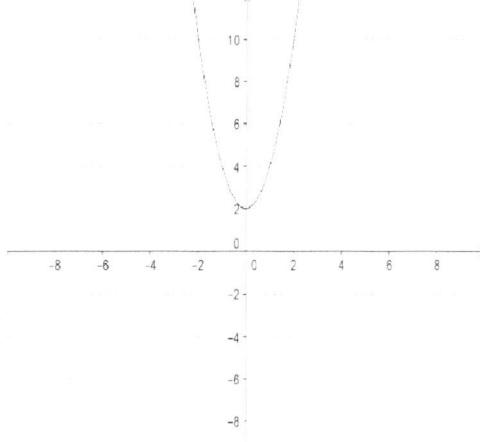

    a. 2
    b. 14
    c. 21
    d. 42

40. Elijah pays a $30 park entrance fee, plus $4 for every ticket purchased. Which of the following equations represents the cost?
    a. $y = 30x + 4$
    b. $y = 34x$
    c. $y = 4x + 30$
    d. $y = 34x + 30$

41. What is the solution to the system of linear equations graphed below?

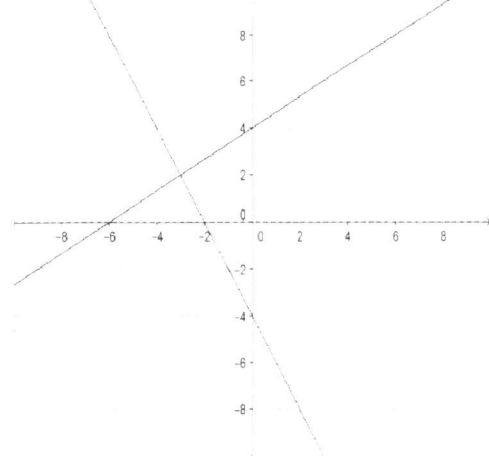

    a. $(2, -3)$
    b. $(-3, -2)$
    c. $(-2, 3)$
    d. $(-3, 2)$

42. What is the solution to the system of linear equations below?
$$4x - 2y = -38$$
$$2x + 3y = 17$$

    a. $(-5, 9)$
    b. $(-2, 11)$
    c. $(-3, 7)$
    d. $(-4, 11)$

43. Which of the following graphs represents the solution to the system of inequalities below?
$$2x - 3y \geq -11$$
$$-2x + 4y \geq 14$$

a.

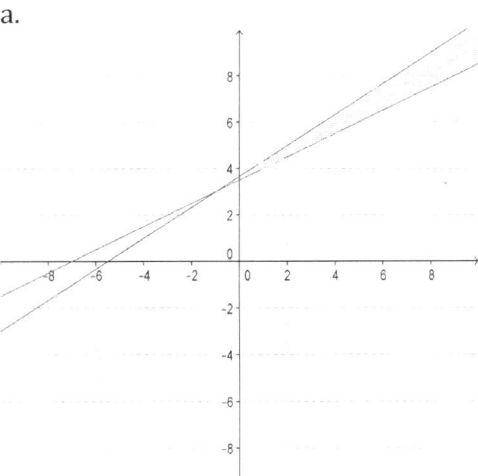

b.

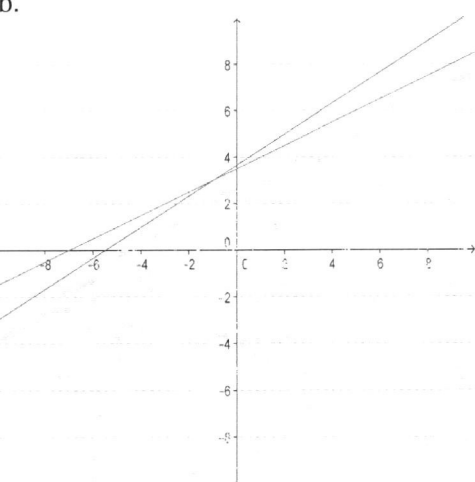

c.

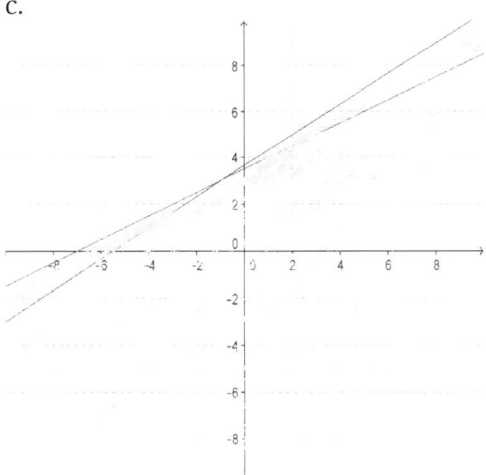

d.

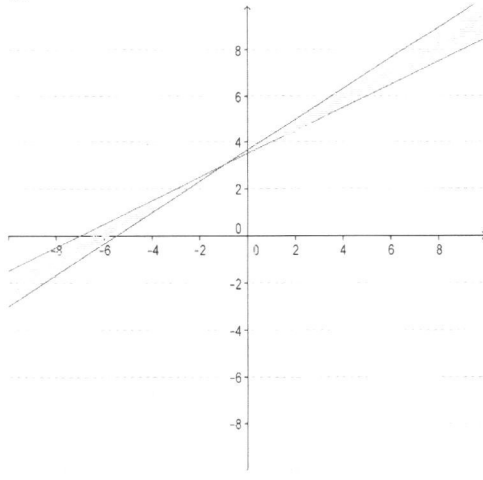

44. Robert drops a ball from his balcony. The height of the ball is modeled by the function $f(x) = -2x^2 + x + 11$, where $f(x)$ represents the height of the ball and x represents the number of seconds. Which of the following best represents the number of seconds that will pass before the ball reaches the ground?

  a. 1.4
  b. 1.9
  c. 2.1
  d. 2.6

45. Which type of function is represented by the table of values below?

x	y
−2	0.25
−1	0.5
0	1
1	2
2	4

  a. linear
  b. quadratic
  c. cubic
  d. exponential

46. What linear equation includes the data in the table below?

x	y
−3	1
1	−11
3	−17
5	−23
9	−35

  a. $y = -3x - 11$
  b. $y = -6x - 8$
  c. $y = -3x - 8$
  d. $y = -12x - 11$

47. Which of the following equations represents a line perpendicular to the one graphed below and passing through the point $(3, 2)$?

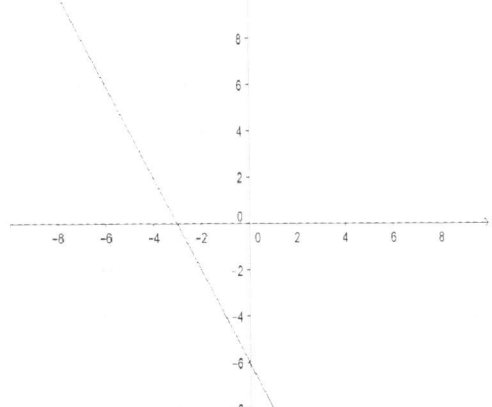

    a. $y = \frac{1}{2}x + 2$
    b. $y = \frac{1}{2}x + \frac{1}{2}$
    c. $y = \frac{3}{2}x + \frac{1}{2}$
    d. $y = 2x + 2$

48. Which of the following equations represents a line parallel to the one graphed below and passing through the point $(-1, 4)$?

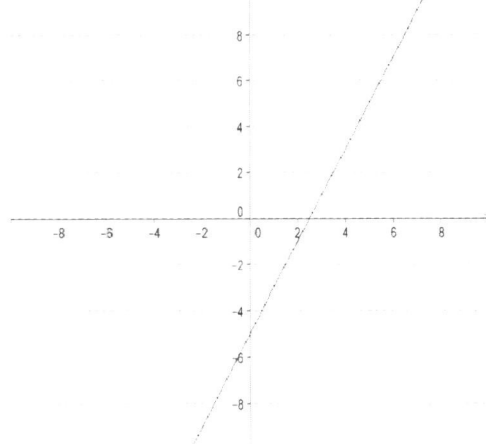

    a. $y = 2x - 2$
    b. $y = 3x + 6$
    c. $y = 3x - 4$
    d. $y = 2x + 6$

49. Hannah's monthly gym membership cost is represented by the graph shown below. Which of the following statements is correct?

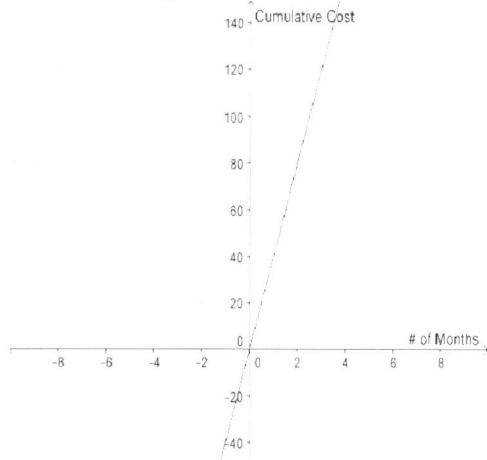

a. The cost is linear, but not proportional.
b. The cost is linear and proportional.
c. The cost is proportional, but not linear.
d. The cost represents an inverse proportional relationship.

50. Amanda saves $0.02 during Month 1. During each subsequent month, she plans to save twice as much as she did the previous month. Which of the following equations represents the amount she will save during the nth month?
a. $a_n = 0.02 \cdot 2^{n-1}$
b. $a_n = 0.02 + 2^n$
c. $a_n = 0.02 \cdot 2^n$
d. $a_n = 2n - 1.98$

51. Kevin saves $3 during Month 1. During each subsequent month, he plans to save 4 more dollars than he saved during the previous month. Which of the following equations represents the amount he will save during the nth month?
a. $a_n = 3n - 1$
b. $a_n = 3n + 4$
c. $a_n = 4n + 3$
d. $a_n = 4n - 1$

52. What is $\lim_{n \to \infty} \frac{n^2+1}{n}$?
a. 0
b. 1
c. 2
d. There is no limit.

53. What is $\lim_{n \to \infty} \frac{5n+2}{n}$?

    a. 0

    b. 2

    c. 5

    d. There is no limit.

54. The initial term of a sequence is 3. Each term in the sequence is $\frac{2}{3}$ the amount of the previous term. What is the sum of the terms, as n approaches infinity?

    a. 6

    b. 9

    c. 12

    d. 15

55. Mandy can buy 4 containers of yogurt and 3 boxes of crackers for $9.55. She can buy 2 containers of yogurt and 2 boxes of crackers for $5.90. How much does one box of crackers cost?

    a. $1.75

    b. $2.00

    c. $2.25

    d. $2.50

56. What is the derivative of $f(x) = 9x^2$?

    a. 3x

    b. 9x

    c. 18x

    d. $18x^2$

57. Which of the following functions converges?

    a. $f(x) = \frac{x^2}{x}$

    b. $f(x) = 2x$

    c. $f(x) = \frac{4x}{x} + 1000$

    d. $f(x) = \frac{3x^2 + 100}{x}$

58. McKenzie shades $\frac{1}{5}$ of a piece of paper. Then, she shades an additional area $\frac{1}{5}$ the size of what she just shaded. Next, she shades another area $\frac{1}{5}$ as large as the previous one. As she continues the process to infinity, what is the limit of the shaded fraction of the paper?

    a. $\frac{1}{5}$

    b. $\frac{1}{4}$

    c. $\frac{1}{3}$

    d. $\frac{1}{2}$

59. Which of the following functions has a limit of 0?
    a. $f(x) = 2x$
    b. $f(x) = \frac{4}{x}$
    c. $f(x) = \frac{x}{8}$
    d. $f(x) = \frac{3x+1}{x}$

60. What is the derivative of $g(x) = x^{ab}$?
    a. $ab \cdot x^{ab}$
    b. $ab \cdot x^{ab-1}$
    c. $a \cdot x^{ab}$
    d. $b \cdot x^{ab-1}$

61. Which of the following graphs represents an inverse proportional relationship?

a.

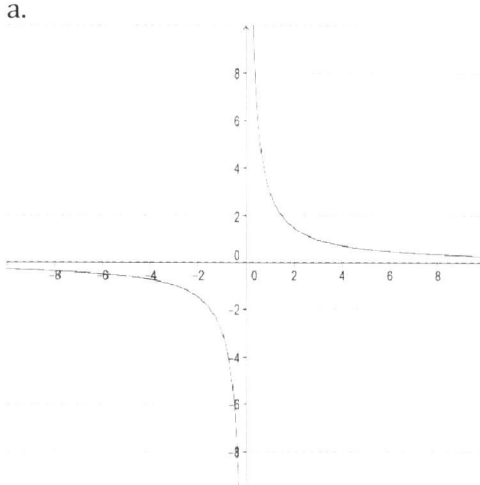

b.

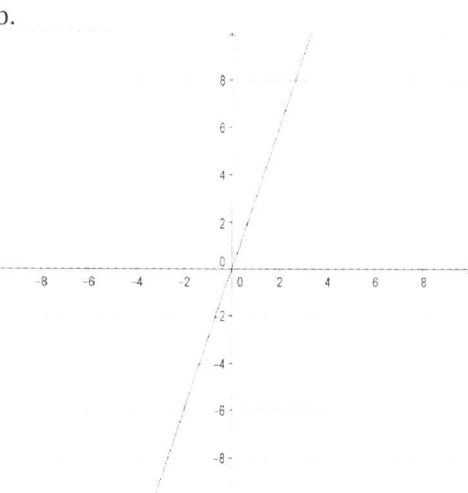

c.

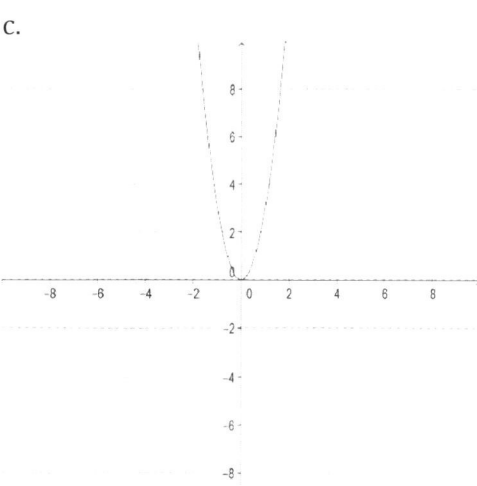

d.

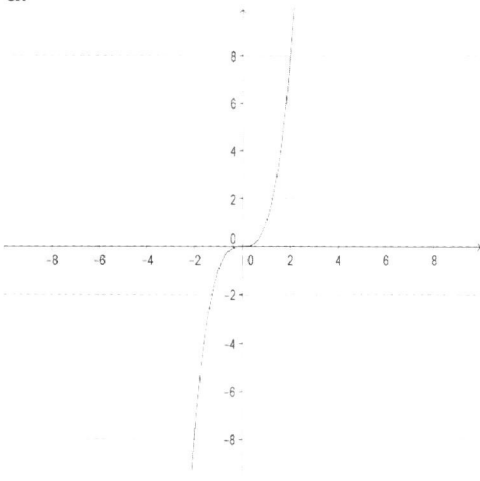

62. What is the sum of the first 50 even, positive integers?
    a. 1,250
    b. 2,025
    c. 2,550
    d. 3,250

63. The graph of the parent function $y = x^2$ is shifted 5 units to the left and 4 units down. Which of the following equations represents the transformed function?
    a. $y = (x - 5)^2 - 4$
    b. $y = (x + 5)^2 - 4$
    c. $y = (x - 5)^2 + 4$
    d. $y = (x + 5)^2 + 4$

64. Which of the following represents a function?
    a. $\{(2, 9), (3, 4), (6, 8), (-1, 5), (3, -1)\}$
    b. $\{(8, 7), (7, 9), (2, 1), (4, 3), (3, 6)\}$
    c. $\{(-4, 6), (2, 1), (-4, -2), (3, 8), (9, 2)\}$
    d. $\{(2, 6), (6, 5), (5, 9), (2, 0), (-3, 1)\}$

65. A car is accelerated. Which of the following accurately describes the appearance of the position-time graph?
    a. It is a line with a positive slope.
    b. It is a line with a negative slope.
    c. It is a curve with an increasing slope.
    d. It is a curve with a decreasing slope.

66. Tom needs to buy ink cartridges and printer paper. Each ink cartridge costs $30. Each ream of paper costs $5. He has $100 to spend. Which of the following inequalities may be used to find the combinations of ink cartridges and printer paper that he may purchase?
    a. $30c + 5p \leq 100$
    b. $30c + 5p < 100$
    c. $30c + 5p > 100$
    d. $30c + 5p \geq 100$

67. Hannah spends at least $16 on 4 packages of coffee. Which of the following inequalities represents the possible costs?
    a. $16 \geq 4p$
    b. $16 < 4p$
    c. $16 > 4p$
    d. $16 \leq 4p$

68. $f(x) = \frac{x+1}{2x}$. What is the equation of the horizontal asymptote?
    a. $y = \frac{1}{4}$
    b. $y = \frac{1}{2}$
    c. $y = 0$
    d. $y = 2$

69. $g(x) = \frac{x}{x+3}$. What is the equation of the horizontal asymptote?
   a. y = 0
   b. y = 0.5
   c. y = 1
   d. y = 3

70. What is $\lim_{x \to -\infty} \frac{4x^2}{x+2}$?
   a. −4000
   b. −400
   c. 0
   d. There is no limit.

71. What is $\lim_{x \to -2}(3x^3 - 6x^2 + 4)$?
   a. −44
   b. −42
   c. 4
   d. 52

72. Jackson can decorate a cake in 3 hours. Eli can decorate the same cake in 2 hours. If they work together, how long will it take them to decorate the cake?
   a. 0.8 hours
   b. 1.2 hours
   c. 1.5 hours
   d. 1.8 hours

73. Robert needs to buy milk and bread. Each gallon of milk costs $3. Each loaf of bread costs $2. He intends to spend at least $20. Which of the following graphs represents the possible combinations of gallons of milk and loaves of bread that he may purchase?

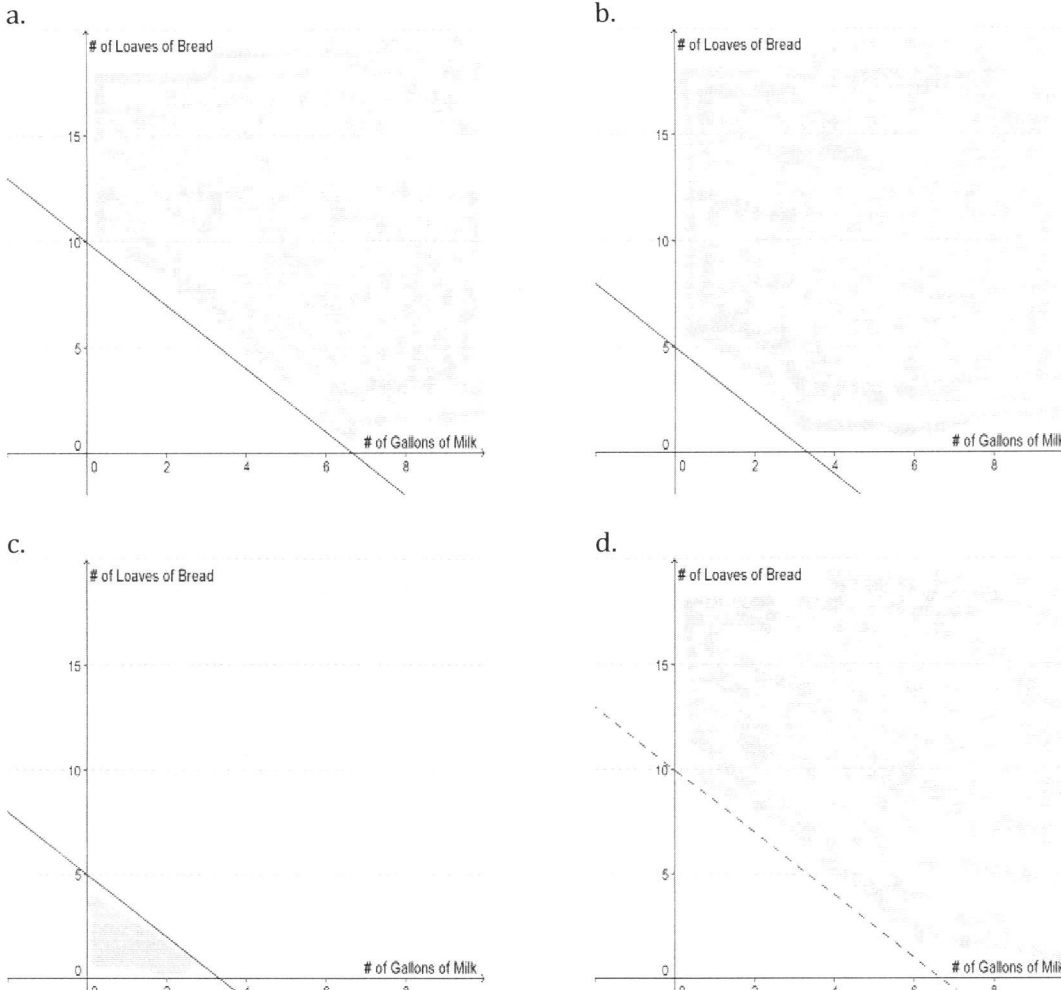

a.

b.

c.

d.

74. Kayla has a $75 budget to purchase gifts for her colleagues. She wants to buy coffee mugs and note pads. She may purchase a maximum of 30 items. Each coffee mug costs $6 and each note pad costs $3. Which of the following graphs correctly shows the possible combinations of coffee mugs and note pads that she may buy?

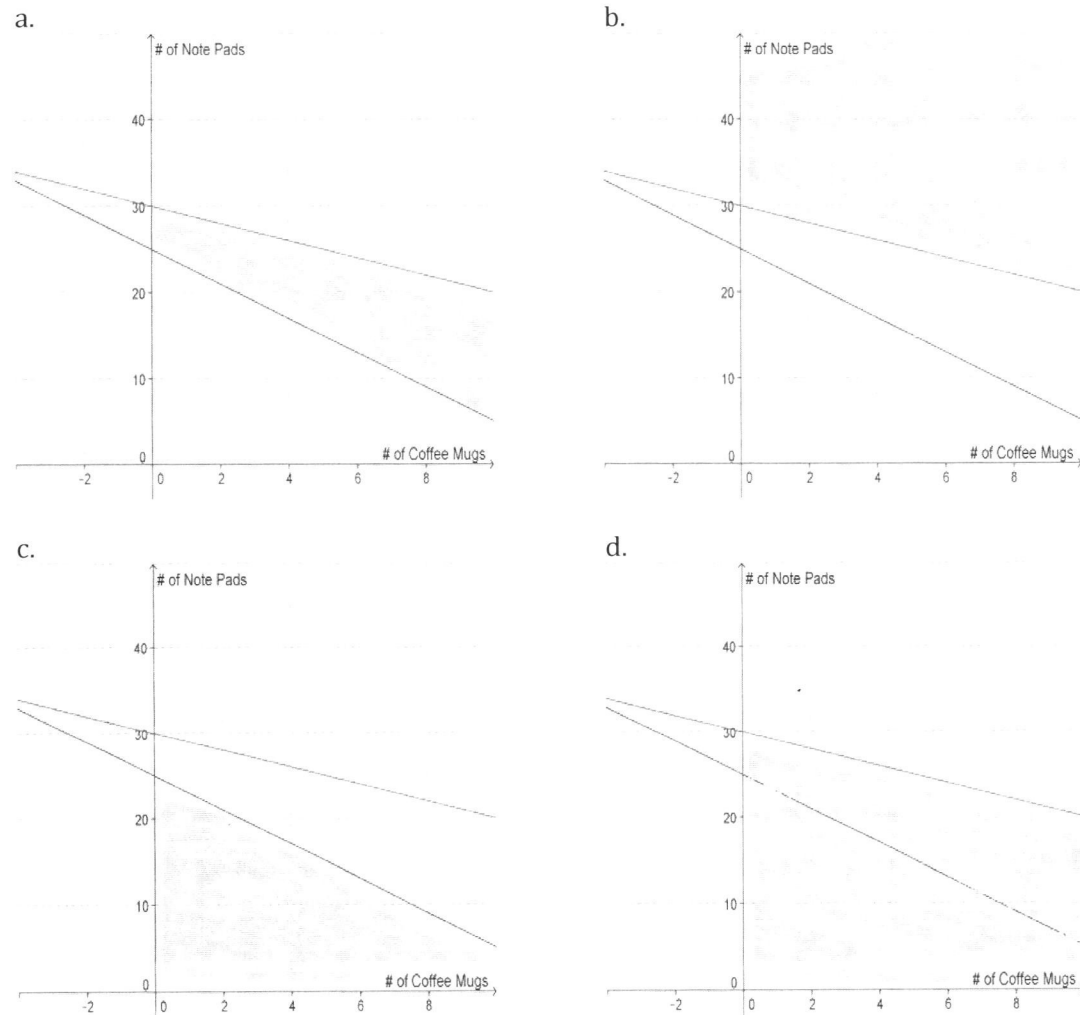

a.

b.

c.

d.

75. Which of the following tables contains points in an exponential function?

a.

x	y
−2	−24
1	12
3	36
5	60
8	96

b.

x	y
−2	12
0	0
2	12
4	48
6	108

c.

x	y
−1	−1
1	1
3	27
5	125
6	216

d.

x	y
−1	0.5
0	1
3	8
5	32
6	64

Measurement and Geometry

76. A city is at an elevation of 6,700 feet. Which of the following best represents the elevation in miles?

a. 0.77 miles
b. 1.27 miles
c. 1.56 miles
d. 1.89 miles

77. A can has a radius of 1.5 inches and a height of 3 inches. Which of the following best represents the volume of the can?
    a. 17.2 in^3
    b. 19.4 in^3
    c. 21.2 in^3
    d. 23.4 in^3

78. A ball has a diameter of 7 inches. Which of the following best represents the volume?
    a. 165.7 in^3
    b. 179.6 in^3
    c. 184.5 in^3
    d. 192.3 in^3

79. A gift box has a length of 14 inches, a height of 8 inches, and a width of 6 inches. How many square inches of wrapping paper are needed to wrap the box?
    a. 56
    b. 244
    c. 488
    d. 672

80. Aidan has a plastic container in the shape of a square pyramid. He wants to fill the container with chocolate candies. If the base has a side length of 6 inches and the height of the container is 9 inches, how many cubic inches of space may be filled with candies?
    a. 98
    b. 102
    c. 108
    d. 112

81. Eric has a beach ball with a radius of 9 inches. He is planning to wrap the ball with wrapping paper. Which of the following is the best estimate for the number of square feet of wrapping paper he will need?
    a. 4.08
    b. 5.12
    c. 7.07
    d. 8.14

82. Each base of a triangular prism has a base length of 9 cm and a height of 12 cm. The height of the prism is 15 cm. What is the volume of the prism?
    a. 652 cm^3
    b. 720 cm^3
    c. 792 cm^3
    d. 810 cm^3

83. The two prisms shown below are similar. What is the measurement of x?

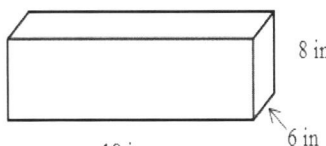 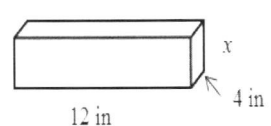

a. $4\frac{3}{4}$ in
b. $5\frac{1}{3}$ in
c. $5\frac{2}{3}$ in
d. $5\frac{3}{4}$ in

84. Given that the two horizontal lines in the diagram below are parallel, which pair of angles is congruent?

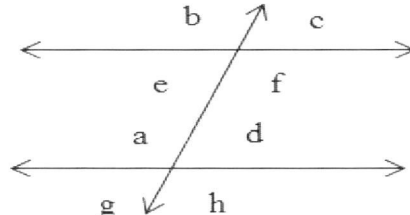

a. e and b
b. d and h
c. g and c
d. d and f

85. Given the diagram below, which of the following theorems may be used to verify that lines a and b are parallel?

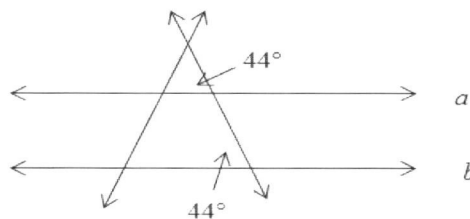

a. Alternate Interior Angles Converse Theorem
b. Alternate Exterior Angles Converse Theorem
c. Consecutive Interior Angles Converse Theorem
d. Corresponding Angles Converse Theorem

86. Given the diagram below, what is the measure of the inscribed angle?

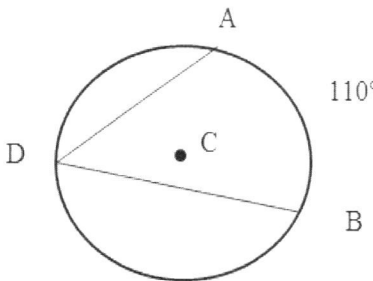

    a. 37°
    b. 45°
    c. 55°
    d. 57°

87. A tree with a height of 15 feet casts a shadow that is 5 feet in length. A man standing at the base of the shadow formed by the tree is 6 feet tall. How long is the shadow cast by the man?
    a. 1.5 feet
    b. 2 feet
    c. 2.5 feet
    d. 3 feet

88. Which of the following best represents the measurement of x, shown in the triangle below?

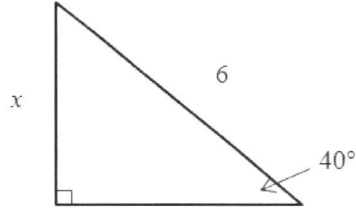

    a. 2.6
    b. 3.1
    c. 3.9
    d. 4.4

89. What is the area of the shaded region in the figure shown below?

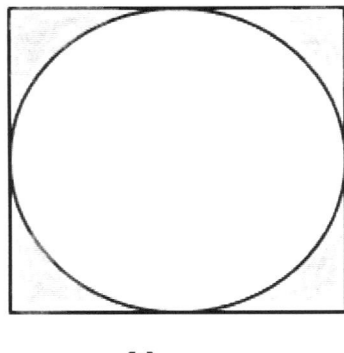

30 cm

30 cm

    a. 177 cm^2
    b. 181 cm^2
    c. 187 cm^2
    d. 193 cm^2

90. Which of the following postulates proves the congruence of the triangles below?

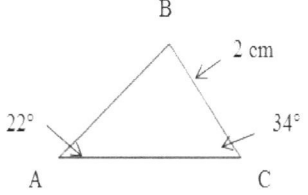 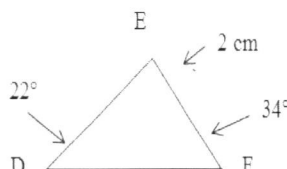

    a. ASA
    b. AAS
    c. SAS
    d. SSS

91. A man standing on a flat, level surface casts a shadow that is 6.2 ft in length. The man is 5.8 ft tall. Which of the following best represents the distance from the top of his head to the end of the shadow?
    a. 7 ft
    b. 7.5 ft
    c. 8 ft
    d. 8.5 ft

92. A cylindrical carrot stick is sliced with a knife. Which of the following shapes is *not* a possible cross-section?
    a. circle
    b. rectangle
    c. ellipse
    d. triangle

93. What is the value of *x*, shown in the diagram below?

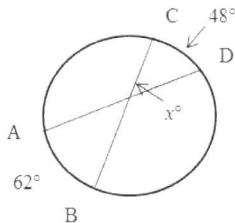

    a. 16
    b. 24
    c. 48
    d. 55

94. What is the value of *x*, shown in the diagram below?

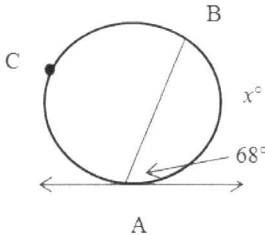

    a. 68°
    b. 76°
    c. 128°
    d. 136°

95. Which of the following represents the net of a triangular prism?

a.

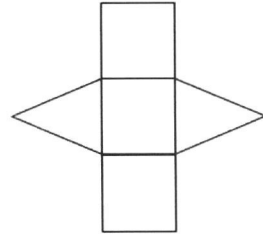

b.

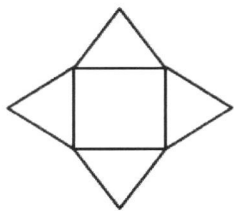

c.

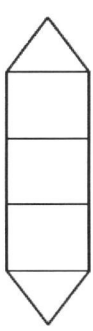

d.

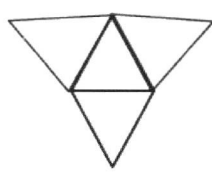

96. A convex three-dimensional figure has 9 edges and 6 vertices. How many faces does it have?
   a. 4
   b. 5
   c. 6
   d. 8

97. Given that the two horizontal lines in the diagram below are parallel, which of the following statements is correct?

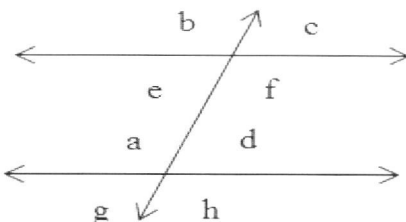

    a. Angles b and g are complementary.
    b. Angles d and c are supplementary.
    c. Angles a and e are supplementary.
    d. Angles e and h are congruent.

98. Which of the following postulates may be used to prove the similarity of $\triangle ABC$ and $\triangle ADE$?

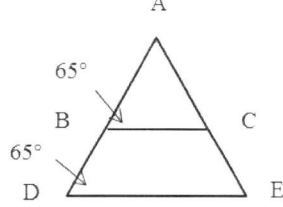

    a. ASA
    b. AA
    c. SAS
    d. SSS

99. Which of the following transformations has been applied to $\triangle ABC$?

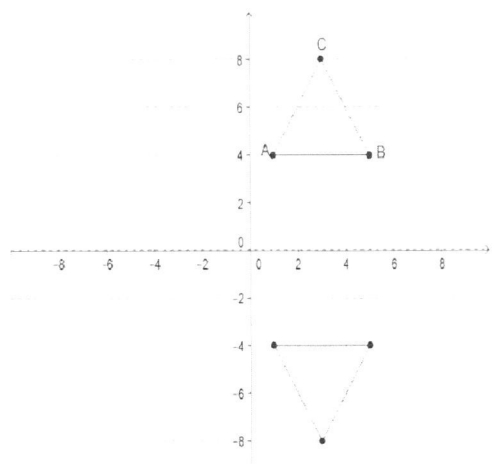

    a. translation
    b. rotation of 90 degrees
    c. reflection
    d. dilation

100. Which of the following steps were applied to $\triangle ABC$?

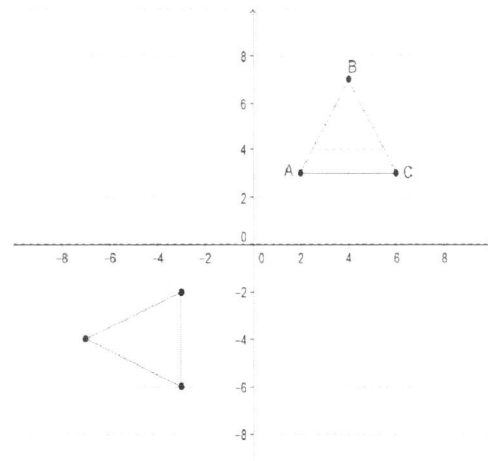

    a. reflection across the x-axis and rotation of 90 degrees
    b. reflection across the x-axis and rotation of 180 degrees
    c. reflection across the x-axis and rotation of 270 degrees
    d. reflection across the y-axis and rotation of 180 degrees

101. What is the midpoint of the line segment below?

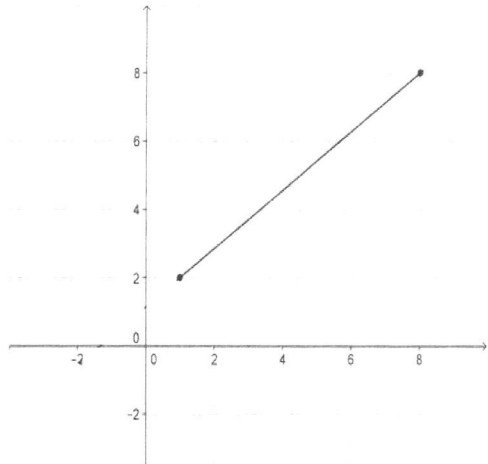

    a. (3.5, 4)
    b. (4, 4)
    c. (4.5, 5)
    d. (5, 5)

102. What is the distance on a coordinate plane from (−8, 6) to (4, 3)?
    a. $\sqrt{139}$
    b. $\sqrt{147}$
    c. $\sqrt{153}$
    d. $\sqrt{161}$

103. What is the perimeter of the trapezoid graphed below?

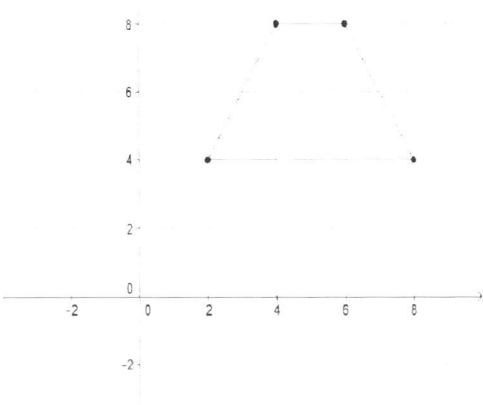

a. $4 + \sqrt{10}$
b. $8 + 4\sqrt{5}$
c. $4 + 2\sqrt{5}$
d. $8 + 2\sqrt{22}$

104. What is the area of the figure graphed below?

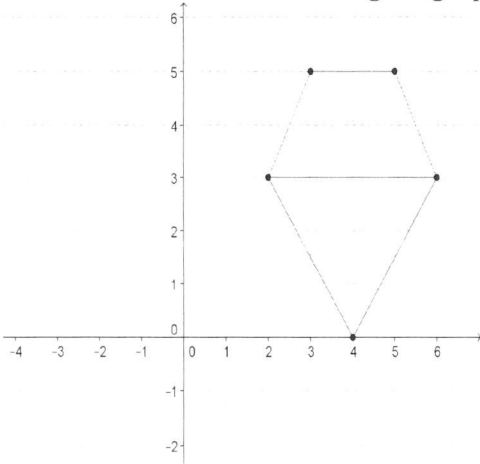

a. 11 units^2
b. 11.5 units^2
c. 12 units^2
d. 12.5 units^2

105. What scale factor was applied to the larger triangle to obtain the smaller triangle below?

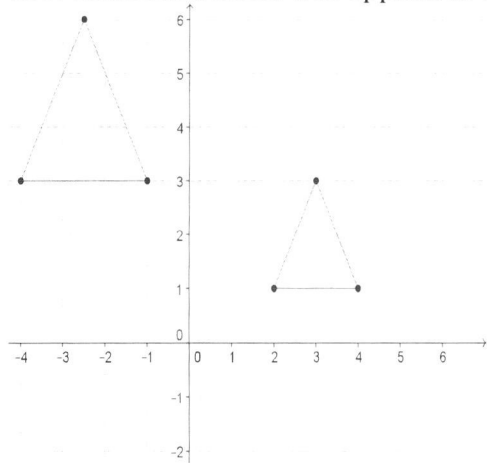

a. $\frac{1}{4}$

b. $\frac{1}{3}$

c. $\frac{1}{2}$

d. $\frac{2}{3}$

106. Which of the following pairs of equations represents the lines of symmetry in the figure below?

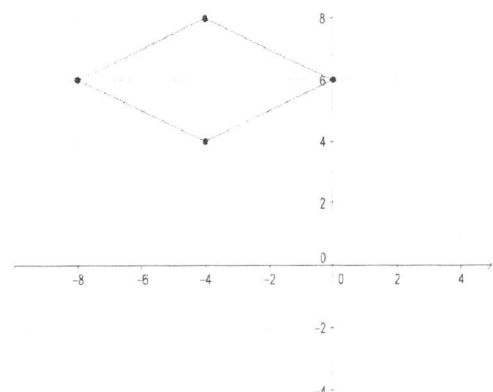

a. $x = -4, y = 6$
b. $x = 4, y = 6$
c. $y = -4, x = 6$
d. $y = 4, x = -6$

107. Which of the following pairs of shapes may tessellate a plane?
  a. regular pentagons and squares
  b. regular pentagons and equilateral triangles
  c. equilateral triangles and regular hexagons
  d. regular octagons and equilateral triangles

108. Andrea must administer $\frac{1}{12}$ of a medicine bottle to a patient. If the bottle contains $3\frac{4}{10}$ fluid ounces of medicine, how much medicine should be administered?

    a. $\frac{17}{60}$ fluid ounces

    b. $\frac{15}{62}$ fluid ounces

    c. $\frac{3}{19}$ fluid ounces

    d. $\frac{17}{67}$ fluid ounces

109. What is the slope of the leg marked x in the triangle graphed below?

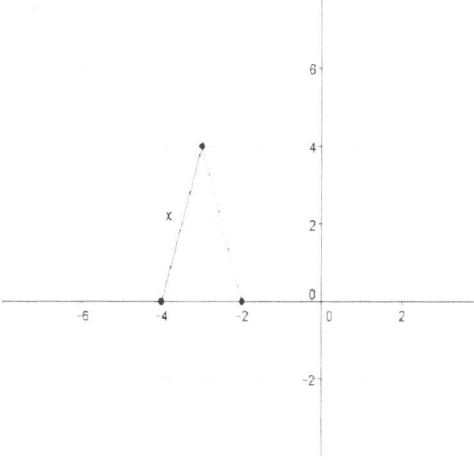

    a. 2
    b. 3.5
    c. 4
    d. 4.5

110. Ann must walk from Point A to Point B and then to Point C. Finally, she will walk back to Point A. If each unit represents 5 miles, which of the following best represents the total distance she will have walked?

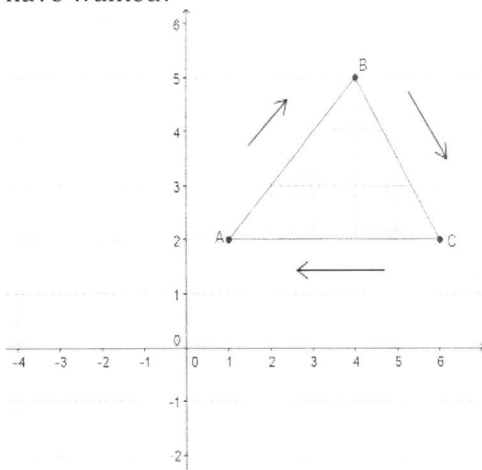

   a. 42 miles
   b. 48 miles
   c. 56 miles
   d. 64 miles

111. Which of the following measurements is the best approximation of 2,012 square inches?
   a. 11.85 ft^2
   b. 12.28 ft^2
   c. 13.97 ft^2
   d. 15.29 ft^2

112. What is the length of the hypotenuse in the triangle shown below?

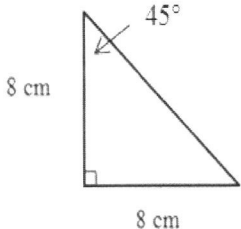

   a. 4 cm
   b. $8\sqrt{3}$ cm
   c. 16 cm
   d. $8\sqrt{2}$ cm

Statistics, Probability, and Discrete Mathematics

113. For which of the following data sets would the mean be an appropriate measure of center to use?
  a. 7, 15, 20, 24, 27, 28, 31, 36, 41, 50
  b. 6, 7, 8, 8, 9, 9, 10, 20, 34, 50
  c. 5, 18, 30, 42, 43, 44, 46, 48, 49, 50
  d. 8, 10, 12, 13, 14, 16, 20, 22, 24, 2200

114. A student scores 82 on a final exam. The class average is 87, with a standard deviation of 2 points. How many standard deviations below the class average is the student's score?
  a. 1.5
  b. 2
  c. 2.5
  d. 3

115. A student scores 61 on a test. The class average is 81, with a standard deviation of 10 points. What percentage of the class scored below this student?
  a. 1.26%
  b. 1.43%
  c. 1.96%
  d. 2.28%

116. A student scores 96 on a test. The class average is 84, with a standard deviation of 4 points. What percentage of the class scored below this student?
  a. 78.89%
  b. 82.77%
  c. 92.67%
  d. 99.87%

117. A student scores 68 on a final exam. Another student scores 84 on the exam. The class average is 80, with a standard deviation of 8 points. What percentage of the class scored within the range of these two students' scores?
  a. 44.32%
  b. 48.54%
  c. 58.39%
  d. 62.47%

118. Class A, with a total of 28 students, had a final exam average of 85 and a standard deviation of 4.5 points. Class B, with a total of 30 students, had a final exam average of 88, with a standard deviation of 4 points. Which of the following statements is true?
  a. There is no significant difference between the classes, as evidenced by a p-value greater than 0.05.
  b. There is no significant difference between the classes, as evidenced by a p-value less than 0.05.
  c. There is a significant difference between the classes, as evidenced by a p-value greater than 0.05.
  d. There is a significant difference between the classes, as evidenced by a p-value less than 0.05.

119. A beverage manufacturer claims to include 20 ounces in each bottle. A random sample of 30 bottles shows a mean of 19.8 ounces, with a standard deviation of 0.2 ounces. Which of the following statements is correct?

    a. The manufacturer's claim is likely true, as evidenced by a p-value less than 0.01.
    b. The manufacturer's claim is likely true, as evidenced by a p-value greater than 0.01.
    c. The manufacturer's claim is likely false, as evidenced by a p-value less than 0.01.
    d. The manufacturer's claim is likely false, as evidenced by a p-value greater than 0.01.

120. An oatmeal manufacturer claims to include 18 ounces in each container, with a standard deviation of 0.3 ounces. A random sample of 25 containers shows a mean of 17.9 ounces. Which of the following statements is true?

    a. The manufacturer's claim is likely true, as evidenced by a p-value less than 0.05.
    b. The manufacturer's claim is likely true, as evidenced by a p-value greater than 0.05.
    c. The manufacturer's claim is likely false, as evidenced by a p-value less than 0.05.
    d. The manufacturer's claim is likely false, as evidenced by a p-value greater than 0.05.

121. A professor claims that the average on his final exam is 82. A random sample of 30 students shows an exam mean of 83 and a standard deviation of 2 points. Which of the following statements is true?

    a. The professor's claim is likely true, as evidenced by a p-value less than 0.05.
    b. The professor's claim is likely false, as evidenced by a p-value less than 0.05.
    c. The professor's claim is likely true, as evidenced by a p-value greater than 0.05.
    d. The professor's claim is likely false, as evidenced by a p-value greater than 0.05.

122. Which of the following describes a sampling technique that will likely increase the sampling error?

    a. choosing every 5th person from a list
    b. grouping a sample according to gender and then choosing every 10th person from a list
    c. using an intact group
    d. assigning numbers to a sample and then using a random number generator to choose numbers

123. What is the area under the normal curve between ±2 standard deviations?

    a. approximately 68%
    b. approximately 90%
    c. approximately 95%
    d. approximately 99%

124. Which of the following best represents the standard deviation of the data below?
3, 4, 4, 5, 6, 12, 12, 15

    a. 2.9
    b. 3.4
    c. 4.1
    d. 4.6

125. Given the boxplots below, which of the following statements is correct?

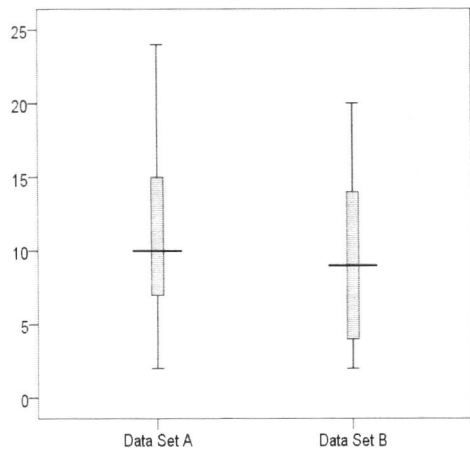

    a. Data Set A has a larger range and a larger median.
    b. Data Set A has a smaller range and a larger median.
    c. Data Set A has a larger range and a smaller median.
    d. Data Set A has a smaller range and a smaller median.

126. What is the interquartile range of the data below?
2, 4, 6, 8, 10, 12, 14, 16, 18, 20
    a. 10
    b. 11
    c. 12
    d. 13

127. According to the scatter plot below, which of the following is the *best* estimate for the earnings received for 20 hours of work?

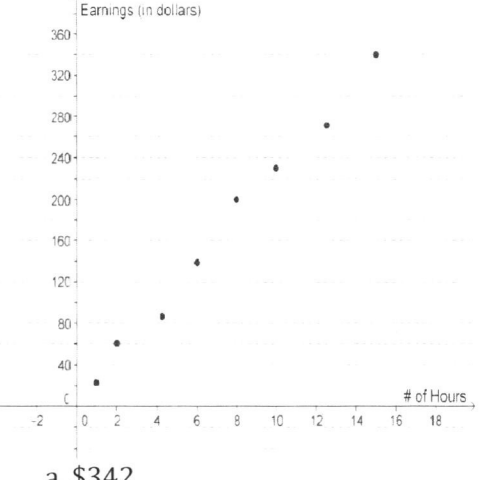

    a. $342
    b. $446
    c. $528
    d. $602

128. Which of the following statements is *not* true?
    a. In a skewed distribution, the mean is pulled towards the tail.
    b. In a skewed distribution, the mean is pulled towards the area with a higher frequency of scores.
    c. In a normal distribution, the mean, median, and mode are the same value.
    d. The area under a normal curve is 1.

129. Given the two-way frequency table below, which of the following *best* represents P(male or graduate)?

	Undergraduate	Graduate	Total
Male	2940	2045	4985
Female	3026	2068	5094
Total	5966	4113	10,079

    a. 55%
    b. 60%
    c. 70%
    d. 75%

130. Adam rolls a standard six-sided die. What is the probability he rolls a number greater than or equal to 5?
    a. $\frac{1}{6}$
    b. $\frac{1}{5}$
    c. $\frac{1}{4}$
    d. $\frac{1}{3}$

131. Kayla rolls a die and tosses a coin. What is the probability she gets an even number and heads?
    a. $\frac{1}{6}$
    b. $\frac{1}{4}$
    c. $\frac{1}{3}$
    d. 1

132. Eli rolls a die and tosses a coin. What is the probability he gets a prime number or tails?
    a. $\frac{1}{2}$
    b. $\frac{2}{3}$
    c. $\frac{3}{4}$
    d. $\frac{5}{6}$

133. Andrew rolls a die. What is the probability he gets a 4 or an even number?
    a. $\frac{1}{4}$
    b. $\frac{1}{2}$
    c. $\frac{2}{3}$
    d. $\frac{3}{4}$

134. The simulation of a coin toss is completed 300 times. Which of the following best represents the number of tosses you can expect to show heads?
    a. 50
    b. 100
    c. 150
    d. 200

135. How many ways can you arrange the letters below, if order does not matter?
HANNAH
    a. 30
    b. 60
    c. 90
    d. 120

136. How many ways can 1st – 3rd place winners be chosen from 6 people?
    a. 120
    b. 60
    c. 30
    d. 20

137. How many ways can the numerals 0 – 9 be arranged?
    a. 36,045
    b. 182,492
    c. 1,048,644
    d. 3,628,800

138. What is the limit of the series below?
$$1 + \frac{1}{2} + \frac{1}{4} + \frac{1}{8} + \frac{1}{16} + \cdots$$

    a. 2
    b. $2\frac{1}{4}$
    c. $2\frac{3}{4}$
    d. 3

139. What is the size of the sample space for tossing four coins?
    a. 8
    b. 12
    c. 16
    d. 20

140. 320 students are surveyed. 120 of the students like only Dallas. 150 of the students like only Houston. 48 of the students like neither city. How many students like Dallas *and* Houston?
    a. 2
    b. 3
    c. 4
    d. 5

141. $A = \{5, 9, 2, 3, -1, 8\}$ and $B = \{2, 0, 4, 5, 6, 8\}$. What is $A \cap B$?
    a. $\{5, 2, 8\}$
    b. $\{-1, 0, 2, 3, 4, 5, 6, 8, 9\}$
    c. $\varnothing$
    d. $\{5, 8\}$

142. $A = \{9, 4, -3, 8, 6, 0\}$ and $B = \{-4, 2, 8, 9, 0\}$. What is $A \cup B$?
    a. $\{9, 8, 0\}$
    b. $\{9, 4, -3, 8, 6, 0, -4, 2\}$
    c. $\varnothing$
    d. $\{9, 8, 0, 2, 4\}$

143. $A = \{3, -4, 1\}$ and $B = \{0, 5, 9, 2\}$. What is $A \cap B$?
    a. $\{3, -4, 1, 0, 5, 9, 2\}$
    b. $\{-4, 2, 3\}$
    c. $\{0, 1, 2, 3, 5, 9\}$
    d. $\varnothing$

144. What is the contrapositive of the statement below?
If I get paid, then I go to the beach.
    a. If I get paid, then I do not go to the beach.
    b. If I go to the beach, then I get paid.
    c. If I do not get paid, then I go to the beach.
    d. If I do not go to the beach, then I do not get paid.

145. What is the converse of the statement below?
If I go skiing, then it is winter.
    a. If it is not winter, then I do not go skiing.
    b. If it is winter, then I go skiing.
    c. If it is not winter, then I go skiing.
    d. If I go skiing, then it is not winter.

146. Using logic, when is $p \vee q$ false?
    a. When p is true and q is true.
    b. When p is true and q is false.
    c. When p is false and q is true.
    d. When p is false and q is false.

147. Using logic, when is $p \wedge q$ true?
    a. When p is true and q is true.
    b. When p is true and q is false.
    c. When p is false and q is true.
    d. When p is false and q is false.

148. Which of the following is logically equivalent to $p \rightarrow q$?
    a. $q \rightarrow p$
    b. $\sim p \rightarrow \sim q$
    c. $\sim q \rightarrow \sim p$
    d. $p \wedge q$

149. Eric's dietary plan consists of 4 different entrées, 5 different appetizers, and 3 different desserts. How many possible meals may he create containing one entrée, one appetizer, and one dessert?

    a. 12
    b. 24
    c. 60
    d. 120

150. Which of the following represents a tautology?

    a. $p \wedge \sim p$
    b. $p \vee \sim p$
    c. $p \vee \sim q$
    d. $p \vee q$

Constructed Response

1. A family bought a new car for a purchase price of $32,000. The car will lose 15% of its value the day it is purchased and the car will depreciate at a constant rate following that. The value of the car as a function of time can be modeled by $y = c - 0.09cx$, where y is the value of the car x years after the car was purchased and c is the value of the car after the initial 15% depreciation.

   A. What is the value of the car 2 years after its purchase date? Show your work.
   B. On an xy-grid, graph the value, y, of the car, as a function of x, where x represents the number of years after the purchase date, for $0 \le x \le 7$ years. Label the axes and show the scales used for the graph.
   C. Use your graph to estimate the number of years, x, after the purchase date that the value of the car is $15,000. Label this point on your graph and indicate the approximate coordinates of the point.
   D. Algebraically find the number of years, x, after the purchase date that the value of the car is exactly $15,000. Round your solution to the nearest tenth of a year. Show your work.

2.

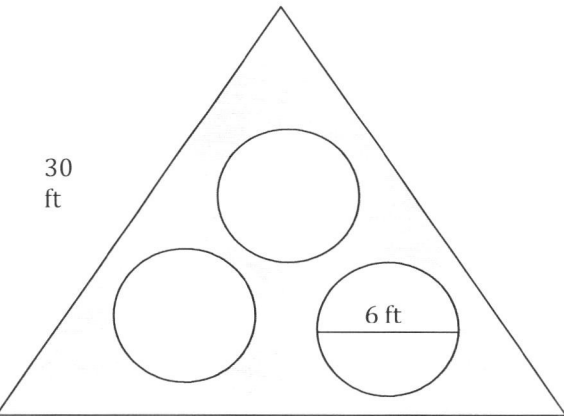

The diagram above shows the plan Berenice has for a triangular splash pad in a local city park. There will be three circles, each with a diameter of 6 feet, and the circles will be enclosed by an equilateral triangle with a side length of 30 feet. Berenice plans to have splash areas/fountains within the circles and walkways in the shaded areas of the triangle.

   A. According to the diagram, what is the maximum area, in square feet, available for Berenice to have for splash/fountain areas in the triangle? Show your work.
   B. According to the diagram, what percentage of the triangle will be set aside for walkways? Show your work.
   C. If a ball were to fall on a random point within the triangular splash pad, what is the probability that the ball would fall where Berenice plans to have splash areas? Show your work or explain your reasoning.

3. Below are listed the heights in centimeters of the 19 students in a class.

48, 53, 53, 54, 55, 56, 59, 60, 60, 63, 63, 63, 64, 65, 66, 67, 69, 71, 73

- A. For the numbers above, define and identify the median and the range.
- B. Define and calculate the mean for the list of numbers above.
- C. Draw a stem and leaf plot of the data using the tens digits as the stems and the units digits as the leaves.

Answers and Explanations

Number Sense and Operations

1. C: The sum is written as:

```
  2222
+  303
  3030
```

The sum of 2 and 3 equals 5, which must be represented as a 10. In the base-5 number system, a number cannot contain any 5's. The 1 of each 10 is carried to the next column to the left.

2. D: The percent increase is represented as $\frac{1100-800}{800}$, which equals 0.375 or 37.5%.

3. C: The set of integers is contained within the set of rational numbers, and is hence, a subset. A rational number may be written as the ratio, $\frac{a}{b}$, where a and b are integers and $b \neq 0$.

4. D: You first divide 2 into 55, recording the remainder. You then divide 2 into each resulting quotient, until the quotient is smaller than 2. Next, you put the final quotient as the first digit. You then go backwards and write the remainders and place them as digits, in order from left to right.

5. D: The original cost may be represented by the equation $45 = x - 0.25x$ or $45 = 0.75x$. Dividing both sides of the equation by 0.75 gives $x = 60$.

6. A: If a number is divisible by 2 and 3, it is also divisible by the lowest common multiple of these two factors. The lowest common multiple of 2 and 3 is their product, 6.

7. B: The decimal expansion of an irrational number does not terminate or repeat. The decimal expansion of $\sqrt{2}$ does not terminate or repeat.

8. C: The original price may be represented by the equation $24,210 = x - 0.10x$ or $24,210 = 0.9x$. Dividing both sides of the equation by 0.9 gives $x = 26,900$.

9. C: His monthly salary may be modeled as $\frac{1}{8}x = 320$. Multiplying both sides of the equation by 8 gives $x = 2,560$.

10. C: Division of a nonzero rational number by another nonzero rational number will always result in a nonzero rational number.

11. D: The set of integers is represented as $\{..., -3, -2, -1, 0, 1, 2, 3, ...\}$. The numbers 1, 2, 3, ..., are counting numbers, or natural numbers. Thus, the set contains the counting numbers, zero, and the negations of the counting numbers.

12. C: The set of irrational numbers is separate from the set of rational numbers. A rational number cannot be irrational, and an irrational number cannot be rational.

13. B: The multiplicative inverse property states that the product of a number and its reciprocal is 1.

14. A: If $a|b$ and $a|c$, it does not necessary follow that $b|c$. One counterexample is $3|6$ and $3|15$, but 6 does not divide 15.

15. A: The repeating decimal may be converted to a fraction by writing:

$$10x = 4.\overline{4}$$
$$-\quad x = 0.\overline{4}$$

which simplifies as $10x - x = 4.\overline{4} - 0.\overline{4}$.

16. C: The amount he donates is equal to $0.01(45,000)$. Thus, he donates \$450.

17. B: The amount she spends on rent and utilities is equal to $0.38(40,000)$, or \$15,200, which is approximately \$15,000.

18. D: The 8 is in the tenths place, the 6 in the hundredths place, and the 7 in the thousandths place. Thus, 0.867 is equal to the sum of the product of 8 and $\frac{1}{10}$, the product of 6 and $\frac{1}{100}$, and the product of 7 and $\frac{1}{1000}$.

19. D: The rectangular array represents the product of the side lengths of 7 and $(4 + 2)$.

20. A: $b|a$ means that a is divisible by b: that is, that a is equal to the product of b and some quotient, q.

21. C: Subtraction of a natural number from another natural number may result in an integer that is not a natural number. For example, $1 - 2 = -1$, which is not a natural number.

22. C. The original price may be modeled by the equation, $(x - 0.45x) + 0.0875(x - 0.45x) = 39.95$, which simplifies to $0.598125x = 39.95$. Dividing each side of the equation by the coefficient of x gives $x \approx 66.79$.

23. C: There are 36 months in 3 years. The following proportion may be written: $\frac{450}{3} = \frac{x}{36}$. The equation $3x = 16200$, may be solved for x. Dividing both sides of the equation by 3 gives $x = 5,400$.

24. D: The total rainfall is 25.38 inches. Thus, the ratio $\frac{4.5}{25.38}$, represents the percentage of rainfall received during October. $\frac{4.5}{25.38} \approx 0.177$ or 17.7%.

25. D: The decimal point is 4 places to the right of the first digit, 3. Thus, $30,490 = 3.049 \times 10^4$.

Algebra and Functions

26. C: The ratio between successive terms is constant (2), so this is a geometric series. A geometric sequence is represented by an exponential function.

27. A: The sum of 3 and the product of each term number and 5 equals the term value. For example, for term number 4, the value of 23 is equal to 5(4) + 3, or 23.

28. B: A vertical line will cross the graph at more than one point. Thus, it is not a function.

29. B: The graph is a straight line that passes through the origin, or point (0, 0).

30. C: This graph is shifted 4 units to the right and 3 units up from that of the parent function, $y = x^2$.

31. D: The product of $(x - 5)(2x + 6)$ equals $2x^2 + 6x - 10x - 30$, which simplifies to $2x^2 - 4x - 30$.

32. D: The constant of proportionality is equal to the slope. Using the points, (2, –8) and (5, –20), the slope may be written as $\frac{-20-(-8)}{5-2}$, which equals –4.

33. C: An inverse proportional relationship is written in the form $y = \frac{k}{x}$, thus the equation $y = \frac{3}{x}$ shows that y is inversely proportional to x.

34. D: The expression $(x - 2)^2$ may be expanded as $x^2 - 4x + 4$. Multiplication of $-3x$ by this expression gives $-3x^3 + 12x^2 - 12x$.

35. A: This graph shows a slope of 3, a y-intercept of –6, and the correct shading above the line. Using the test point (0, 0), the equation $0 \geq 0 - 6$ may be written. Since $0 \geq -6$, the solution is the shaded area above the line, which contains the point (0, 0).

36. C: Substituting 2 for each x-value gives $f(2) = \frac{2^3-2(2)+1}{3(2)}$, which simplifies to $f(2) = \frac{5}{6}$.

37. D: The table shows the y-intercept to be –5. The slope is equal to the ratio of change in y-values to change in corresponding x-values. As each x-value increases by 1, each y-value increases by 3. Thus, the slope is $\frac{3}{1}$, or 3. This graph represents the equation $y = 3x - 5$.

38. B: Each of the graphs shows the correct y-intercept of –6, but only graph B shows the correct slope. Using the points (0, –6) and (–2, 2), the slope of graph B may be written as $m = \frac{2-(-6)}{-2-0}$, which simplifies to $m = -4$.

39. B: The graph shows $f(2) = 10$. Since the y-intercept of the parabola is 2, the following equation may be written: $10 = a(2)^2 + 2$, which simplifies to $10 = 4a + 2$. Subtracting 2 from both sides gives $8 = 4a$. Dividing both sides of the equation by 4 gives $a = 2$. Thus the graph represents the function, $f(x) = 2x^2 + 2$. Evaluating this function for an x-value of 5 gives $f(5) = 2(5)^2 + 2$ or $f(5) = 52$. The average rate of change may be written as $A(x) = \frac{52-10}{5-2}$, which simplifies to $A(x) = 14$.

40. C: The slope is equal to 4, since each ticket costs $4. The y-intercept is represented by the constant fee of $30. Substituting 4 for m and 30 for b into the equation $y = mx + b$ gives $y = 4x + 30$.

41. D: The lines cross at the point with an x-value of –3 and a y-value of 2. Thus, the solution is (–3, 2).

42. A: On a graph, the lines intersect at the point, (–5, 9). Thus, (–5, 9) is the solution to the system of linear equations.

43. A: The test point of (0, 0) indicates that shading should occur below the line with the steeper slope. The same test point indicates that shading should occur above the other line. The overlapped shading occurs between these two lines, in the upper right.

44. D: A graph of the function shows the positive x-intercept to occur at approximately (2.6, 0). Thus, the ball will reach the ground after approximately 2.6 seconds.

45. D: The table represents a geometric sequence, with a common ratio of 2. Geometric sequences are modeled by exponential functions.

46. C: Using the points (–3, 1) and (1, –11), the slope may be written as $m = \frac{-11-1}{1-(-3)}$ or $m = -3$. Substituting the slope of –3 and the x- and y-values from the point (–3, 1), into the slope-intercept form of an equation gives $1 = -3(-3) + b$, which simplifies to $1 = 9 + b$. Subtracting 9 from both sides of the equation gives $b = -8$. Thus, the linear equation that includes the data in the table is $y = -3x - 8$.

47. B: The slope of the graphed line is –2. A line perpendicular to this one will have a slope of $\frac{1}{2}$. Substituting the slope and the x- and y-values from the point (3, 2), into the slope-intercept form of an equation gives: $2 = \frac{1}{2}(3) + b$, which simplifies to $2 = \frac{3}{2} + b$. Subtracting $\frac{3}{2}$ from each side of the equation gives $b = \frac{1}{2}$. So the equation of a line perpendicular to this one and passing through the point (3, 2) is $y = \frac{1}{2}x + \frac{1}{2}$.

48. D: The slope of the graphed line is 2. A line parallel to this one will also have a slope of 2. Substituting the slope and the x- and y-values from the point (–1, 4), into the slope-intercept form of an equation gives: $4 = 2(-1) + b$, which simplifies to $4 = -2 + b$. Adding 2 to both sides of the equation gives $b = 6$. So the equation of a line parallel to this one and passing through the point (–1, 4) is $y = 2x + 6$.

49. B: The graph is a straight line that passes through the origin, or (0, 0). Thus, it is linear and proportional.

50. A: This situation may be modeled by a geometric sequence, with a common ratio of 2 and initial value of 0.02. Substituting the common ratio and initial value into the formula $a_n = a_1 \cdot r^{n-1}$, gives $a_n = 0.02 \cdot 2^{n-1}$.

51. D: This situation may be modeled by an arithmetic sequence, with a common difference of 4 and initial value of 3. Substituting the common difference and initial value into the formula, $a_n = a_1 + (n-1)d$, gives $a_n = 3 + (n-1)4$, which simplifies to $a_n = 4n - 1$.

52. D: If we divide both terms in the numerator by n, the expression reduces to $n + \frac{1}{n}$. Although $\frac{1}{n}$ converges to 0, n increases without bound. The expression therefore has no limit.

53. C: The limit is simply the quotient of $5n$ divided by n, or 5.

54. B: The sum of an infinite geometric series may be modeled by the formula $S = \frac{a}{1-r}$, where a represents the initial value and r represents the common ratio. Substituting the initial value of 3 and common ratio of $\frac{2}{3}$ into the formula, gives $= \frac{3}{1-\frac{2}{3}}$, which simplifies to $S = \frac{3}{\frac{1}{3}}$ or 9.

55. C: The situation may be modeled by the system $\begin{matrix} 4x + 3y = 9.55 \\ 2x + 2y = 5.90 \end{matrix}$. Multiplying the bottom equation by -2 gives $\begin{matrix} 4x + 3y = 9.55 \\ -4x - 4y = -11.80 \end{matrix}$. Addition of the two equations gives $-y = -2.25$ or $y = 2.25$. Thus, one box of crackers costs \$2.25.

56. C: The derivative of an equation of the form $y = ax^n$ is equal to $(n \cdot a)x^{n-1}$. So the derivative of $y = 9x^2$ is equal to $(2 \cdot 9)x^{2-1}$ or $18x$.

57. C: The limit of the expression $\frac{4x}{x}$, is 4, so the limit of the entire function is 1,004. The function converges.

58. B: The sequence $\frac{1}{5}, \frac{1}{25}, \frac{1}{125}, \frac{1}{625}, \ldots$, may be used to represent the situation. Substituting the initial value of $\frac{1}{5}$ and common ratio of $\frac{1}{5}$ into the formula $S = \frac{a}{1-r}$ gives $= \frac{\frac{1}{5}}{1-\frac{1}{5}}$, which simplifies to $S = \frac{\frac{1}{5}}{\frac{4}{5}}$ or $S = \frac{1}{4}$.

59. B: As the denominator approaches infinity, the value of the function will get smaller and smaller and converge to 0.

60. B: The derivative of an equation of the form $y = x^n$ is equal to $n \cdot x^{n-1}$. So the derivative of $g(x) = x^{ab}$ is equal to $ab \cdot x^{ab-1}$.

61. A: An inverse proportional relationship is represented by an equation in the form $y = \frac{k}{x}$, where k represents some constant of proportionality. The graph of this equation is a hyperbola with diagonal axes, symmetric about the lines $y = x$ and $y = -x$.

62. C: The value of the 50th term may be found using the formula $a_n = a_1 + (n-1)d$. Substituting the number of terms for n, the initial value of 2 for a, and the common difference of 2 for d gives: $a_{50} = 2 + (50-1)(2)$, which simplifies to $a_{50} = 100$. Now, the value of the 50th term may be substituted into the formula, $S_n = \frac{n(a_1 + a_n)}{2}$, which gives: $S_{50} = \frac{50(2+100)}{2}$, which simplifies to $S_{50} = 2{,}550$.

63. B: The sign of the constant, inside the squared term, is positive for a shift to the left and negative for a shift to the right. Thus, a movement of 5 units left is indicated by the expression $y = (x + 5)^2$. A shift of 4 units down is indicated by subtraction of 4 units from the squared term.

64. B: Relation B is the only one in which there is not any x-value that is mapped to more than one y-value. Thus, this relation represents a function.

65. C: The position of an accelerating car is changing according to a non-constant speed. Thus, the graph will show a curve with an increasing slope. The slope is increasing since it represents the velocity, and the velocity is increasing.

66. A: The inequality will be less than or equal to, since he may spend $100 or less on his purchase.

67. D: Since she spends at least $16, the relation of the number of packages of coffee to the minimum cost may be written as $4p \geq 16$. Alternatively, the inequality may be written as $16 \leq 4p$.

68. B: The horizontal asymptote is equal to the ratio of the coefficient of x to the coefficient of $2x$, or $\frac{1}{2}$.

69. C: The horizontal asymptote is equal to the ratio of the two coefficients of x, or $\frac{1}{1}$, which equals 1.

70. D: As x goes to positive or negative infinity, only the leading term of a polynomial function of x matters. Therefore, we can ignore the "+2" in the denominator; $\lim_{x \to -\infty} \frac{4x^2}{x+2} = \lim_{x \to -\infty} \frac{4x^2}{x} = \lim_{x \to -\infty} 4x$. As x goes to negative infinity, $4x$ decreases without bound. The expression therefore has no limit.

71. A: Evaluation of the expression for an x-value of –2 gives: $(3(-2)^3 - 6(-2)^2 + 4)$, which equals –44.

72. B: The situation may be modeled with the equation $\frac{1}{3} + \frac{1}{2} = \frac{1}{t}$, which simplifies to $\frac{5}{6} = \frac{1}{t}$. Thus, $t = \frac{6}{5}$. If working together, it will take them 1.2 hours to decorate the cake.

73. A: The situation may be modeled by the inequality $3x + 2y \geq 20$. Isolating the y-term gives $2y \geq -3x + 20$. Solving for y gives $y \geq -\frac{3}{2}x + 10$. Thus, the y-intercept will be 10, the line will be solid, and a test point of (0, 0) indicates the shading should occur above the line.

74. C: The situation may be modeled by the following system of inequalities: $\begin{array}{l} 6x + 3y \leq 75 \\ x + y \leq 30 \end{array}$. A test point of (0, 0) indicates shading should occur below the blue line and below the red line. The overlapped shading occurs below the blue line. Thus, graph C represents the correct combinations of items that she may buy, given her budget.

75. D: The table represents part of a geometric sequence, with a common ratio of 2, so it also represents points of an exponential function.

Measurement and Geometry

76. B: The following proportion may be written and solved for x: $\frac{5,280}{1} = \frac{6,700}{x}$. Thus, $x \approx 1.27$.

- 154 -

77. C: The volume of a cylinder may be calculated using the formula $V = \pi r^2 h$, where r represents the radius and h represents the height. Substituting 1.5 for r and 3 for h gives $V = \pi(1.5)^2(3)$, which simplifies to $V \approx 21.2$.

78. B: The volume of a sphere may be calculated using the formula $V = \frac{4}{3}\pi r^3$, where r represents the radius. Substituting 3.5 for r gives $V = \frac{4}{3}\pi(3.5)^3$, which simplifies to $V \approx 179.6$.

79. C: The surface area of a rectangular prism may be calculated using the formula $SA = 2lw + 2wh + 2hl$. Substituting the dimensions of 14 inches, 6 inches, and 8 inches gives $SA = 2(14)(6) + 2(6)(8) + 2(8)(14)$. Thus, the surface area is 488 square inches.

80. C: The volume of a pyramid may be calculated using the formula $V = \frac{1}{3}Bh$, where B represents the area of the base and h represents the height. Since the base is a square, the area of the base is equal to 6^2, or 36 square inches. Substituting 36 for B and 9 for h gives $V = \frac{1}{3}(36)(9)$, which simplifies to $V = 108$.

81. C: The surface area of a sphere may be calculated using the formula $SA = 4\pi r^2$. Substituting 9 for r gives $SA = 4\pi(9)^2$, which simplifies to $SA \approx 1017.36$. So the surface area of the ball is approximately 1017.36 square inches. There are twelve inches in a foot, so there are $12^2 = 144$ square inches in a square foot. In order to convert this measurement to square feet, then, the following proportion may be written and solved for x: $\frac{1}{144} = \frac{x}{1017.36}$. So $x \approx 7.07$. He needs approximately 7.07 square feet of wrapping paper.

82. D: The volume of a prism may be calculated using the formula $V = Bh$, where B represents the area of the base and h represents the height of the prism. The area of each triangular base is represented by $A = \frac{1}{2}(9)(12)$. So the area of each base is equal to 54 square centimeters. Substituting 54 for the area of the base and 15 for the height of the prism gives $V = (54)(15)$ or $V = 810$. The volume of the prism is 810 cm^3.

83. B: Since the figures are similar, the following proportion may be written and solved for x: $\frac{6}{4} = \frac{8}{x}$. Thus, $x = \frac{32}{6}$ or $5\frac{1}{3}$.

84. C: Angles g and c are alternate exterior angles. Thus, they are congruent.

85. D: The corresponding angles have congruent angle measures, each measuring 44°. According to the Corresponding Angles Converse Theorem, two lines are parallel if a transversal, intersecting the lines, forms congruent corresponding angles.

86. C: The measure of the inscribed angle is half of the measure of the intercepted arc. Since the intercepted arc measures 110°, the inscribed angle is equal to $\frac{110°}{2}$ or 55°.

87. B: The following proportion may be written and solved for x: $\frac{15}{5} = \frac{6}{x}$. Solving for x gives $x = 2$. Thus, the shadow cast by the man is 2 feet in length.

88. C: The following equation may be written and solved for x: $\sin 40° = \frac{x}{6}$. Multiplying both sides of the equation by 6 gives: $6 \cdot \sin 40° = x$, or $x \approx 3.9$.

89. D: The area of the square is equal to $(30)^2$, or 900 square centimeters. The area of the circle is equal to $\pi(15)^2$, or approximately 707 square centimeters. The area of the shaded region is equal to the difference of the area of the square and the area of the circle, or 900 cm^2 – 707 cm^2, which equals 193 cm^2. So the area of the shaded region is about 193 cm^2.

90. B: Two of the angles, plus one side, not included between the angles, are congruent to the corresponding angles and side of the other triangle. Thus, the AAS (Angle-Angle-Side) Theorem may be used to prove the congruence of the triangles.

91. D: The Pythagorean Theorem may be used to find the diagonal distance from the top of his head to the base of the shadow. The following equation may be written and solved for c: $5.8^2 + 6.2^2 = c^2$. Thus, $c \approx 8.5$. The distance is approximately 8.5 ft.

92. D: The cross-section of a cylinder will never be a triangle.

93. D: The measure of an angle formed by intersecting chords inside a circle is equal to one-half of the sum of the measures of the intercepted arcs. Thus, $x = \frac{1}{2}(48° + 62°)$, or 55°.

94. D: The measure of the angle formed by the chord and the tangent is equal to one-half of the measure of the intercepted arc. Since the measure of the angle is 68°, the measure of the intercepted arc may be found by writing $68° = \frac{1}{2}x$. Dividing both sides of the equation by $\frac{1}{2}$ gives $x = 136°$. The measure of the intercepted arc may also be found by multiplying 68° by 2. Thus, the value of x is 136°.

95. A: The net of a triangular prism has three rectangular faces and two triangular faces. This is true of both A and C, but net C cannot be folded into a triangular prism, because the two rectangular faces on the end cannot be made to join each other. So only A can be folded into a triangular prism.

96. B: The relationship between number of faces, edges, and vertices is represented by Euler's Formula, $E = F + V - 2$. Substituting 9 for E and 6 for V gives: $9 = F + 6 - 2$, which simplifies to $9 = F + 4$. Thus, $F = 5$.

97. C: When two parallel lines are cut by a transversal, the consecutive angles formed inside the lines are supplementary.

98. B: The two triangles are similar because they each have an angle measuring 65°, and the measurement of Angle A is the same for both triangles, due to the Reflexive Property. So the two triangles are similar according to the AA (Angle-Angle) Similarity Postulate.

99. C: The original triangle was reflected across the x-axis. When reflecting across the x-axis, the x-values of each point remain the same, but the y-values of the points will be opposites. $(1, 4) \rightarrow (1, -4), (5, \ 4) \rightarrow (5, -4), (3, 8) \rightarrow (3, -8)$.

100. C: A reflection across the x-axis will result in a triangle with vertices at $(2, -3)$, $(4, -7)$, and $(6, -3)$. A rotation of 270 degrees is denoted by the following: $(a, b) \rightarrow (b, -a)$. Thus, a rotation of the

reflected triangle by 270 degrees will result in a figure with vertices at (−3, −2), (−7, −4), and (−3, −6). The transformed triangle indeed has these coordinates as its vertices.

101. C: The midpoint may be calculated by using the formula $m = \left(\frac{x_1+x_2}{2}, \frac{y_1+y_2}{2}\right)$. Thus, the midpoint of the line segment shown may be written as $m = \left(\frac{1+8}{2}, \frac{2+8}{2}\right)$, which simplifies to m = (4.5, 5).

102. C: The distance may be calculated using the distance formula, $d = \sqrt{(x_2 - x_1)^2 + (y_2 - y_1)^2}$. Substituting the given coordinates, the following equation may be written: $d = \sqrt{(4 - (-8))^2 + (3 - 6)^2}$, which simplifies to $d = \sqrt{153}$.

103. B: The perimeter is equal to the sum of the lengths of the two bases, 2 and 6 units, and the diagonal distances of the other two sides. Using the distance formula, each side length may be represented as $d = \sqrt{20} = 2\sqrt{5}$. Thus, the sum of the two sides is equal to $2\sqrt{20}$, or $4\sqrt{5}$. The whole perimeter is equal to $8 + 4\sqrt{5}$.

104. C: The area of a trapezoid may be calculated using the formula, $A = \frac{1}{2}(b_1 + b_2)h$. Thus, the area of the trapezoid is represented as $A = \frac{1}{2}(4 + 2)(2)$, which simplifies to A = 6. The area of the triangle is represented as $A = \frac{1}{2}(4)(3)$, which also simplifies to A = 6. Thus, the total area is 12 square units.

105. D: The larger triangle has a base length of 3 units and a height of 3 units. The smaller triangle has a base length of 2 units and a height of 2 units. Thus, the dimensions of the larger triangle were multiplied by a scale factor of $\frac{2}{3}$. Note that $3 \cdot \left(\frac{2}{3}\right) = 2$.

106. A: The vertical line of symmetry is represented by an equation of the form $x = a$. The horizontal line of symmetry is represented by an equation of the form $y = a$. One line of symmetry occurs at x = −4. The other line of symmetry occurs at y = 6.

107. C: Equilateral triangles and regular hexagons may tessellate a plane. Each triangle may be attached to each side of a hexagon, leaving no gaps in the plane.

108. A: The amount to be administered may be written as $\frac{1}{12} \cdot \frac{34}{10}$, which equals $\frac{17}{60}$. Thus, she should administer $\frac{17}{60}$ fluid ounces of medicine.

109. C: The slope may be written as $m = \frac{4-0}{-3-(-4)}$, which simplifies to m = 4.

110. D: The perimeter of the triangle is equal to the sum of the side lengths. The length of the longer diagonal side may be represented as $d = \sqrt{(4 - 1)^2 + (5 - 2)^2}$, which simplifies to $d = \sqrt{18}$. The length of the shorter diagonal side may be represented as $d = \sqrt{(6 - 4)^2 + (2 - 5)^2}$, which simplifies to $d = \sqrt{13}$. The base length is 5 units. Thus, the perimeter is equal to $5 + \sqrt{18} + \sqrt{13}$, which is approximately 12.85 units. Since each unit represents 5 miles, the total distance she will have walked is equal to the product of 12.85 and 5, or approximately 64 miles.

111. C: The following proportion may be written and solved for x: $\frac{144}{1} = \frac{2012}{x}$. $144x = 2012$. Dividing both sides of the equation by 144 gives $x \approx 13.97$. Thus, 2,012 square inches is approximately equal to 13.97 square feet.

112. D: The triangle is a 45-45-90 right triangle. Thus, if each leg is represented by x, the hypotenuse is represented by $x\sqrt{2}$. Thus, the hypotenuse is equal to $8\sqrt{2}$ cm.

Statistics, Probability, and Discrete Mathematics

113. A: Data sets B and C are asymmetrical: data set B is skewed toward lower values, and data set C is skewed toward higher values. This makes the mean a poor measure of center. Data set D is mostly symmetrical, but has a large outlier. The mean is very sensitive to outliers, and is not an appropriate measure of center for data sets that include them. Data set A is roughly symmetrical and has no outliers; the mean would be an appropriate measure of center here.

114. C: A z-score may be calculated using the formula $z = \frac{X-\mu}{\sigma}$. Substituting the score of 82, class average of 87, and class standard deviation of 2 into the formula gives: $z = \frac{82-87}{2}$, which simplifies to $z = -2.5$. Thus, the student's score is 2.5 standard deviations below the mean.

115. D: The z-score is written as $z = \frac{61-81}{10}$, which simplifies to $z = -2$. A z-score with an absolute value of 2 shows a mean to z area of 0.4772. Subtracting this area from 0.5 gives 0.0228, or 2.28%.

116. D: The z-score is written as $z = \frac{96-84}{4}$, which simplifies to $z = 3$. A z-score of 3 shows a mean to z area of 0.4987. Adding 0.5 to this area gives 0.9987, or 99.87%.

117. D: Two z-scores should be calculated, one for each student's score. The first z-score may be written as $z = \frac{68-80}{8}$, which simplifies to $z = -1.5$. The second z-score may be written as $z = \frac{84-80}{8}$, which simplifies to $z = 0.5$. The percentage of students scoring between these two scores is equal to the sum of the two mean to z areas. A z-score with an absolute value of 1.5 shows a mean to z area of 0.4332. A z-score of 0.5 shows a mean to z area of 0.1915. The sum of these two areas is 0.6247, or 62.47%.

118. D: A two-sample t-test should be used. Entering the sample mean, sample standard deviation, and sample size of each group into a graphing calculator reveals a p-value that is less than 0.05, so a significant difference between the groups may be declared.

119. C: A t-test should be used. A t-score may be calculated using the formula $t = \frac{\bar{X}-\mu}{\frac{s}{\sqrt{n}}}$. Substituting the sample mean, population mean, sample standard deviation, and sample size into the formula gives $t = \frac{19.8-20}{\frac{0.2}{\sqrt{30}}}$, which simplifies to $t \approx -5.48$. For degrees of freedom of 29, any t-value greater than 3.659 will have a p-value less than 0.001. Thus, there is a significant difference between what the manufacturer claims and the actual amount included in each bottle. The claim is likely false, due to a p-value less than 0.01.

120. B: A z-test may be used, since the population standard deviation is known. A z-score may be calculated using the formula $z = \frac{\bar{X} - \mu}{\frac{\sigma}{\sqrt{n}}}$. Substituting the sample mean, population mean, population standard deviation, and sample size into the formula gives $z = \frac{17.9 - 18}{\frac{0.3}{\sqrt{25}}}$, which simplifies to $z \approx -1.67$. The p-value is approximately 0.1, which is greater than 0.05. Thus, there does not appear to be a significant difference between what the manufacturer claims and the actual number of ounces found in each container. The claim is likely true, due to a p-value greater than 0.05.

121. B: A t-test should be used. A t-score may be calculated using the formula $t = \frac{\bar{X} - \mu}{\frac{s}{\sqrt{n}}}$. Substituting the sample mean, population mean, sample standard deviation, and sample size into the formula gives $t = \frac{83 - 82}{\frac{2}{\sqrt{30}}}$, which simplifies to $t \approx 2.74$. For degrees of freedom of 29, the p-value is approximately 0.01. Thus, there is a significant difference between what the professor claimed to be the final exam average and what the actual sample average showed. His claim is likely false, as evidenced by a p-value less than 0.05.

122. C: Use of an intact group is called a convenience sample. Such a sample increases sampling error, since randomization was not employed. The other described techniques utilize random sampling.

123. C: A z-score of 2 has a mean to z area of 0.4772, or 47.72%. Twice this percentage is about 95%.

124. D: The standard deviation is equal to the square root of the ratio of the sum of the squares of the deviation of each score from the mean to the square root of the difference of n and 1. The mean of the data set is 7.625. The deviations are −4.625, −3.625, −3.625, −2.625, −1.625, 4.375, 4.375, and 7.375. The sum of the squares of the deviations may be written as 21.39 + 13.14 + 13.14 + 6.89 + 2.64 + 19.14 + 19.14 + 54.39, which equals 149.87. Division of this sum by 7 ($n - 1$) gives 21.41. The square root of this quotient is approximately 4.6.

125. A: The ends of Data Set A are farther apart, indicating a larger range. The horizontal line in the middle of a boxplot represents the median, so Data Set A also has a larger median.

126. A: The median of the lower half of the scores is 6. The median of the upper half of the scores is 16. The interquartile range is equal to the difference in the first and third quartiles. Thus, the interquartile range is 10.

127. B: The points may be entered into a graphing calculator or Excel spreadsheet to find the least-squares regression line. This line is approximately $y = 22x + 6$. Substituting 20 for x gives $y = 22(20) + 6$, or $y = 446$. Thus, $446 is a good estimate for the earnings received after 20 hours of work. If a line of best fit is predicted visually, the slope between points near that line is around 20, and the line passes near the origin. Thus, another good estimate would be $400. The estimate of $446 is closer to $400 than any of the other choices.

128. B: The mean is pulled towards the tail of a skewed distribution. It is not pulled towards the area with the larger frequency of scores. Outliers pull the mean towards those outliers.

129. C: The probability may be written as $P(M \text{ or } G) = P(M) + P(G) - P(M \text{ and } G)$. Substituting the probabilities, the following may be written: $P(M \text{ or } G) = \frac{4985}{10,079} + \frac{4113}{10,079} - \frac{2045}{10,079}$, which simplifies to $P(M \text{ or } G) = \frac{7053}{10,079}$ or approximately 70%.

130. D: The number of outcomes in the event is 2 (rolling a 5 or 6), and the sample space is 6 (numbers 1 – 6). Thus, the probability may be written as $\frac{2}{6}$, which simplifies to $\frac{1}{3}$.

131. B: The probability may be written as $P(E \text{ and } H) = P(E) \cdot P(H)$. Substituting the probability of each event gives $(E \text{ and } H) = \frac{1}{2} \cdot \frac{1}{2}$, which simplifies to $\frac{1}{4}$.

132. D: Since they are not mutually exclusive events, the probability may be written as $P(P \text{ or } T) = P(P) + P(T) - P(P \text{ and } T)$. Because the events are independent, $P(P \text{ and } T) = P(P) \cdot P(T)$. Substituting the probability of each event gives $(P \text{ or } T) = \frac{1}{2} + \frac{1}{2} - \left(\frac{1}{2} \cdot \frac{1}{2}\right)$, or 3/4.

133. B: Since they are not mutually exclusive events, the probability may be written as $P(4 \text{ or } E) = P(4) + P(E) - P(4 \text{ and } E)$. Substituting the probability of each event gives $(4 \text{ or } E) = \frac{1}{6} + \frac{1}{2} - \frac{1}{6}$, or $\frac{1}{2}$.

134. C: The theoretical probability is $\frac{1}{2}$, and $\frac{1}{2}(300) = 150$.

135. C: The number of ways the letters can be arranged may be represented as $\frac{6!}{2!2!2!}$, which equals 90.

136. A: This situation describes a permutation, since order matters. The formula for calculating a combination is $P(n,r) = \frac{n!}{(n-r)!}$. This situation may be represented as $P(6,3) = \frac{6!}{(6-3)!}$, which equals 120.

137. D: Since there are 10 numerals, the answer is equal to 10!, or 3,628,800.

138. A: The series is an infinite geometric series. The sum may be calculated using the formula $S = \frac{a}{1-r}$, where a represents the value of the first term and r represents the common ratio. Substituting 1 for a and $\frac{1}{2}$ for r gives $S = \frac{1}{1-\frac{1}{2}}$ or 2.

139. C: The number in the sample space is equal to the number of possible outcomes for one coin toss, 2, raised to the power of the number of coin tosses, or 4. $2^4 = 16$.

140. A: A Venn diagram such as the one shown below may be drawn to assist in finding the answer.

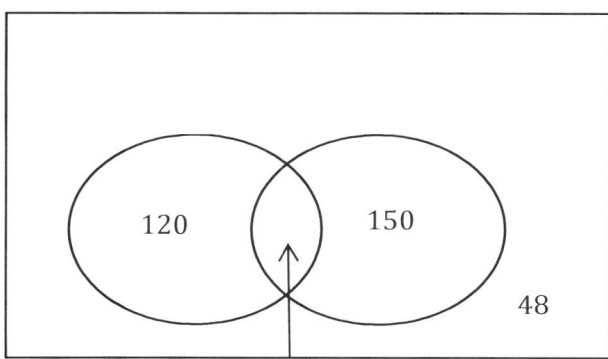

Since the set contains 320 total people, the solution is equal to $320 - (120 + 150 + 48)$ or 2 people.

141. A: $A \cap B$ means "A intersect B," or the elements that are common to both sets. "A intersect B" represents "A and B," that is, an element is in the intersection of A and B if it is in A *and* it is in B. The elements 2, 5, and 8 are common to both sets.

142. B: $A \cup B$ means "A union B," or all of the elements in either of the two sets. "A union B" represents "A or B," that is, an element is in the union of A and B if it is in A *or* it is in B. The elements in sets A and B are 9, 4, −3, 8, 6, 0, −4, and 2.

143. D: The intersection of the two sets is empty, denoted by the symbol, ∅. There are not any elements common to both sets.

144. D: If the statement is written in the form $p \rightarrow q$, then the contrapositive is represented as $\sim q \rightarrow \sim p$. Thus, the contrapositive should read, "If I do not go to the beach, then I do not get paid."

145. B: If the statement is written in the form $p \rightarrow q$, then the converse is represented as $q \rightarrow p$. Thus, the converse should read, "If it is winter, then I go skiing."

146. D: Only when both p and q are false is the union of p and q false.

147. A: Both p and q must be true in order for the intersection to be true.

148. C: A conditional statement $p \rightarrow q$ and its contrapositive $\sim q \rightarrow \sim p$ are logically equivalent because of the identical values in a truth table. See below.

p	q	$\sim p$	$\sim q$	$p \rightarrow q$	$\sim q \rightarrow \sim p$
T	T	F	F	T	T
T	F	F	T	F	F
F	T	T	F	T	T
F	F	T	T	T	T

149. C: This is a counting problem. The possible number of meals is equal to the product of the possibilities for each category. The product of 4, 5, and 3 is 60. Thus, there are 60 meals that he may create.

150. B: A tautology will shows all true values in a truth table column. Look at the table below:

p	q	$\sim p$	$\sim q$	p or $\sim p$	p and $\sim p$	p or $\sim q$	p or q
T	T	F	F	T	F	T	T
T	F	F	T	T	F	T	T
F	T	T	F	T	F	F	T
F	F	T	T	T	F	T	F

Only the statement $p \lor \sim p$ shows all T's in the column.

Secret Key #1 - Time is Your Greatest Enemy

Pace Yourself

Wear a watch. At the beginning of the test, check the time (or start a chronometer on your watch to count the minutes), and check the time after every few questions to make sure you are "on schedule."

If you are forced to speed up, do it efficiently. Usually one or more answer choices can be eliminated without too much difficulty. Above all, don't panic. Don't speed up and just begin guessing at random choices. By pacing yourself, and continually monitoring your progress against your watch, you will always know exactly how far ahead or behind you are with your available time. If you find that you are one minute behind on the test, don't skip one question without spending any time on it, just to catch back up. Take 15 fewer seconds on the next four questions, and after four questions you'll have caught back up. Once you catch back up, you can continue working each problem at your normal pace.

Furthermore, don't dwell on the problems that you were rushed on. If a problem was taking up too much time and you made a hurried guess, it must be difficult. The difficult questions are the ones you are most likely to miss anyway, so it isn't a big loss. It is better to end with more time than you need than to run out of time.

Lastly, sometimes it is beneficial to slow down if you are constantly getting ahead of time. You are always more likely to catch a careless mistake by working more slowly than quickly, and among very high-scoring test takers (those who are likely to have lots of time left over), careless errors affect the score more than mastery of material.

Secret Key #2 - Guessing is not Guesswork

You probably know that guessing is a good idea - unlike other standardized tests, there is no penalty for getting a wrong answer. Even if you have no idea about a question, you still have a 20-25% chance of getting it right.

Most test takers do not understand the impact that proper guessing can have on their score. Unless you score extremely high, guessing will significantly contribute to your final score.

Monkeys Take the Test

What most test takers don't realize is that to insure that 20-25% chance, you have to guess randomly. If you put 20 monkeys in a room to take this test, assuming they answered once per question and behaved themselves, on average they would get 20-25% of the questions correct. Put

20 test takers in the room, and the average will be much lower among guessed questions. Why?
1. The test writers intentionally write deceptive answer choices that "look" right. A test taker has no idea about a question, so picks the "best looking" answer, which is often wrong. The monkey has no idea what looks good and what doesn't, so will consistently be lucky about 20-25% of the time.
2. Test takers will eliminate answer choices from the guessing pool based on a hunch or intuition. Simple but correct answers often get excluded, leaving a 0% chance of being correct. The monkey has no clue, and often gets lucky with the best choice.

This is why the process of elimination endorsed by most test courses is flawed and detrimental to your performance- test takers don't guess, they make an ignorant stab in the dark that is usually worse than random.

$5 Challenge

Let me introduce one of the most valuable ideas of this course- the $5 challenge:

You only mark your "best guess" if you are willing to bet $5 on it.
You only eliminate choices from guessing if you are willing to bet $5 on it.

Why $5? Five dollars is an amount of money that is small yet not insignificant, and can really add up fast (20 questions could cost you $100). Likewise, each answer choice on one question of the test will have a small impact on your overall score, but it can really add up to a lot of points in the end.

The process of elimination IS valuable. The following shows your chance of guessing it right:

If you eliminate wrong answer choices until only this many remain:	Chance of getting it correct:
1	100%
2	50%
3	33%

However, if you accidentally eliminate the right answer or go on a hunch for an incorrect answer, your chances drop dramatically: to 0%. By guessing among all the answer choices, you are GUARANTEED to have a shot at the right answer.

That's why the $5 test is so valuable- if you give up the advantage and safety of a pure guess, it had better be worth the risk.

What we still haven't covered is how to be sure that whatever guess you make is truly random. Here's the easiest way:

Always pick the first answer choice among those remaining.

Such a technique means that you have decided, **before you see a single test question**, exactly how you are going to guess- and since the order of choices tells you nothing about which one is correct, this guessing technique is perfectly random.

This section is not meant to scare you away from making educated guesses or eliminating choices- you just need to define when a choice is worth eliminating. The $5 test, along with a pre-defined random guessing strategy, is the best way to make sure you reap all of the benefits of guessing.

Secret Key #3 - Practice Smarter, Not Harder

Many test takers delay the test preparation process because they dread the awful amounts of practice time they think necessary to succeed on the test. We have refined an effective method that will take you only a fraction of the time.

There are a number of "obstacles" in your way to succeed. Among these are answering questions, finishing in time, and mastering test-taking strategies. All must be executed on the day of the test at peak performance, or your score will suffer. The test is a mental marathon that has a large impact on your future.

Just like a marathon runner, it is important to work your way up to the full challenge. So first you just worry about questions, and then time, and finally strategy:

Success Strategy

1. Find a good source for practice tests.
2. If you are willing to make a larger time investment, consider using more than one study guide- often the different approaches of multiple authors will help you "get" difficult concepts.
3. Take a practice test with no time constraints, with all study helps "open book." Take your time with questions and focus on applying strategies.
4. Take a practice test with time constraints, with all guides "open book."
5. Take a final practice test with no open material and time limits

If you have time to take more practice tests, just repeat step 5. By gradually exposing yourself to the full rigors of the test environment, you will condition your mind to the stress of test day and maximize your success.

Secret Key #4 - Prepare, Don't Procrastinate

Let me state an obvious fact: if you take the test three times, you will get three different scores. This is due to the way you feel on test day, the level of preparedness you have, and, despite the test writers' claims to the contrary, some tests WILL be easier for you than others.

Since your future depends so much on your score, you should maximize your chances of success. In order to maximize the likelihood of success, you've got to prepare in advance. This means taking practice tests and spending time learning the information and test taking strategies you will need to succeed.

Never take the test as a "practice" test, expecting that you can just take it again if you need to. Feel free to take sample tests on your own, but when you go to take the official test, be prepared, be focused, and do your best the first time!

Secret Key #5 - Test Yourself

Everyone knows that time is money. There is no need to spend too much of your time or too little of your time preparing for the test. You should only spend as much of your precious time preparing as is necessary for you to get the score you need.

Once you have taken a practice test under real conditions of time constraints, then you will know if you are ready for the test or not.

If you have scored extremely high the first time that you take the practice test, then there is not much point in spending countless hours studying. You are already there.

Benchmark your abilities by retaking practice tests and seeing how much you have improved. Once you score high enough to guarantee success, then you are ready.

If you have scored well below where you need, then knuckle down and begin studying in earnest. Check your improvement regularly through the use of practice tests under real conditions. Above all, don't worry, panic, or give up. The key is perseverance!

Then, when you go to take the test, remain confident and remember how well you did on the practice tests. If you can score high enough on a practice test, then you can do the same on the real thing.

General Strategies

The most important thing you can do is to ignore your fears and jump into the test immediately- do not be overwhelmed by any strange-sounding terms. You have to jump into the test like jumping into a pool- all at once is the easiest way.

Make Predictions

As you read and understand the question, try to guess what the answer will be. Remember that several of the answer choices are wrong, and once you begin reading them, your mind will immediately become cluttered with answer choices designed to throw you off. Your mind is typically the most focused immediately after you have read the question and digested its contents.

If you can, try to predict what the correct answer will be. You may be surprised at what you can predict.

Quickly scan the choices and see if your prediction is in the listed answer choices. If it is, then you can be quite confident that you have the right answer. It still won't hurt to check the other answer choices, but most of the time, you've got it!

Answer the Question

It may seem obvious to only pick answer choices that answer the question, but the test writers can create some excellent answer choices that are wrong. Don't pick an answer just because it sounds right, or you believe it to be true. It MUST answer the question. Once you've made your selection, always go back and check it against the question and make sure that you didn't misread the question, and the answer choice does answer the question posed.

Benchmark

After you read the first answer choice, decide if you think it sounds correct or not. If it doesn't, move on to the next answer choice. If it does, mentally mark that answer choice. This doesn't mean that you've definitely selected it as your answer choice, it just means that it's the best you've seen thus far. Go ahead and read the next choice. If the next choice is worse than the one you've already selected, keep going to the next answer choice. If the next choice is better than the choice you've already selected, mentally mark the new answer choice as your best guess.

The first answer choice that you select becomes your standard. Every other answer choice must be benchmarked against that standard. That choice is correct until proven otherwise by another answer choice beating it out. Once you've decided that no other answer choice seems as good, do one final check to ensure that your answer choice answers the question posed.

Valid Information

Don't discount any of the information provided in the question. Every piece of information may be necessary to determine the correct answer. None of the information in the question is there to throw you off (while the answer choices will certainly have information to throw you off). If two seemingly unrelated topics are discussed, don't ignore either. You can be confident there is a relationship, or it wouldn't be included in the question, and you are probably going to have to determine what is that relationship to find the answer.

Avoid "Fact Traps"

Don't get distracted by a choice that is factually true. Your search is for the answer that answers the question. Stay focused and don't fall for an answer that is true but incorrect. Always go back to the question and make sure you're choosing an answer that actually answers the question and is not just a true statement. An answer can be factually correct, but it MUST answer the question asked. Additionally, two answers can both be seemingly correct, so be sure to read all of the answer choices, and make sure that you get the one that BEST answers the question.

Milk the Question

Some of the questions may throw you completely off. They might deal with a subject you have not been exposed to, or one that you haven't reviewed in years. While your lack of knowledge about the subject will be a hindrance, the question itself can give you many clues that will help you find the correct answer. Read the question carefully and look for clues. Watch particularly for adjectives and nouns describing difficult terms or words that you don't recognize. Regardless of if you completely understand a word or not, replacing it with a synonym either provided or one you more familiar with may help you to understand what the questions are asking. Rather than wracking your mind about specific detailed information concerning a difficult term or word, try to use mental substitutes that are easier to understand.

The Trap of Familiarity

Don't just choose a word because you recognize it. On difficult questions, you may not recognize a number of words in the answer choices. The test writers don't put "make-believe" words on the test; so don't think that just because you only recognize all the words in one answer choice means that answer choice must be correct. If you only recognize words in one answer choice, then focus on that one. Is it correct? Try your best to determine if it is correct. If it is, that is great, but if it doesn't, eliminate it. Each word and answer choice you eliminate increases your chances of getting the question correct, even if you then have to guess among the unfamiliar choices.

Eliminate Answers

Eliminate choices as soon as you realize they are wrong. But be careful! Make sure you consider all of the possible answer choices. Just because one appears right, doesn't mean that the next one won't be even better! The test writers will usually put more than one good answer choice for every question, so read all of them. Don't worry if you are stuck between two that seem right. By getting down to just two remaining possible choices, your odds are now 50/50. Rather than wasting too much time, play the odds. You are guessing, but guessing wisely, because you've been able to knock out some of the answer choices that you know are wrong. If you are eliminating choices and realize that the last answer choice you are left with is also obviously wrong, don't panic. Start over and consider each choice again. There may easily be something that you missed the first time and will realize on the second pass.

Tough Questions

If you are stumped on a problem or it appears too hard or too difficult, don't waste time. Move on! Remember though, if you can quickly check for obviously incorrect answer choices, your chances of guessing correctly are greatly improved. Before you completely give up, at least try to knock out a couple of possible answers. Eliminate what you can and then guess at the remaining answer choices before moving on.

Brainstorm

If you get stuck on a difficult question, spend a few seconds quickly brainstorming. Run through the complete list of possible answer choices. Look at each choice and ask yourself, "Could this answer the question satisfactorily?" Go through each answer choice and consider it independently of the other. By systematically going through all possibilities, you may find something that you would otherwise overlook. Remember that when you get stuck, it's important to try to keep moving.

Read Carefully

Understand the problem. Read the question and answer choices carefully. Don't miss the question because you misread the terms. You have plenty of time to read each question thoroughly and make sure you understand what is being asked. Yet a happy medium must be attained, so don't waste too much time. You must read carefully, but efficiently.

Face Value

When in doubt, use common sense. Always accept the situation in the problem at face value. Don't read too much into it. These problems will not require you to make huge leaps of logic. The test writers aren't trying to throw you off with a cheap trick. If you have to go beyond creativity and make a leap of logic in order to have an answer choice answer the question, then you should look at the other answer choices. Don't overcomplicate the problem by creating theoretical relationships or explanations that will warp time or space. These are normal problems rooted in reality. It's just that the applicable relationship or explanation may not be readily apparent and you have to figure things out. Use your common sense to interpret anything that isn't clear.

Prefixes

If you're having trouble with a word in the question or answer choices, try dissecting it. Take advantage of every clue that the word might include. Prefixes and suffixes can be a huge help. Usually they allow you to determine a basic meaning. Pre- means before, post- means after, pro - is positive, de- is negative. From these prefixes and suffixes, you can get an idea of the general meaning of the word and try to put it into context. Beware though of any traps. Just because con is the opposite of pro, doesn't necessarily mean congress is the opposite of progress!

Hedge Phrases

Watch out for critical "hedge" phrases, such as likely, may, can, will often, sometimes, often, almost, mostly, usually, generally, rarely, sometimes. Question writers insert these hedge phrases to cover every possibility. Often an answer choice will be wrong simply because it leaves no room for exception. Avoid answer choices that have definitive words like "exactly," and "always".

Switchback Words

Stay alert for "switchbacks". These are the words and phrases frequently used to alert you to shifts in thought. The most common switchback word is "but". Others include although, however, nevertheless, on the other hand, even though, while, in spite of, despite, regardless of.

New Information

Correct answer choices will rarely have completely new information included. Answer choices typically are straightforward reflections of the material asked about and will directly relate to the question. If a new piece of information is included in an answer choice that doesn't even seem to relate to the topic being asked about, then that answer choice is likely incorrect. All of the information needed to answer the question is usually provided for you, and so you should not have to make guesses that are unsupported or choose answer choices that require unknown information that cannot be reasoned on its own.

Time Management

On technical questions, don't get lost on the technical terms. Don't spend too much time on any one question. If you don't know what a term means, then since you don't have a dictionary, odds are you aren't going to get much further. You should immediately recognize terms as whether or not you know them. If you don't, work with the other clues that you have, the other answer choices and terms provided, but don't waste too much time trying to figure out a difficult term.

Contextual Clues

Look for contextual clues. An answer can be right but not correct. The contextual clues will help you find the answer that is most right and is correct. Understand the context in which a phrase or statement is made. This will help you make important distinctions.

Don't Panic

Panicking will not answer any questions for you. Therefore, it isn't helpful. When you first see the question, if your mind goes blank, take a deep breath. Force yourself to mechanically go through the steps of solving the problem and using the strategies you've learned.

Pace Yourself

Don't get clock fever. It's easy to be overwhelmed when you're looking at a page full of questions, your mind is full of random thoughts and feeling confused, and the clock is ticking down faster than you would like. Calm down and maintain the pace that you have set for yourself. As long as you are on track by monitoring your pace, you are guaranteed to have enough time for yourself. When you get to the last few minutes of the test, it may seem like you won't have enough time left, but if you only have as many questions as you should have left at that point, then you're right on track!

Answer Selection

The best way to pick an answer choice is to eliminate all of those that are wrong, until only one is left and confirm that is the correct answer. Sometimes though, an answer choice may immediately look right. Be careful! Take a second to make sure that the other choices are not equally obvious. Don't make a hasty mistake. There are only two times that you should stop before checking other answers. First is when you are positive that the answer choice you have selected is correct. Second is when time is almost out and you have to make a quick guess!

Check Your Work

Since you will probably not know every term listed and the answer to every question, it is important that you get credit for the ones that you do know. Don't miss any questions through careless mistakes. If at all possible, try to take a second to look back over your answer selection and make sure you've selected the correct answer choice and haven't made a costly careless mistake (such as marking an answer choice that you didn't mean to mark). This quick double check should more than pay for itself in caught mistakes for the time it costs.

Beware of Directly Quoted Answers

Sometimes an answer choice will repeat word for word a portion of the question or reference section. However, beware of such exact duplication – it may be a trap! More than likely, the correct choice will paraphrase or summarize a point, rather than being exactly the same wording.

Slang

Scientific sounding answers are better than slang ones. An answer choice that begins "To compare the outcomes…" is much more likely to be correct than one that begins "Because some people insisted…"

Extreme Statements

Avoid wild answers that throw out highly controversial ideas that are proclaimed as established fact. An answer choice that states the "process should be used in certain situations, if…" is much more likely to be correct than one that states the "process should be discontinued completely." The first is a calm rational statement and doesn't even make a definitive, uncompromising stance, using a hedge word "if" to provide wiggle room, whereas the second choice is a radical idea and far more extreme

Answer Choice Families

When you have two or more answer choices that are direct opposites or parallels, one of them is usually the correct answer. For instance, if one answer choice states "x increases" and another answer choice states "x decreases" or "y increases," then those two or three answer choices are very similar in construction and fall into the same family of answer choices. A family of answer choices is when two or three answer choices are very similar in construction, and yet often have a directly opposite meaning. Usually the correct answer choice will be in that family of answer choices. The "odd man out" or answer choice that doesn't seem to fit the parallel construction of the other answer choices is more likely to be incorrect.

Special Report: How to Overcome Test Anxiety

The very nature of tests caters to some level of anxiety, nervousness or tension, just as we feel for any important event that occurs in our lives. A little bit of anxiety or nervousness can be a good thing. It helps us with motivation, and makes achievement just that much sweeter. However, too much anxiety can be a problem; especially if it hinders our ability to function and perform.

"Test anxiety," is the term that refers to the emotional reactions that some test-takers experience when faced with a test or exam. Having a fear of testing and exams is based upon a rational fear, since the test-taker's performance can shape the course of an academic career. Nevertheless, experiencing excessive fear of examinations will only interfere with the test-takers ability to perform, and his/her chances to be successful.

There are a large variety of causes that can contribute to the development and sensation of test anxiety. These include, but are not limited to lack of performance and worrying about issues surrounding the test.

Lack of Preparation

Lack of preparation can be identified by the following behaviors or situations:

Not scheduling enough time to study, and therefore cramming the night before the test or exam
Managing time poorly, to create the sensation that there is not enough time to do everything
Failing to organize the text information in advance, so that the study material consists of the entire text and not simply the pertinent information
Poor overall studying habits

Worrying, on the other hand, can be related to both the test taker, or many other factors around him/her that will be affected by the results of the test. These include worrying about:

Previous performances on similar exams, or exams in general
How friends and other students are achieving
The negative consequences that will result from a poor grade or failure

There are three primary elements to test anxiety. Physical components, which involve the same typical bodily reactions as those to acute anxiety (to be discussed below). Emotional factors have to do with fear or panic. Mental or cognitive issues concerning attention spans and memory abilities.

Physical Signals

There are many different symptoms of test anxiety, and these are not limited to mental and emotional strain. Frequently there are a range of physical signals that will let a test taker know that he/she is suffering from test anxiety. These bodily changes can include the following:
Perspiring
Sweaty palms
Wet, trembling hands
Nausea
Dry mouth
A knot in the stomach
Headache
Faintness
Muscle tension
Aching shoulders, back and neck
Rapid heart beat
Feeling too hot/cold

To recognize the sensation of test anxiety, a test-taker should monitor him/herself for the following sensations:

The physical distress symptoms as listed above
Emotional sensitivity, expressing emotional feelings such as the need to cry or laugh too much, or a sensation of anger or helplessness
A decreased ability to think, causing the test-taker to blank out or have racing thoughts that are hard to organize or control.

Though most students will feel some level of anxiety when faced with a test or exam, the majority can cope with that anxiety and maintain it at a manageable level. However, those who cannot are faced with a very real and very serious condition, which can and should be controlled for the immeasurable benefit of this sufferer.

Naturally, these sensations lead to negative results for the testing experience. The most common effects of test anxiety have to do with nervousness and mental blocking.

Nervousness

Nervousness can appear in several different levels:

The test-taker's difficulty, or even inability to read and understand the questions on the test
The difficulty or inability to organize thoughts to a coherent form
The difficulty or inability to recall key words and concepts relating to the testing questions (especially essays)
The receipt of poor grades on a test, though the test material was well known by the test taker

Conversely, a person may also experience mental blocking, which involves:

Blanking out on test questions

Only remembering the correct answers to the questions when the test has already finished.

Fortunately for test anxiety sufferers, beating these feelings, to a large degree, has to do with proper preparation. When a test taker has a feeling of preparedness, then anxiety will be dramatically lessened.

The first step to resolving anxiety issues is to distinguish which of the two types of anxiety are being suffered. If the anxiety is a direct result of a lack of preparation, this should be considered a normal reaction, and the anxiety level (as opposed to the test results) shouldn't be anything to worry about. However, if, when adequately prepared, the test-taker still panics, blanks out, or seems to overreact, this is not a fully rational reaction. While this can be considered normal too, there are many ways to combat and overcome these effects.

Remember that anxiety cannot be entirely eliminated, however, there are ways to minimize it, to make the anxiety easier to manage. Preparation is one of the best ways to minimize test anxiety. Therefore the following techniques are wise in order to best fight off any anxiety that may want to build.

To begin with, try to avoid cramming before a test, whenever it is possible. By trying to memorize an entire term's worth of information in one day, you'll be shocking your system, and not giving yourself a very good chance to absorb the information. This is an easy path to anxiety, so for those who suffer from test anxiety, cramming should not even be considered an option.

Instead of cramming, work throughout the semester to combine all of the material which is presented throughout the semester, and work on it gradually as the course goes by, making sure to master the main concepts first, leaving minor details for a week or so before the test.

To study for the upcoming exam, be sure to pose questions that may be on the examination, to gauge the ability to answer them by integrating the ideas from your texts, notes and lectures, as well as any supplementary readings.

If it is truly impossible to cover all of the information that was covered in that particular term, concentrate on the most important portions, that can be covered very well. Learn these concepts as best as possible, so that when the test comes, a goal can be made to use these concepts as presentations of your knowledge.

In addition to study habits, changes in attitude are critical to beating a struggle with test anxiety. In fact, an improvement of the perspective over the entire test-taking experience can actually help a test taker to enjoy studying and therefore improve the overall experience. Be certain not to overemphasize the significance of the grade - know that the result of the test is neither a reflection of self worth, nor is it a measure of intelligence; one grade will not predict a person's future success.

To improve an overall testing outlook, the following steps should be tried:

Keeping in mind that the most reasonable expectation for taking a test is to expect to try to demonstrate as much of what you know as you possibly can.

Reminding ourselves that a test is only one test; this is not the only one, and there will be others.

The thought of thinking of oneself in an irrational, all-or-nothing term should be avoided at all costs.

A reward should be designated for after the test, so there's something to look forward to. Whether it be going to a movie, going out to eat, or simply visiting friends, schedule it in advance, and do it no matter what result is expected on the exam.

Test-takers should also keep in mind that the basics are some of the most important things, even beyond anti-anxiety techniques and studying. Never neglect the basic social, emotional and biological needs, in order to try to absorb information. In order to best achieve, these three factors must be held as just as important as the studying itself.

Study Steps

Remember the following important steps for studying:

Maintain healthy nutrition and exercise habits. Continue both your recreational activities and social pass times. These both contribute to your physical and emotional well being.
Be certain to get a good amount of sleep, especially the night before the test, because when you're overtired you are not able to perform to the best of your best ability.
Keep the studying pace to a moderate level by taking breaks when they are needed, and varying the work whenever possible, to keep the mind fresh instead of getting bored.
When enough studying has been done that all the material that can be learned has been learned, and the test taker is prepared for the test, stop studying and do something relaxing such as listening to music, watching a movie, or taking a warm bubble bath.

There are also many other techniques to minimize the uneasiness or apprehension that is experienced along with test anxiety before, during, or even after the examination. In fact, there are a great deal of things that can be done to stop anxiety from interfering with lifestyle and performance. Again, remember that anxiety will not be eliminated entirely, and it shouldn't be. Otherwise that "up" feeling for exams would not exist, and most of us depend on that sensation to perform better than usual. However, this anxiety has to be at a level that is manageable.

Of course, as we have just discussed, being prepared for the exam is half the battle right away. Attending all classes, finding out what knowledge will be expected on the exam, and knowing the exam schedules are easy steps to lowering anxiety. Keeping up with work will remove the need to cram, and efficient study habits will eliminate wasted time. Studying should be done in an ideal location for concentration, so that it is simple to become interested in the material and give it complete attention. A method such as SQ3R (Survey, Question, Read, Recite, Review) is a wonderful key to follow to make sure that the study habits are as effective as possible, especially in the case of learning from a textbook. Flashcards are great techniques for memorization. Learning to take good notes will mean that notes will be full of useful information, so that less sifting will need to be done to seek out what is pertinent for studying. Reviewing notes after class and then again on occasion will keep the information fresh in the mind. From notes that have been taken summary sheets and outlines can be made for simpler reviewing.

A study group can also be a very motivational and helpful place to study, as there will be a sharing of ideas, all of the minds can work together, to make sure that everyone understands, and the studying will be made more interesting because it will be a social occasion.

Basically, though, as long as the test-taker remains organized and self confident, with efficient study habits, less time will need to be spent studying, and higher grades will be achieved.

To become self confident, there are many useful steps. The first of these is "self talk." It has been shown through extensive research, that self-talk for students who suffer from test anxiety, should be well monitored, in order to make sure that it contributes to self confidence as opposed to sinking the student. Frequently the self talk of test-anxious students is negative or self-defeating, thinking that everyone else is smarter and faster, that they always mess up, and that if they don't do well, they'll fail the entire course. It is important to decreasing anxiety that awareness is made of self talk. Try writing any negative self thoughts and then disputing them with a positive statement instead. Begin self-encouragement as though it was a friend speaking. Repeat positive statements to help reprogram the mind to believing in successes instead of failures.

Helpful Techniques

Other extremely helpful techniques include:

Self-visualization of doing well and reaching goals
While aiming for an "A" level of understanding, don't try to "overprotect" by setting your expectations lower. This will only convince the mind to stop studying in order to meet the lower expectations.
Don't make comparisons with the results or habits of other students. These are individual factors, and different things work for different people, causing different results.
Strive to become an expert in learning what works well, and what can be done in order to improve. Consider collecting this data in a journal.
Create rewards for after studying instead of doing things before studying that will only turn into avoidance behaviors.
Make a practice of relaxing - by using methods such as progressive relaxation, self-hypnosis, guided imagery, etc - in order to make relaxation an automatic sensation.
Work on creating a state of relaxed concentration so that concentrating will take on the focus of the mind, so that none will be wasted on worrying.
Take good care of the physical self by eating well and getting enough sleep.
Plan in time for exercise and stick to this plan.

Beyond these techniques, there are other methods to be used before, during and after the test that will help the test-taker perform well in addition to overcoming anxiety.

Before the exam comes the academic preparation. This involves establishing a study schedule and beginning at least one week before the actual date of the test. By doing this, the anxiety of not having enough time to study for the test will be automatically eliminated. Moreover, this will make the studying a much more effective experience, ensuring that the learning will be an easier process. This relieves much undue pressure on the test-taker.

Summary sheets, note cards, and flash cards with the main concepts and examples of these main concepts should be prepared in advance of the actual studying time. A topic should never be eliminated from this process. By omitting a topic because it isn't expected to be on the test is only setting up the test-taker for anxiety should it actually appear on the exam. Utilize the course syllabus for laying out the topics that should be studied. Carefully go over the notes that were made in class, paying special attention to any of the issues that the professor took special care to emphasize while lecturing in class. In the textbooks, use the chapter review, or if possible, the chapter tests, to begin your review.

It may even be possible to ask the instructor what information will be covered on the exam, or what the format of the exam will be (for example, multiple choice, essay, free form, true-false). Additionally, see if it is possible to find out how many questions will be on the test. If a review sheet or sample test has been offered by the professor, make good use of it, above anything else, for the preparation for the test. Another great resource for getting to know the examination is reviewing tests from previous semesters. Use these tests to review, and aim to achieve a 100% score on each of the possible topics. With a few exceptions, the goal that you set for yourself is the highest one that you will reach.

Take all of the questions that were assigned as homework, and rework them to any other possible course material. The more problems reworked, the more skill and confidence will form as a result. When forming the solution to a problem, write out each of the steps. Don't simply do head work. By doing as many steps on paper as possible, much clarification and therefore confidence will be formed. Do this with as many homework problems as possible, before checking the answers. By checking the answer after each problem, a reinforcement will exist, that will not be on the exam. Study situations should be as exam-like as possible, to prime the test-taker's system for the experience. By waiting to check the answers at the end, a psychological advantage will be formed, to decrease the stress factor.

Another fantastic reason for not cramming is the avoidance of confusion in concepts, especially when it comes to mathematics. 8-10 hours of study will become one hundred percent more effective if it is spread out over a week or at least several days, instead of doing it all in one sitting. Recognize that the human brain requires time in order to assimilate new material, so frequent breaks and a span of study time over several days will be much more beneficial.

Additionally, don't study right up until the point of the exam. Studying should stop a minimum of one hour before the exam begins. This allows the brain to rest and put things in their proper order. This will also provide the time to become as relaxed as possible when going into the examination room. The test-taker will also have time to eat well and eat sensibly. Know that the brain needs food as much as the rest of the body. With enough food and enough sleep, as well as a relaxed attitude, the body and the mind are primed for success.

Avoid any anxious classmates who are talking about the exam. These students only spread anxiety, and are not worth sharing the anxious sentimentalities.

Before the test also involves creating a positive attitude, so mental preparation should also be a point of concentration. There are many keys to creating a positive attitude. Should fears become rushing in, make a visualization of taking the exam, doing well, and seeing an A written on the paper. Write out a list of affirmations that will bring a feeling of confidence, such as "I am doing well in my English class," "I studied well and know my material," "I enjoy this class." Even if the affirmations aren't believed at first, it sends a positive message to the subconscious which will result in an alteration of the overall belief system, which is the system that creates reality.

If a sensation of panic begins, work with the fear and imagine the very worst! Work through the entire scenario of not passing the test, failing the entire course, and dropping out of school, followed by not getting a job, and pushing a shopping cart through the dark alley where you'll live. This will place things into perspective! Then, practice deep breathing and create a visualization of the opposite situation - achieving an "A" on the exam, passing the entire course, receiving the degree at a graduation ceremony.

On the day of the test, there are many things to be done to ensure the best results, as well as the most calm outlook. The following stages are suggested in order to maximize test-taking potential:

Begin the examination day with a moderate breakfast, and avoid any coffee or beverages with caffeine if the test taker is prone to jitters. Even people who are used to managing caffeine can feel jittery or light-headed when it is taken on a test day.

Attempt to do something that is relaxing before the examination begins. As last minute cramming clouds the mastering of overall concepts, it is better to use this time to create a calming outlook.

Be certain to arrive at the test location well in advance, in order to provide time to select a location that is away from doors, windows and other distractions, as well as giving enough time to relax before the test begins.

Keep away from anxiety generating classmates who will upset the sensation of stability and relaxation that is being attempted before the exam.

Should the waiting period before the exam begins cause anxiety, create a self-distraction by reading a light magazine or something else that is relaxing and simple.

During the exam itself, read the entire exam from beginning to end, and find out how much time should be allotted to each individual problem. Once writing the exam, should more time be taken for a problem, it should be abandoned, in order to begin another problem. If there is time at the end, the unfinished problem can always be returned to and completed.

Read the instructions very carefully - twice - so that unpleasant surprises won't follow during or after the exam has ended.

When writing the exam, pretend that the situation is actually simply the completion of homework within a library, or at home. This will assist in forming a relaxed atmosphere, and will allow the brain extra focus for the complex thinking function.

Begin the exam with all of the questions with which the most confidence is felt. This will build the confidence level regarding the entire exam and will begin a quality momentum. This will also create encouragement for trying the problems where uncertainty resides.

Going with the "gut instinct" is always the way to go when solving a problem. Second guessing should be avoided at all costs. Have confidence in the ability to do well.

For essay questions, create an outline in advance that will keep the mind organized and make certain that all of the points are remembered. For multiple choice, read every answer, even if the correct one has been spotted - a better one may exist.

Continue at a pace that is reasonable and not rushed, in order to be able to work carefully. Provide enough time to go over the answers at the end, to check for small errors that can be corrected.

Should a feeling of panic begin, breathe deeply, and think of the feeling of the body releasing sand through its pores. Visualize a calm, peaceful place, and include all of the sights, sounds and sensations of this image. Continue the deep breathing, and take a few minutes to continue this with closed eyes. When all is well again, return to the test.

If a "blanking" occurs for a certain question, skip it and move on to the next question. There will be time to return to the other question later. Get everything done that can be done, first, to guarantee all the grades that can be compiled, and to build all of the confidence possible. Then return to the weaker questions to build the marks from there.

Remember, one's own reality can be created, so as long as the belief is there, success will follow. And remember: anxiety can happen later, right now, there's an exam to be written!

After the examination is complete, whether there is a feeling for a good grade or a bad grade, don't dwell on the exam, and be certain to follow through on the reward that was promised...and enjoy it! Don't dwell on any mistakes that have been made, as there is nothing that can be done at this point anyway.

Additionally, don't begin to study for the next test right away. Do something relaxing for a while, and let the mind relax and prepare itself to begin absorbing information again.

From the results of the exam - both the grade and the entire experience, be certain to learn from what has gone on. Perfect studying habits and work some more on confidence in order to make the next examination experience even better than the last one.

Learn to avoid places where openings occurred for laziness, procrastination and day dreaming.

Use the time between this exam and the next one to better learn to relax, even learning to relax on cue, so that any anxiety can be controlled during the next exam. Learn how to relax the body. Slouch in your chair if that helps. Tighten and then relax all of the different muscle groups, one group at a time, beginning with the feet and then working all the way up to the neck and face. This will ultimately relax the muscles more than they were to begin with. Learn how to breathe deeply and comfortably, and focus on this breathing going in and out as a relaxing thought. With every exhale, repeat the word "relax."

As common as test anxiety is, it is very possible to overcome it. Make yourself one of the test-takers who overcome this frustrating hindrance.

Additional Bonus Material

Due to our efforts to try to keep this book to a manageable length, we've created a link that will give you access to all of your additional bonus material.

Please visit http://www.mometrix.com/bonus948/mtelmsmath to access the information.